Multi-Dimensional Therapy with Families, Children and Adults

Multi-Dimensional Therapy with Families, Children and Adults: The Diamond Model is a comprehensive introduction to a model of multi-systemic, integrative, culturally competent, child and family-oriented psychotherapy: The Diamond Model.

This model integrates a great number of concepts, methods and techniques, found in diverse fields such as the various branches of psychology and psychotherapy, cultural anthropology, biology, linguistics and more, into a single linguistically unified theoretical and methodological framework. Through this model, the author presents clinical cases to help explore various internal and external factors that lead individuals and families to seek out therapy. The book also reserves a special place for examining play therapeutic and culturally competent techniques.

With vivid clinical examples throughout, *Multi-Dimensional Therapy with Families, Children and Adults* serves both as a theory-to-practice guide and as a reference book for therapists working with children and families in training and practice.

Dr. Shlomo Ariel is a senior clinical psychologist and family therapist, an international trainer of therapists and Director of the Integrative Psychotherapy Center and the Israel Play Therapy Institute in Ramat Gan, Israel.

Multi-Dimensional Therapy with Families, Children and Adults

The Diamond Model

Shlomo Ariel

LONDON AND NEW YORK

First published 2018
by Routledge
2 Park Square, Milton Park, Abingdon, Oxon OX14 4RN

and by Routledge
711 Third Avenue, New York, NY 10017

Routledge is an imprint of the Taylor & Francis Group, an informa business

© 2018 Shlomo Ariel

The right of Shlomo Ariel to be identified as author of this work has been asserted by him in accordance with sections 77 and 78 of the Copyright, Designs and Patents Act 1988.

All rights reserved. No part of this book may be reprinted or reproduced or utilised in any form or by any electronic, mechanical, or other means, now known or hereafter invented, including photocopying and recording, or in any information storage or retrieval system, without permission in writing from the publishers.

Trademark notice: Product or corporate names may be trademarks or registered trademarks, and are used only for identification and explanation without intent to infringe.

British Library Cataloguing in Publication Data
A catalogue record for this book is available from the British Library

Library of Congress Cataloging in Publication Data
Names: Ariel, Shlomo, author.
Title: Multidimensional therapy with families, children and adults :
the diamond model / Shlomo Ariel.
Description: Abingdon, Oxon ; New York, NY : Routledge, 2018. |
Includes index.
Identifiers: LCCN 2017055176 | ISBN 9781138244238 (hardback) |
ISBN 9781138282513 (pbk.) | ISBN 9781315101057 (master) |
ISBN 9781351587952 (web) | ISBN 9781351587945 (epub) |
ISBN 9781351587938 (mobipocket)
Subjects: | MESH: Family Therapy–methods | Case Reports
Classification: LCC RC455.4.F3 | NLM WM 430.5.F2 | DDC 616.89/156–dc23
LC record available at https://lccn.loc.gov/2017055176

ISBN: 978-1-138-24423-8 (hbk)
ISBN: 978-1-138-28251-3 (pbk)
ISBN: 978-1-315-10105-7 (ebk)

Typeset in Times New Roman
by Out of House Publishing

Disclaimer: The cases included in this book are inspired by real cases, but the original cases are unrecognizable, because they are far removed from the original cases in many crucial details.

Contents

Preface	xi
Acknowledgments	xiii
Introduction	1

PART I
Theoretical and methodological foundations   **5**

1   The Diamond Model – essentials   7
Case 1.1 Nonny 7
What is The Diamond Model? 10
A model vs. an idiographic theory 16
The procedure of creating and validating The Diamond Model 16
Summary of Chapter 1 21

**2   The sublanguages of information processing, cybernetics
and semiotics**   26
The sublanguage of information processing 26
The sublanguage of cybernetics 34
The sublanguage of semiotics 36
Summary of Chapter 2 40

**3   The synchronic and diachronic perspectives and the concept
of simplicity**   43
Loss of simplicity in periods of change or crisis 43
Restoring simplicity partially 44
Summary of Chapter 3 48

viii   Contents

PART 2
The internal and external subsystems

51

4   The internal subsystems

53

Developmental lines and dimensions 54
The cognitive and psychomotor subsystems 56
The subsystem of emotions 62
Personality and social development 65
Summary of Chapter 4 72

5   The external subsystems

77

Important life events 77
The external and internalized culture 77
The family and other social systems 93
Summary of Chapter 5 101

PART 3
Multi-systemic diagnosis

105

6   Collecting and analyzing diagnostic data

107

The stages of therapy 107
Preliminary diagnostic evaluation 107
*Observations of free or structured play and non-play behaviors of
    individuals, groups and families 118*
Analyzing and interpreting the observed behavior 125
Context-Dependent Componential Analysis 133
Summary of Chapter 6 137

7   Organizing the multi-systemic diagnostic data

139

Putting it all together 140
Summary of Chapter 7 149

PART 4
Therapy

151

8   Planning and carrying out the therapy

153

Strategy 153
The therapeutic alliance 156
Carrying out the therapy 157
Summary of Chapter 8 167

Contents ix

9 The healing power of various therapeutic techniques 169
Types of mechanisms of change 169
*A survey of therapeutic techniques, classified according to their main
    change mechanisms 172*
Summary of Chapter 9 198

10 Make-believe play as a therapeutic instrument 204
The advantages of play therapy 204
The functions of play therapy 204
A formal, explicit definition of the concept of make-believe play 205
Make-believe play as a language, a semiotic system 205
Make-believe play as a cognitive-affective regulative mechanism 207
Make-believe play as a cybernetic social regulative device 208
Make-believe play as a product of culture 209
Play development and the child's general development 210
The therapeutic power of play 210
Emotion balancing by means of play 211
Play as a debugging instrument 214
The role of the play therapist 218
Summary of Chapter 10 224

11 Monitoring the therapeutic process 227
Changes in sessions and between sessions 227
Termination 234
Summary of Chapter 11 235

Epilogue 238
List of cases, examples and observations 239
Index 241

Preface

Once upon a time, I had been a researcher and lecturer of linguistics. My areas of specialization included theoretical linguistics, semiotics, children's language development, anthropological linguistics and philosophy of language.

One day, I had the good fortune of being invited, as an expert on child language, to participate in a cross-cultural research project, in which samples of spontaneous play and social behavior of preschoolers of all sections of the Israeli population were videotaped and analyzed. I soon found out that the knowledge I had acquired as a linguist was readily applicable to the task of recording and analyzing the verbal and non-verbal behavior of those kids. Their individual and social play could be looked at as a language – a semiotic system, a culture-prescribed medium of expression and communication. I was captivated by the children's creativity and imagination. I was fascinated by the ingenious ways in which they were using play as a means of expressing their inner world, of solving emotional difficulties and interpersonal conflicts.

My way from there to the decision to undergo training as a psychotherapist, specializing in play therapy for individuals, groups and families, was short.

I found the new realm I entered enchanting, but not easy to adapt myself to. My mind had already been conditioned to examine the new field with the critical, pedantic eye of a linguist. I found quite a few areas of overlap between my previous fields of specialization and the new ones, but in the latter, most of the concepts and methodologies seemed to lack the systematic rigor of the former. I was exposed to many jargons spoken or written by zealots of numerous different, sometimes mutually hostile, tribes and sects. To my ears, some of these nomenclatures sounded esoteric, some multiply ambiguous, obscure and vague. Different tribes appeared to use different terms for the same notion or the same term for different notions. I was fascinated by many brilliant ideas that seemed to me, however, half-baked. Other ideas I found pitifully simplistic, attempts to force a genie into a bottle, to reduce Shakespeare's Hamlet to a simple formula.

When I began practicing, I experienced the world of psychotherapy as overwhelming and confusing. How could I put together all these poorly understood concepts and methods in working with a specific case, attempting to make sense of it and navigate it to a safe harbor?

I soon realized that my previous training in the various subfields of linguistics had equipped me with invaluable tools for charting a clear road map that could help me orient myself in my practice. It dawned on me that my wish to be released from the straightjacket of scientific discipline and only enjoy the fresh air of warm human relations, intuition and creativity would not be fully fulfilled. My previous academic background would not let me go. I could not just learn a new language and use it by sheer practice. I needed to learn its grammar or, if its grammar had not yet been researched, it was my task, as a linguist to be the one who would reveal and formulate it.

I then began to explicate and reformulate those various theoretical concepts and clinical methods that I had found particularly useful and orchestrate them into a coherent, organized system. It took time and significant effort before this endeavor began to bear fruit. The budding version of what I later termed The Diamond Model really helped me to know what I was doing and why I was doing it, especially in working with complex cases. Thanks to that effort, I became a much more efficacious psychotherapist.

To my relief, I soon realized that the rigor of the model did not stifle my intuition and creativity at all. On the contrary, the clear theoretical and methodological framework helped intuition, imagination and creativity come to fuller expression.

When I felt ready, I mustered the courage to publish parts of this model and began training therapists to apply it in their practice.

I have continued developing, elaborating and crystalizing The Diamond Model through the years. Two sub-models have been developed within its general framework: integrative play therapy and culturally competent psychotherapy. The effectiveness of The Diamond Model and of these two sub-models has been tested, beyond my own practice, in full and partial international training programs, although validating it by formal research is still a task for the future. This book is a comprehensive introduction to its current stage of development.

The Diamond Model may be said to belong to the rapidly growing psychotherapy integration tradition. Theorists of this relatively new tradition have identified three different approaches to psychotherapy integration: looking for factors common to various therapy models; assimilating concepts and methods borrowed from various therapy schools into one single model; and amalgamating various model into a single overall theory (theoretical integration). The Diamond Model constitutes an attempt to achieve the latter.

Acknowledgments

Of the many individuals who have contributed to this work, directly or indirectly, I would like to express my special thanks to the following persons.

In 1979, I worked in the Psychology Department of Yale University, where I was in close contact with Professor Jerome L. Singer. I am deeply indebted to Professor Singer not just for the opportunity to have direct access to his pioneering, highly inspiring work on play, but also for his personal support and encouragement.

I must also mention the late Professor Brian Sutton-Smith, with whom I had long-term exchanges and who wrote an insightful foreword to my book *Children's Imaginative Play: A Visit to Wonderland*.

I would like to express my gratitude to Dr. Florence Kaslow for her support and encouragement and for having taken the time to write a foreword to my book *Culturally Competent Family Therapy*.

In 2010, I was given a unique opportunity to train a first generation of systemic family therapists in Kosovo for five years. In this program, sponsored by the International Family Therapy Association, The Kosova Health Foundation and the Child and Adolescent Psychiatry Unit, The University Clinical Center of Kosova, trainees learned to apply The Diamond Model in their practice. I am grateful to all my colleagues and trainees who took part in this program, and in particular to Phoebe Prosky, Fried Didden, Mirjam Palsma and Dr. Mimoza Shahini.

Professor David Keith and Dr. Arnon Bentovim read an earlier version of this work. I am grateful to each of them for their encouraging and useful reviews.

Finally, I am deeply indebted to my wife, Ruti, and my daughter, Nana, for their unbending support and encouragement and for their insightful critiques of my work.

Introduction

This book is a complete, comprehensive introduction to a model of multi-dimensional, integrative, culturally competent psychotherapy – The Diamond Model. In my mind, this model is, like a diamond, multi-faceted, translucent and well-shaped. The Diamond Model synthesizes numerous theoretical concepts, methods and techniques drawn from diverse sources: the various branches of psychology and psychotherapy, cultural anthropology, linguistics, philosophy, biology and more. Parts of it have been published in books and articles. Novices and professional therapists have been trained to apply this model in their practice in full and partial training programs and workshops, in universities, training institutes and professional organizations in Israel, various European countries and the USA.

The Diamond Model is based on the following principles:

- Every case brought to therapy is multi-determined. It is a product of a complex interaction between factors (termed *programs* below) that belong to systems residing within the person and outside the person. Therefore, an integrative model of psychotherapy should be multi-systemic.
- Constructing and validating a universally applicable model is a challenging, exciting endeavor. It is an endless process of formulating empirically refutable concepts and generalizations and testing whether they apply to all cases or just to some cases.
- All concepts and generalizations that belong to each of the internal and external subsystems are or can be formulated in a fairly rigorous, explicit formal language. The choice or construction of the theoretical language is not arbitrary but empirically based. The language chosen includes three sublanguages: human information processing, cybernetics (the science of regulation and control mechanisms, using concepts such as homeostasis, feedback and feed-forward) and semiotics (the science of signs and symbols). Such reformulations are not just replacing one jargon with

2   Introduction

another. They explicate, formalize and systematize the original concepts and expose their communalities.

- The external and internal systems can be looked at *diachronically* (from the past to the present) or *synchronically* (simultaneously, a cross-section at a specific time).
- The central principle that explains the etiology of a case as well as spontaneous or therapeutic change is *simplicity*. Well-functioning information processing programs in any subsystem are, for all practical purposes, optimally simple; that is, *comprehensive* (able to process all the information needed for proper functioning), *parsimonious* (process only the information relevant to good functioning), *consistent* (process the relevant information in a self-consistent manner) and *plausible* (do not misinterpret input data or data retrieved from memory and do not draw erroneous inferences that hamper good functioning).

The meaning of *well-functioning* in this context is not self-explanatory. It will be discussed in Chapters 1–3.

In some cases, one encounters programs that have never been optimally simple in this sense. In many cases, however, optimally simple programs lose their simplicity mainly in periods of change and crisis that generate emotional distress. The unbalanced emotions mobilize efforts to preserve partial simplicity (only comprehensiveness, only consistency, only parsimony or only plausibility). The partial simplicity infects the programs with *bugs* (i.e. lack of information crucial for good functioning, irrelevant information that interferes with proper functioning, misinterpretations of information that result in ineffective or damaging responses or harmful inconsistent functioning). The bugs prevent the programs from enlisting corrective feedback. They lead to deviations from the needed homeostasis, to dangerous feed-forward.

The main purpose of therapy is therefore to remove or weaken the bugs by *bug-busters* that mobilize corrective feedback and restore a well-functioning homeostasis. To achieve this, emotions that got off-balance should be rebalanced.

Rebalancing the emotions and fixing the bugs by bug-busters can be achieved by applying the principle of *systematic technical eclecticism*. Any technique borrowed from any source or invented by the therapist can be employed, as long as it can effectively achieve emotion balancing and remove or weaken the bugs. Many modern and traditional therapeutic and healing techniques share the same change mechanisms (i.e. the mechanisms that makes them effective). Understanding the change mechanism that successfully accomplishes a specific therapeutic task can help the therapist choose or make up the right technique. In Chapter 9, numerous techniques are briefly surveyed and classified according to the change mechanisms they activate. Special attention is given in The Diamond Model to emotion-balancing techniques and bug-busters using play therapy. Such techniques are described and illustrated in Chapter 10.

The book begins with a detailed account of the above principles. This is followed by a description and analysis of a sample of subsystems and their development. Then comes the practical applications part: collecting and analyzing diagnostic data; designing and evaluating multi-systemic, integrative therapeutic strategies; forming a culturally sensitive therapeutic alliance; and managing individual, family or group therapeutic sessions through play and other methods. Emotion balancing and other therapeutic techniques from various sources, notably play therapeutic techniques, are listed and explained. Finally, methods for monitoring the process of therapy and its outcomes and termination methods are described and discussed.

Each chapter of the book includes vivid case examples and is followed by a summary of its main contents, by home assignments and by a classified list of publications. It should be noted that the lists of references do not purport to be comprehensive and exhaustive. A review of the relevant literature is not one of the goals of this book. Such review requires a different publication.

This book can serve as a complete introductory textbook for both novices in psychotherapy and experienced psychotherapists who would like to expand their professional education and enrich their professional toolbox: clinical, educational and rehabilitation psychologists, child and family therapists, clinical social workers, creative arts therapists, play therapists, special educators, psychiatrists, etc. It can serve, internationally, as a basic text in graduate- and postgraduate-level training programs of therapists in universities, colleges and training institutes, psychotherapy organizations and clinics. Its scope is wide enough to fit into various schools of psychotherapy: dynamic, cognitive-behavioral, systemic and more. It can also be used as a reference book for psychotherapists. Secondary audiences can be doctoral and postdoctoral students, researchers and theorists interested in recent developments in psychotherapy integration, family therapy, applied linguistics, human ethology, semiotics and other relevant fields. I should point out, however, that this book, despite the considerable room allotted in it to theoretical discussions, is primarily a practice-oriented training textbook. It has not been intended to be a book of academic theoretical or empirical research.

The Diamond Model, being multi-dimensional and culturally informed, is particularly useful in working with complex cases and with non-mainstream clients.

Part I

Theoretical and methodological foundations

Chapter 1

The Diamond Model – essentials

Case 1.1 Nonny

His mother pushed him lightly into my office, as if his legs refused to carry him. He was slim, pale. He had a strange look: gray eyes, staring inwards, expressionless face, except for a vague smile that seemed to me slightly mocking. He stood motionless, limp, his arms hanging. He wore a long-sleeved winter shirt, buttoned to the neck, though it was a very hot, end-of-summer day.

Nonny, a nickname for Noam, thirteen years old.

Nonny's father did not show up. He told Nonny's mother that he "didn't believe in psychology."

When I asked Nonny to sit down, he did not respond, and when I tried to engage him in a conversation, he did not cooperate.

I was a clinical psychology intern in a community mental health center in Jerusalem.

After further attempts to secure the father's cooperation had failed, my supervisor, Daphna, instructed me to interview just the mother. I was required to fill in a standard intake questionnaire, of which the purpose was to obtain data on the child's symptoms, milestones in his development, his family and the circumstances of his life. The standard intake procedure was also to include administering a battery of psychological tests, but in Nonny's case this was impossible.

Nonny's mother, Tanya, looked exhausted. She spoke in a barely audible voice, with a Russian accent. She immigrated to Israel with her mother from Ukraine when she was sixteen. She was the one who decided to seek therapy for Nonny. Since the beginning of the school summer vacation, he had been locking himself up in his room, refusing to come out. In the safety of his room, he would spend the time obsessively writing in notebooks in tiny, dense, unreadable characters, which looked like an illegible, meaningless scrawl. Only after his mother had pressed him over and over again to tell her what he was writing, he said,

8 Theoretical and methodological foundations

"TV series," and when she asked him why in such dense script and tiny letters, he said, "To save paper." Indeed, his mother had to buy him scores of notebooks. He insisted on eating in his room and would barely touch the food. His mother would put a tray of food on his table and he would nod her out. Social ties and activities out of home were of course out of the question.

Nonny was born with hypotonia ("floppy baby syndrome"), a state of low muscle tone, which impaired his motor development and therefore his social development as well. As a preschooler, he spoke a mixture of Hebrew and Russian, because his mother could not speak Hebrew fluently. This was another stumbling block on his way to social adjustment.

Tanya evaded, not so skillfully, probing questions about her husband, Shalom, and her relationship with him. From that first and later conversations with her, however, I managed to learn that Shalom had the habit of spending money obsessively on the soccer lottery. In this way, he compensated himself for the loss of his status as a soccer star. His gambling addiction got him entangled in heavy debts. There were rumors that he had embezzled some sport club money and that this affair was hushed up. The family was forced to sell their apartment and move to rented apartments in "bad" neighborhoods. Shalom used to borrow money from loan sharks. Often creditors were knocking on the door, making threats. Tanya was making desperate efforts to cover the debts. She worked as an accountant and, after work hours, she cleaned homes. These efforts put her under great physical and mental strain, but also strengthened her position vis-à-vis her husband. She accused and criticized Shalom scathingly, and he reacted by being on the defensive, making all kinds of excuses. He also poured unsolicited gifts on her, which only increased the family's debts.

Shalom grew up in Tel Aviv in a low socioeconomic area. As a child, he often failed to attend school, spending most of his time playing soccer. He had barely finished elementary school.

My supervisor, Daphna, qualified herself as a Rogerian humanistic, person-centered, non-directive psychotherapist (see Rogers, 1942). She had read Virginia Axline's *Play therapy* (1947) and *Dibs in search of self* (1964) and was deeply impressed by Axline's approach. She said that Nonny's symptoms were his way of asserting his autonomous, independent self in a difficult, stormy family situation. She suggested that in my work with Nonny I adopt a non-directive, child-centered approach. I should let him write his "TV series" in my office and have on my table all sorts of objects such as games, books and even a soccer ball that could remind him of his father. My only role would be to provide him with an accepting and empathetic human environment, without suggesting anything to do and without interfering in his

The Diamond Model – essentials 9

own choices. I should only use non-judgmental reflections to give Nonny the message that I am there for him. The therapeutic process would take care of itself, she predicted.

I lacked a more in-depth analysis of the complexity of this case, nor was I convinced that the treatment method Daphna suggested was the right one for this case. I suspected that Nonny would experience my presence as intrusive. I was afraid I would feel like a Peeping Tom. The assumption that the process would happen without my active involvement seemed to me unfounded. Furthermore, our workplace was a public clinic. We could not have all the time in the world to work with each case.

What I did, eventually, was suggest to Nonny for us to write his "TV series" together. To my pleasant surprise, he agreed. Our conjoint creation, at first in writing and later orally, was, for all intents and purposes, a fruitful therapeutic dialogue, disguised as dramatic scenes in an "American TV crime series", which, as expected, related allegorically to the realities of Nonny's life. That metaphorical dialogue opened new and unexpected avenues for continued multi-systemic therapy. Individual sessions with Tanya led to Shalom's consent to participate in couple therapy, followed by family play therapy (see Chapter 9). Shalom joined a gambling addiction therapeutic group. That drama series terminated in a happy ending. In the final scene, Nonny was seen riding toward the horizon, a mentally healthy and normative adolescent.

But let us go back to what directly followed the intake. Nonny's case was discussed in a multi-disciplinary team meeting. The clinic director, a psychiatrist, said that although he still had no conclusive diagnosis, his impression was that this was a case of simple-type schizophrenia, settled on a pervasive developmental disorder infrastructure, perhaps the first step toward catatonia. He said he had not yet decided on the suitable medication, but suggested that the patient be hospitalized for observation. A cognitive-behavior therapy (CBT) expert proposed behavior therapy, using positive and negative reinforcement (e.g. giving Nonny a notebook and a pen only if he comes out of his room for five minutes and, if he did so, he would get one pen and one notebook for every minute he was out of his room). A family therapist with a strategic, solution-focused leaning suggested using paradoxical injunctions such as prescribing the symptoms and endorsing the triangulation of Nonny by his parents. A psychoanalyst spoke in a complicated, obscure Kleinian and Winnicottian jargon that I couldn't make head or tail of. The discussion was like the dialogue of the deaf. I came out of that meeting utterly confused.

It was such mental state of bewilderment and disorientation, experienced by myself in the early stage of my retraining as a mental health professional and later by my trainees, that led me to develop The Diamond Model.

Students of mine, especially in the initial stages of their training, were expressing difficulty with the systematic rigor of the model, which they experienced as being "dry" and "cold". It seemed to them inconsistent with

10 Theoretical and methodological foundations

the richness and inherent vagueness of the clinical encounter. They expressed concern that internalizing the model would extinguish their intuition, imagination and creativity. My standard answer used to be that the model was like the "dry" and "cold" grammar of a language, or the theory of music, which serve as frameworks for endless possibilities of creating original productions. I like to quote the title of the book *The Structure of Magic* by the founders of Neuro-Linguistic Programming, Bandler and Grinder (1975). They explicated the "grammar" underlying the work of gifted psychotherapists such as Virginia Satir and Milton Erickson to make their methods and techniques available to less gifted psychotherapists.

What is The Diamond Model?

The Diamond Model is a complete guide to integrative psychotherapy in general and to integrative play therapy in particular.

The attributes of The Diamond Model are that it is multi-systemic, integrative, linguistically uniform, rigorous up to a certain extent, explanatory and technically eclectic.

The Diamond Model is multi-systemic

Every case brought to therapy, whatever the presenting difficulties, is multideterminded, a product of a dynamic interaction between factors (programs) belonging to different internal and external subsystems. Therefore, The Diamond Model is *multi-systemic*. In designing and carrying out the therapy, all the relevant programs and their interrelations must be considered. Ignoring relevant programs found in any of the subsystems can result in understanding the case incorrectly and choosing an ineffective or even harmful therapeutic strategy.

The internal subsystems (within the individual) are: the body (the brain and the nervous system, the genetic, anatomic and physiological subsystems); the cognitive and psychomotor subsystems; conscious or unconscious emotional concerns (*emotives*), emotional conflicts and emotional defenses; the individual and social personality (self and body images and concepts, object relations, self and body boundaries, attachment, egocentricity and narcissism vs. empathy and prosocial attitude, reality testing, self-control, psychosexual development and moral development); and the internalized culture.

The external subsystems are: significant life events; the family and other social systems; the ecosystems (the human and non-human environments at large); and the culture.

Each of the subsystems and all of them can be looked at *synchronically* (a cross-section at a particular time, usually the beginning of therapy) or *diachronically* (from the past to the present, developing through time).

The Diamond Model – essentials 11

Nonny's case, like any other case, is multi-determined in this sense. To understand this case and treat it effectively, a therapist should scrutinize the dynamic interaction between programs belonging to all the above-listed subsystems as they are manifested in this specific case. In this procedure, the therapist will form hypotheses about the various programs and their dynamic interrelations, to be confirmed or refuted by further data. Attending only to some of the relevant programs while disregarding other (e.g. treating just Nonny's symptoms while ignoring his hypotonia, his social isolation, his father's addiction to gambling, his entanglement with the conflict between his parents, the absence of his mother in the evenings, her cultural and linguistic background, his cognitive potential, etc.) could lead the therapy astray.

A sample, just a sample, of the relevant programs in Nonny's case and their interrelations is presented below. In a full analysis of a case, the relevant programs will be organized in a different format that displays their dynamic interrelations (see Chapter 7).

In the following informal presentation, the programs are looked at from both a diachronic and a synchronic perspective. Past events are relevant inasmuch as they have a continued impact on the present. The subsystems that each part of this presentation belongs to are placed in square brackets. It should be stressed that most of the following statements are just hypotheses, to be confirmed or refuted by more empirical data.

Shalom, Nonny's father, grew up in a low-socioeconomic neighborhood, where children used to spend a great deal of their free time out on the street [the ecological and culture subsystems]. He did not like school, maybe because he had an undiagnosed ADHD, maybe because his learning abilities were low, maybe because he could not get along with authority [the cognitive, psychomotor and social subsystems]. But he was sporty, with a talent for and powerful attraction to soccer [the psychomotor subsystem; the subsystem of emotions]. Soccer was the arena where he could have high self-esteem and enjoy social prestige [the personality development and social subsystems]. As an adult, he reached the rank of national soccer superstar [the social subsystem]. His career was short-lived, as is always the case, because he grew older [significant life event]. The termination of his career was a major crisis for him because his self-image and self-esteem had depended entirely on his success as a soccer player [personality development subsystem]. He attempted to fill the emptiness inside him, affected by the loss of his previous thrills and glory, with soccer betting, which enabled him to remain close to his favorite environment. His betting habit grew and became an obsession, an addiction [the subsystem of emotions; the subsystem of ecology].

Tanya immigrated to Israel when she was sixteen, with her mother and nobody else [the family subsystem]. For her, Israel was a foreign country. Hebrew was not her mother tongue. This was a culture shock for her. It was not easy for her to adjust to the unfamiliar environment. She was lonely [the culture, ecological and social subsystems and the subsystem of emotions]. She met Shalom when he was still at the height of his fame [significant life event].

12 Theoretical and methodological foundations

Her marriage with him was conceived by her as winning the Grand Prix. The depth of the fall when he lost his status and began being addicted to gambling matched the height of her previous euphoria [significant life events; the subsystem of emotions]. Perhaps because of her difficulty in coping with the loss, she undertook the Sisyphean and frustrating task of covering Shalom's debts. Her efforts to cover the debts only weakened Shalom's motivation and ability to rehabilitate and exacerbated the dysfunctional relationship between the two of them [the subsystem of emotions; the family subsystem]. Apparently, Shalom's fall from his status as a star exposed Tanya's higher academic achievements. From being the inferior partner, she became the superior one.

Nonny was born with hypotonia [the genetic and psychomotor subsystems]. This limited his ability to participate in his peers' motor activities and therefore adversely affected his social adjustment. He preferred to avoid interpersonal exchanges. He felt more comfortable with his social isolation, with his being a lone wolf, and gave up opportunities to acquire social skills [the social subsystem and the subsystem of emotions].

Nonny's physical disability was diametrically opposed to his father's high physical capacity. Subconsciously, he knew he could never acquire physical skills like his father's. Therefore, he avoided connecting with Shalom through physical activities. It is reasonable to assume that Shalom was also disappointed by his inability to impart sports skills, his main asset, to his son, and therefore gave up and kept his distance from Nonny [the family subsystem; the subsystem of emotions]. So, Nonny could not see his father as a role model. He could not internalize his image and form a good attachment with him [the personality development subsystem]. He opted for his mother [the family subsystem]. Over the years, he found it difficult to reach the level of separation-individuation from his mother appropriate for his age [the personality development subsystem]. He was a witness to his father's weakness and to his mother's angry accusations. These imprinted in his mind a negative image of his father [the personality development subsystem; the family subsystem]. All these kept him further away from his father and strengthened his dependence on his mother [the family subsystem].

The decline in the family's standard of living and the frequent moving into new apartments greatly increased Nonny's sense of instability [the ecology subsystem; the subsystem of emotions]. The invasion of creditors, his mother's absence from home after hours and her angry outbursts at his father instilled in him a powerful sense of threat and insecurity [the ecology and social subsystems; the family subsystem. the subsystem of emotions]. He took refuge from all these threats in the safety of his room, where he shut himself up. It was not difficult for him to be isolated, because from early childhood he had chosen isolation as a relatively comfortable defense [the subsystem of emotions; the family subsystem].

Toward the age of thirteen, various signs of gender maturity began to appear, such as pubic hair and hair growing on his arms and chest. Nonny was

The Diamond Model – essentials 13

ashamed of it, because the growing hair marked him as a man, like his father. The internalized image of a man like his father in his mind was characterized by being physically strong, unlike himself, but mentally weak, troublesome and under attack from the side of a woman, Nonny's mother. If he, Nonny, grows up to be a man, will he be rejected and attacked by his mother too? He must differentiate himself from his father by all means. Therefore, to hide the growing hair, he insisted on wearing a long-sleeved winter shirt, buttoned to the neck, even on a sweltering day [the personality development and psychosexual development subsystems; the subsystem of emotions; the family subsystem].

The repressed memory of his childhood peers' mocking his clumsy movements, as well as of his father's dissatisfaction with his clumsiness, coupled with the fear of being attacked, led him to minimize the use of his muscles to almost the point of paralysis. His lack of movements may have stemmed also from an unconscious effort to suppress and conceal his rage and violence drive. His anger with both of his parents was mixed with fear of the creditors' threats and of his mother's aggression. He did not let his mother come near him and was willing to accept only the amount of food necessary for his survival [the psychomotor system; the subsystem of emotions]. Apparently, he displaced the impressions of the traumatic events he had involuntarily been a part and a victim of to writing the "TV series" as a kind of writing therapy. Writing in unreadable handwriting was perhaps a kind of secret code intended to hide his injured inner world from others and maybe even from himself. The reason he gave for his writing in tiny, cramped handwriting – "to save paper" – was probably not just an excuse. It was perhaps a symbolic expression of his attempt to magically undo his father's wastefulness.

In the above analysis, readers will identify eclectic use of concepts from various psychodynamic, cognitive and systemic theories. Later, these different concepts will be integrated into a unified theoretical framework.

The Diamond Model is integrative

Integrative means that The Diamond Model is a product of a theoretical synthesis of concepts, research results, methods and techniques collected from numerous sources such as various branches of psychology and psychotherapy, cultural anthropology, biology, linguistics, philosophy and more. *Integrative* should be distinguished from *eclectic*, which means collecting such entities from various sources under a single roof, without attempting to amalgamate all of them into a new theoretical model.

The Diamond Model is linguistically uniform and rigorous

This means that all of the concepts discussed above have been explicated and reformulated in a single uniform, fairly accurate, theoretical language, purported to be universally applicable. All aspects of the clinical discourse

14 Theoretical and methodological foundations

can be expressed in the vocabulary and grammar of this language. This does not mean that adherents of The Diamond Model never talk about a case in their own natural language. It only means that the technical language of the model is available to them if and when they need or want to talk about a case in more rigorous, exact terms.

The language of The Diamond Model includes three sublanguages: the sublanguage of information processing; the sublanguage of cybernetics (the science of systems of regulation and control, using notions such as homeostasis, corrective feedback and feed-forward); and the sublanguage of semiotics (the science of signs and symbols). All the internal and external subsystems listed above can be reformulated in these three sublanguages. The readers will be familiarized with these sublanguages in Chapter 2.

The Diamond Model is explanatory

This means that the etiology of each case and the mechanisms of therapeutic change are explained by one single concept: *simplicity*. Loss of the previous simplicity of external and internal subsystems in times of change and crisis and abortive attempts to restore simplicity throw the subsystems off-balance, causing emotion dysregulation, loss of homeostasis and an inability to mobilize corrective feedback. The purpose of therapy is to create a new simplicity. The same notion, simplicity, is also the criterion for testing the relative validity of the interpretations given to particular cases.

The notion of simplicity comprises the following four subnotions: *comprehensiveness* (covering all the relevant data), *parsimony* (covering just the relevant data), *consistency* (covering the relevant data in a self-consistent manner) and *plausibility* (interpreting the relevant data correctly). These subnotions are further explained and discussed below and in Chapter 3.

As mentioned in the Introduction, *relevant data* are pieces of information that are needed for the proper functioning of the various programs. In The Diamond Model, well-functioning programs are defined as *programs that are cybernetically sound*; that is to say, programs that can mobilize corrective feedback and restore the lost homeostatic balance of the subsystem to which they belong.

Programs that, temporarily, do not process all and only the input or memory data in a consistent, plausible manner are not necessarily dysfunctional. They are dysfunctional if and only if they are chronically unable to enlist corrective feedback. For example, a quarrel between spouses does not necessarily indicate the existence of dysfunctional programs in the marital subsystem. Such a dispute can even make a positive contribution to the relationship between the members of the couple. The quarrel can bring the couple into contact with data that will help them get to know each other better and accept one another. It can lead to reconciliation and reduce the unpleasant emotional tension. Before and during the quarrel, the spouses have not processed all and

The Diamond Model – essentials   15

only the information related to their relationship in a consistent and plausible manner, but after the quarrel they will. Their marital programs are dysfunctional only if they lead to unstoppable escalation of the quarrel, resulting in ever-mounting animosity, aggression and emotional distress.

Likewise, programs of the subsystem of perception that fail temporarily to process all and only the information needed for a specific task are not necessarily dysfunctional. Consider, for instance, a child with attention deficit disorder, whose attention is diverted to stimuli that are irrelevant to a particular task and who has difficulty processing all the necessarily data. He can still make an effort to concentrate on the task and complete it successfully. His attention programs are dysfunctional only if no effort will overcome the diversion and the difficulty of concentrating, so that any task he undertakes will end in failure.

It should be added that the concept *dysfunction* depends on culture. What is considered dysfunctional in one culture may not be considered as such in another culture (see Chapter 5).

In Nonny's case, the simplicity of various programs was lost in situations of change and crisis, notably Tanya's immigration to Israel, the loss of Shalom's status as a soccer star, his addiction to soccer betting and Nonny's passage from childhood to adolescence. Each of these crises and changes caused loss of simplicity of previous programs. Tanya's immigration to Israel resulted in loss of the comprehensiveness and parsimony of her previous programs. She had to deal with language, culture, people and situations she had never encountered before. Because of her lack of familiarity with the social stratification of Israeli society, she was dazzled by Shalom's achievements as a soccer player and did not take into account his poor academic achievements. Shalom's termination of his soccer career caused loss of comprehensiveness, parsimony and plausibility of some of his previous programs. He did not prepare himself for the expected change, failed to take into account other options besides problematic clinging to the past and interpreted the end of his career as a fatal blow to his self-image rather than as part of a natural process of transformation and growth. Nonny's passage to adolescence also resulted in loss of the comprehensiveness, parsimony and plausibility of his previous programs. His previous over-attachment to his mother was no longer appropriate for his age. He failed to consider options for a fresh relationship with both his parents; that is, independent of the conflict between them and of his father's shortcomings. Nor did he consider the possibility of playing a positive and beneficial role in the family crisis. He also mistakenly imagined that his physical maturity would make him be like his father, with all the disadvantages that this would entail, such as getting entangled in his father's shady affairs and being rejected by his mother.

There are programs that have never been optimally simple in the above sense. Such programs are found, for example, in children whose information processing capacities in any of the internal subsystems are genetically

16 Theoretical and methodological foundations

impaired or in interpersonal subsystems (e.g. the parental one) that have been dysfunctional right from the very beginning. It would be wrong to assume that such programs are hopelessly dysfunctional. In most cases, the right therapeutic interventions can help them become simpler and improve their functioning.

The Diamond Model is technically eclectic

This means that the methods and techniques of intervention in each particular case may be borrowed from numerous sources: the main approaches to psychotherapy, traditional healing techniques, educational methods, etc., or made up by the therapist's creative mind. This eclecticism should not, however, be haphazard or random, but systematic, subject to the overall diagnostic evaluation and the ensuing therapeutic strategy and tactics. A classification of the types of change mechanisms employed by various traditional and modern therapeutic and healing techniques is proposed in Chapter 9. Once a therapist has understood what change mechanism would work for a therapeutic task, he or she can choose or invent a technique in which this change mechanism is activated.

A model vs. an idiographic theory

One should distinguish between a *theoretical model* and an *idiographic theory* (a theory about a single case). A model is a pool of concepts and generalizations (rules and laws, like the rules of grammar or the laws of physics) considered, temporarily, universally applicable, from which one draws the building blocks of an idiographic theory. An idiographic theory about a particular case is a formulation of the rules, or laws, underlying the case in hand. It is a set of hypotheses whose purpose is to explain the difficulties brought to therapy and the spontaneous or therapeutic changes the case in question has been or can be going through.

A theoretical model is, in some sense, an explanation of a certain type of behavior. Its explanatory power is derived from the fact that it exposes the essential properties and the universal rules governing the type of behavior under investigation. The model distils the constant and stable properties underlying what keeps changing and what depends on particular places and times.

The procedure of creating and validating The Diamond Model

Composing The Diamond Model has proceeded through the following stages: collecting; screening; explicating; formalizing and systematizing; creating a tentative model; deciding on a central explanatory principle;

The Diamond Model – essentials 17

formulating alternative idiographic theories for particular cases in terms of the tentative model; testing the relative validity of the alternative idiographic theories by the criterion of relative simplicity; choosing the simplest one; and revising and re-revising the tentative model endlessly.

Here are the stages in more detail:

(a) Collecting concepts, research findings, methods and techniques of intervention relevant to multi-systemic diagnostic evaluation and therapy from many pure and applied sciences and from therapeutic lore.

   As mentioned above, the sources are numerous: sociology and anthropology, biology, brain studies, neurology, cognitive science, linguistics, all branches of psychology in general and clinical psychology in particular, family therapy, management, education, social work and so on.

(b) Screening all these and selecting only the most robust ones.

   Admittedly, the subjective judgment of the developer of the model plays a crucial rule at this stage. This judgment, however, is informed by some general criteria, such as preferring concepts and methods supported by a solid body of accumulating research (e.g. attachment research) and preferring time-honored concepts, methods and techniques universally considered valid and useful. A detailed discussion of the specific entities chosen to be included in the integrative model is beyond the scope of this book.

(c) Explicating, formalizing and systematizing the ingredients selected to be included in the theoretical model.

   Creating an integrative model may be compared to preparing a cake. The cake is not just the sum of its ingredients: flour, oil, butter, sugar and so on. The ingredients are blended and transformed into something else. They become integral parts of a cake. The same applies to the various concepts, findings, methods and techniques incorporated in the tentative model. They are converted into ingredients of a new synthesis.

The philosopher Rudolph Carnap defined the concept of *explication* as follows: "Explication is the task of making more exact a vague or not quite exact concept used in everyday life or in an earlier stage of scientific or logical development, or rather by replacing it by a newly constructed, more exact concept" (Carnap, 1950, pp. 8–9). Many of the ingredients chosen to be included in the integrative cake, the tentative model, are vague, not quite exact, multiply ambiguous, belonging to an earlier stage of scientific development. So, they had to be explicated. The explication involved disambiguation, convergence of terminologies and clarification. To achieve this, the original concepts had to be formalized; that is, translated into a more exact and rigorous formal language. Furthermore, they had to be systematized, embedded in a system that explicitly exposes their interconnectedness. The formal language into which all these ingredients were translated was not arbitrarily chosen. Its choice had to be justified empirically. It had to be a valid representation of the original, pre-scientific concepts, covering roughly the same ground as the original concepts, but in a more exact, less vague or ambiguous manner.

The formal language chosen for explicating and formalizing the ingredients of the tentative model includes, as stated above, three sublanguages: information processing, cybernetics and semiotics.

An argument often put forward by adherents of the psychotherapy integration movement is that translating central concepts from different branches of psychotherapy into a single uniform, universal language is an unattainable task. It is therefore impossible, they claim, to create a universal grand theory of psychotherapy. Although some attempts have been made to integrate various psychotherapy models, notably Wachtel's integration of psychoanalysis, behavior therapy and systemic therapy (Wachtel, 1997), many believe that different models diverge in theoretical tenets, underlying assumptions, philosophies and epistemologies to such an extent that they cannot be combined into a single entity.

The theoretical and methodological issues involved in the question of theoretical and linguistic integration are too complex to get into here. I shall only say that explication in Carnap's sense does not require adherence to the original contexts in which the concept to be explicated has been used. An interesting attempt to reformulate Freud's psychoanalytic concepts in information processing terms is presented by Peterfreund (1971). A crucial step in the Peterfreund's work was replacing Freud's concept *mental energy* with the concept *information*. To my mind, Peterfreund's work is a good example of explication in Carnap's sense. It should be clarified that explication is not just replacing one jargon with another, equally valid, jargon. Nor is it substituting one metaphor for another, equally cogent one. When Peterfreund suggested to replace Freud's representation of the human psyche as a kind of hydraulic system with looking at it as an information processing system, he explicated a rather vague and obscure concept by substituting it with a more accurate concept that covers roughly the same ground as the original one.

(d) Formulating a central explanatory principle that explains the multi-systemic etiology of the difficulties brought to therapy and the power that brings about spontaneous and therapeutically induced change.

The main explanatory principle in The Diamond model is simplicity. As stated above, the central idea is that the best-functioning multi-system is the simplest one. When a multi-system loses its simplicity, becomes unduly complex, it gets out of control and becomes dysfunctional. In cybernetic terms, it loses its homeostasis, its internal balance, its ability to mobilize corrective feedback. The task of therapy is to help the multi-system to regain optimal simplicity so that its proper functioning is restored. The concept of simplicity and related concepts are discussed and explained in Chapter 3.

The Diamond Model – essentials 19

(e) Formulating a tentative multi-systemic model comprising the most robust concepts and generalizations that are considered, for the time being, universally applicable, in a rigorous, exact formal language.
(f) Applying the tentative model in formulating competing idiographic theories about particular cases. Each idiographic theory will be an attempt to capture the rules underlying the case, its recurring patterns.
(g) Testing the relative validity of the alternative idiographic theories by the criterion of simplicity, choosing the simplest (the most comprehensive, parsimonious, consistent and plausible) one.

Chomsky (1957, 1965) claimed that the grammar (set of rules) of a language cannot be revealed by a mechanical *discovery procedure* from a sample of linguistic productions (i.e. a mechanical procedure involving various statistical manipulations of the raw data). He also asserted that there cannot be any *decision procedure*, determining whether a proposed grammar is correct or not. There can only be an *evaluation procedure*, comparing different grammars proposed for the same data and choosing the most empirically valid one. One of the criteria applied in the evaluation procedures is relative simplicity. Such an evaluation procedure will be employed in testing the relative validity of alternative model-informed idiographic theories proposed for the same case.

Applying such an evaluation procedure in working with particular cases is important. All too often, clinicians speculate about the cases they treat without attempting to consider different interpretations or testing their relative validity. They fall in love with their idiographic theories and refuse to part with them. This can cause ineffective or even damaging therapeutic interventions.

Example 1.1 Nonny again

To clarify steps (f) and (g), let us return to Case 1.1 (Nonny). The building blocks for constructing an idiographic theory about this case would be taken from a multi-systemic model that is considered, tentatively, universal. At this stage, the model is still eclectic, not yet integrative.

The model would comprise concepts such as genetic syndromes, physical development, culture shock, self-image, object relations, attachment, social status, gender and age hierarchy in family structure, socioeconomic status, emotional concerns, conflicts and defenses, cognitive development and more.

The model would include generalizations (rules, laws) about interrelations between these concepts; for example:

"A negative parental role-model can delay age-appropriate psychosexual development and separation-individuation."

"A reversal of the culture-dependent hierarchy between spouses is likely to make it difficult for a child to identify with a same-gender parent."

20 Theoretical and methodological foundations

An optimally simple idiographic theory about this case must be comprehensive. It must consider all the relevant concepts and generalizations. An idiographic theory that ignores, for instance, the generalizations concerning the influence of the loss of Shalom's status in the family on Nonny's object relations development would prevent the therapist from fully understanding the case and from choosing an effective therapeutic strategy.

Such an optimally simple idiographic theory must be parsimonious. It shouldn't include dogmatic, far-fetched, redundant hypotheses irrelevant to the case and not backed by the available empirical data, such as, "Nonny, who had regressed to the Oedipal stage, locked himself in his room to protect himself from the danger of being castrated by his father." Such a hypothesis, which ignores, for instance, his fear of his mother's aggression and his rejection of her attempts to approach him, can lead the therapy astray, unless it is backed by strong supportive evidence.

The optimally simple idiographic theory should be consistent. It must not include self-contradictions such as, on the one hand, asserting that Nonny shut himself up in his room as an act of typical adolescent rebellion against his quarreling parents and, on the other hand, claiming that he shut himself up in his room because he was terribly scared of his mother's aggression. Such an inconsistency can confuse the therapist and lead him or her to adopt an inconsistent therapeutic strategy.

The optimally simple idiographic theory must be plausible. It should not include hypotheses that contradict the empirical data, such as that Nonny's symptoms are the result of social learning, which includes modeling.

(h) Concepts and generalizations (laws, rules) considered universal but found inapplicable to all cases will be taken out of the tentative model. Concepts and generalizations found applicable to all cases but not yet included in the tentative model will be introduced into the tentative model.

The qualifier *tentative* means that the model initially constructed is empirically based. It should be continuously revised as more and more empirical evidence from the diagnostic evaluation and treatment of particular cases is accumulated. An idiographic theory about each specific case is constructed, using the concepts and generalizations of the tentative model and formulating them in the model's formal language. As more and more cases are studied in this way, concepts and generalizations of the tentative model previously considered universal can be found to be local; that is to say, applicable only to some cases and inapplicable to other cases, due to individual or cultural differences between the cases. So, the concepts and generalizations no longer considered universal will be taken out of the tentative model, or will be left in the tentative model with the rejoinder that they apply only to cases of such and such a type. The opposite can occur too; that is, phenomena initially not included in the general model can be found

The Diamond Model – essentials 21

to be applicable to every case studied. Then, concepts and generalizations relevant to these phenomena will be formulated and introduced into the model. This process of revising and re-revising the model is, in principle, infinite.

Example 1.2 Autism

In some psychoanalytic models, autism had been explained as a response to environmental deprivation. For example, in 1944, the American psychoanalyst Bruno Bettelheim directed the Chicago-based Orthogenic School for children with emotional problems, placing special emphasis on the treatment of autism. Bettelheim believed that autistic children had been raised in unstimulating environments during the first few years of their lives, when language and motor skills develop. He saw parents being unresponsive to their child as an underlying cause of autistic behavior. Later studies showed that autistic children can grow up in perfectly normal parental environments and that the syndrome has genetic or congenital origins. So, initially a tentative model had considered the generalization that autistic children grow in a depriving environment universally applicable, but later empirical findings showed that it was not and should be taken out of the general model.

Later research results suggested that prenatal environmental factors and parental psychopathology were associated with the risk of autism. So, these causal factors were introduced into the general model.

Summary of Chapter I

This chapter lists the main attributes of The Diamond Model and details the stages by which this model has been constructed and validated. The Diamond Model is multi-systemic. The diagnostic evaluation and treatment of every case should consider factors belonging to various subsystems inside and outside of the individual. The Diamond Model is integrative. It synthesizes robust concepts, research findings, methods and techniques from numerous sources. This model is linguistically uniform and rigorous. Its ingredients have been explicated, formalized and systematized in a theoretical language comprising the sublanguages of information processing, semiotics and cybernetics. It is an explanatory model, in the sense that the multi-systemic etiology of each case and the mechanisms of spontaneous and therapeutic change are explained by the principle of simplicity, comprising the criteria of comprehensiveness, parsimony, consistency and plausibility. It is a systematically eclectic model, admitting any therapeutic methods and techniques of which the change mechanism fits into the multi-systemic diagnostic evaluation and the derived therapeutic strategy and tactics.

22 Theoretical and methodological foundations

The stages of constructing and validating The Diamond Model have been: collecting; screening; explicating; formalizing and systematizing; creating a tentative model; deciding on a central explanatory principle; formulating alternative idiographic theories for particular cases in terms of the tentative model; testing the relative validity of the alternative idiographic theories by the criterion of relative simplicity and choosing the simplest one; and revising and re-revising the tentative model endlessly.

Assignments

Here is a brief case description:

Case 1.2 Joyce

The characters:

Joyce, a happily married twenty-seven-year-old woman.
Ada, Joyce's thirty-three-year-old sister.
Kimberly, Ada's girlfriend.
James, Ada and Joyce's father.
Elisabeth, James' sister.

Joyce came to therapy when she was in her fourth month of pregnancy. In the first session with the therapist, she was in great distress, crying almost incessantly. Her complaint was related to Ada and Kimberly. Ada and Joyce's mother died of breast cancer when Joyce was five and Ada was eleven. Ada and Kimberly were urging Joyce to have a blood test to find out whether Joyce was a carrier of a genetic mutation that increased the probability of contracting breast cancer to 18%. If Joyce was found to be a carrier, then, Ada said, the probability of Ada having this mutation would be lower. After Joyce had refused to go through with this blood test, Ada and Kimberly began flooding her with text messages, formulated in aggressive, threatening language, demanding her to go through with the blood test.

James, the father, had been aloof, passive and absent before his wife's death and remained so after her death. The one who cared for the daughters was his older sister, Elisabeth. When Ada was thirteen, she became anorexic and was hospitalized for half a year. She insisted that the one who was really anorexic was not she but Joyce, although Joyce was not anorexic at all. Ada used to yell at Elisabeth that she should force Joyce to eat. When James told Ada that Joyce was not anorexic, she would curse him and refuse to be on speaking terms with him for months. Joyce was very good at school and Ada was a poor student. Ada used to blame Joyce that she "stole her [Ada's] brain" and that her father helped her to do that because

The Diamond Model – essentials 23

he loved Joyce and hated her, Ada. Elisabeth set Ada strict limits and she was the only one not blamed or attacked by Ada.

After Ada left home, she used to blame her father, James, for all her troubles. When he refused to accept the blame, she would break off all relationship with him. Only her girlfriend, Kimberly, could persuade her to resume her relationship with him.

Joyce said that one of the reasons why she found it difficult to resist the pressures Ada was applying on her was that she grew up without a mother and needed her older sister to be a mother substitute.

(a) Insert, in square brackets, the internal and external subsystems to which each part of this case belongs, as has been done with Nonny's case above.

(b) Indicate, with respect to each of these parts of the case, which of the following theories and therapeutic approaches can explain this part and provide effective treatment methods: Freud's psychoanalysis; object relations theory; attachment theory; classical conditioning; operant conditioning; social learning; CBT; structural family therapy; strategic or solution-focused family therapy; narrative family therapy; creative arts therapies. You do not need to have a deep knowledge of any of these theories to do this assignment. You may find a brief description of each of them on the internet.

(c) Try to reformulate, at this stage informally, five parts of this case in information processing and cybernetic terms.

Example:
"After Ada left home, she used to blame her father, James, for all her troubles. When he refused to accept the blame, she would break off all relationship with him."

Reformulation in information processing terms:

Input: James refuses to take the blame.
Internal processing: James doesn't care about me.
Output: Punishing James by cutting all ties with him.

Reformulation in cybernetic terms:

No corrective feedback. James' refusal to take the blame didn't make Ada change her mind. (Feed-forward, amplified deviation from homeostasis. Escalating the dysfunctional response.)

(d) Specify the main situations of change and crisis in the history of this case. Show how in each of these situations internal and external subsystems lost their previous simplicity (their comprehensiveness, parsimony, consistency or plausibility).

24 Theoretical and methodological foundations

Example:
Crisis situation: "When Ada was thirteen, she became anorexic. ... She insisted that the one who was really anorexic was not she but Joyce, although Joyce was not anorexic at all."

After Ada had become ill, the previous program regulating her relationship with Joyce lost its plausibility.

(e) The concept of *idiographic theory* is defined above as "a formulation of the rules, or laws, underlying the case in hand. It is a set of hypotheses whose purpose is to explain the difficulties brought to therapy and the spontaneous or therapeutic changes the case in question has been or can be going through." Write two alternative idiographic theories for the case of Joyce. Decide which of these two idiographic theories is simpler (more comprehensive, parsimonious, consistent and plausible). Explain your decision.

A classified list of publications

Person-centered psychotherapy

Axline, V. (1947). *Play therapy*. New York, NY: Ballantine.
Axline, V. (1964). *Dibs in search of self.* New York, NY: Ballantine.
Rogers, C. (1942). *Counseling and psychotherapy*. Boston, MA: Houghton Mifflin.

Multi-systemic psychotherapy and psychotherapy integration

Brooks-Harris, J.E. (2008). *Integrative multitheoretical psychotherapy*. Boston, MA: Houghton-Mifflin.
Casonguay, L., Eubanks, C.F., Goldfried, M.R., Muran, J.C. and Lutz, W. (2015). Research on psychotherapy integration: Building on the past, looking for the future. *Psychotherapy Research*, 25(3), pp.365–382.
Norcross, J.C. and Goldfried, M.R., eds. (2005). *Handbook of psychotherapy integration*. Oxford, UK: Oxford University Press.
Wachtel, P.L. (1997). *Psychoanalysis, behavior therapy, and the relational world*. Washington, DC: American Psychological Association.

Human information-processing

Ariel, S. (1987). An information processing theory of family dysfunction. *Psychotherapy, Theory, Research, Practice, Training*, 24(3S), pp.477–494.
Lindsay, P.H. and Norman, D.A. (2013). *Human information processing: An introduction to psychology*. New York, NY: Academic Press.

The Diamond Model – essentials 25

Cybernetics

Maltz, M. (2015). *Psycho-Cybernetics*. New York, NY: TarcherPerigee.

Semiotics

Cobley, P. and Jansz, L. (2014). *Introducing semiotics: A graphic guide*. London, UK: Icon Books.

Explication, systematization and formalization

Bandler, R. and Grinder, J. (1975). *The structure of magic: A book about language and therapy*. Palo Alto, CA: Science and Behavior Books.
Carnap, R. (1950). *Logical foundations of probability*. London, UK: Routledge and Kegan Paul.
Okasha, S. (2016). *Philosophy of science: A very short introduction*. Oxford, UK: Oxford University Press.
Peterfreund, E. (1971). Information, systems, and psychoanalysis. An evolutionary biological approach to psychoanalytic theory. *Psychological Issues* 7(1), pp.1–397.

Constructing and validating a theoretical model

Chomsky, N. (1957). *Syntactic structures*. The Hague, the Netherlands: Mouton.
Chomsky, N. (1965). *Aspects of the theory of syntax*. Cambridge, MA: MIT Press.
Jaccard, J. and Jacoby, J. (2009). *Theory construction and model-building skills: A practical guide for social scientists*. New York, NY: Guilford.
Richmond, S.A. (1996). A simplification of the theory of simplicity. *Synthese*, 107(3), pp.373–393.

Chapter 2

The sublanguages of information processing, cybernetics and semiotics

As stated in Chapter 1, all the concepts and generalizations of The Diamond Model, belonging to all the internal and external subsystems, can be explicated, formalized and systematized in a single uniform theoretical language that has three sublanguages: information processing, cybernetics and semiotics.

The sublanguage of information processing

In information processing terms, concepts and generalizations belonging to each of the internal and external subsystems are formulated as programs – human computer programs, so to speak. Each such program describes regular, patterned ways by which *input* information (data taken in from outside) or information retrieved from memory is processed. The processed information goes out as *output*. Processing means assigning the input or the retrieved information various meanings and functions, restructuring the information by dismantling it and combining its various pieces into a variety of structures. In the processing stage, various levels of arousal of emotions evoked by the information are identified. Human information processing programs are goal-oriented. They are designed to achieve specific goals (see Chapters 4 and 5).

The information processing programs included in The Diamond Model may be viewed as formulas applying not to specific items of information (constants), but to whole types of information (variables: X, Y, Z, etc.). When an idiographic theory about a particular case is constructed, these variables are replaced by constants (i.e. by the specific data of the case in hand).

Example 2.1 Jill

A generalization in the model:

If an input of type INP1 causes in the internal processing of person P1 a heightened level of a specific emotion EM1, then images associated in P1's mind with INP1 are more likely to be retrieved from P1's memory than images not associated with INP1 in P1's memory.

In an idiographic theory about a specific person, Jill, the variables of this generalization will be replaced by constants, for instance:

If Jill sees a neglected puppy and hears it whimpering desperately and this arouses in her intense emotions of pity and compassion, then associated memories (e.g. of babies in an orphanage she used to work in) are more likely to be retrieved to her mind than memories not associated with the neglected puppy (see Chapter 4).

Let us look at the following case:

Case 2.1 Linda

When Linda (thirty-two years old) was ten, her father disappeared without warning and then sent a message to Linda's mother that he had left her for another woman. For a full year, he didn't maintain any contact with Linda and her mother. A year later, he came back home. He had a heart condition and died of a heart attack some weeks afterwards.

Two months before the beginning of therapy Linda moved to an apartment together with her new boyfriend, Sam. When Sam was a little late coming home from work, Linda used to call him over and over again, worried. Usually, he wasn't available on the phone and wouldn't answer her text messages, because he was busy working. When he was back home, she would scold him and lecture at him for hours, threatening to leave home. This was a recurring pattern.

Let me try to analyze this case, still informally, in information processing terms. A more formal analysis will be attempted further on. The analysis will necessarily include some inferences and conjectures not manifest in the case report. The latter, however, are not pure speculations, but empirically testable, refutable hypotheses.

The input to which Linda responded was Sam's being late from work and failing to respond to her calls and text messages. Her output was calling or texting him obsessively and, later, when he was back home, scolding him, lecturing at him for hours and threatening to leave home. Obviously, her output was inappropriate and dysfunctional. Apparently, this output was triggered by traumatic childhood memories related to her late father that she retrieved and projected on Sam's behavior. In her internal processing, Sam's being late and unresponsive were associated with her father's disappearance without warning and leaving her mother for another woman. This was mixed with worry that Sam might have contracted a fatal disease like her father. She also thought that her father had returned not because he missed her and her mother, but because he was ill and could not rely on his girlfriend to take

28 Theoretical and methodological foundations

good care of him. She projected all that on Sam's input. All these pieces of information aroused in her turbulent emotions of anxiety, bitterness, anger and sadness. These emotions caused her to respond (output) in an obsessive-compulsive, uncontrolled manner.

Linda's internal processing of the input and her output were infested with information processing errors that in computer jargon are termed *bugs*. For instance, identifying Sam with her father and his misbehavior was totally wrong, based on no evidence whatsoever. Her output could only push him to break up with her – a self-fulfilling prophesy, or perhaps an unconscious wish.

A formal analysis, in the technical language of information processing, of Linda's internal processing and the bugs hosted in it will have several advantages over an informal analysis in common, natural language. A technical formulation in a language that is shared by other professionals reduces the likelihood that the analysis will be overly subjective and biased. A technical formulation will pinpoint the stages and parts of the information processing where the bugs reside and thus enable putting into effect therapeutic interventions of which the targets are clearly delimited, like a laser beam operation.

The following is a presentation of the main building blocks of the information processing language employed in The Diamond Model.

The vocabulary, grammar and syntax of the information processing language

Here is a semi-formal presentation of the information processing language that serves the purpose of explicating and formalizing programs in all the internal and external subsystems. A full formal elaboration of this language will require much more than its partial, simplified presentation below, but the following rudimentary presentation will suffice for our purposes here.

The language includes the following types of expressions:

(a) Expressions applying to sources and targets of information (written in capital letters):
INPUT, RETRIEVAL FROM MEMORY, STORING IN MEMORY, OUTPUT.

(b) Expressions describing internal processing operations:
connectors. Expressions connecting pieces of information (written in capital italics): *IF...THEN, AND, BOTH...AND, (EITHER) OR, AND/ OR, IS/ARE, NOT, ALL, EACH, BUT, SAME AS*.
operators. Expressions performing various types of operations on pieces of information (written in ordinary italics).

Here are the main types of operators:

Logical connoters:
IF X THEN necessarily Y.

Pragmatic connoters:
IF X THEN probably Y.

Denoters:
X denotes Y (i.e. stands for, signifies, represents, like a sign in a map that denotes a real entity in the terrain the map represents).

Effectors:
X is the cause of Y.

Qualifiers:
Operators of this type assign a piece of information a qualification, an attribute (e.g. *qualifying* an act as stupid).

Evaluators:
Operators of this type assess various properties of a piece of information that are likely to affect the self. The difference between a qualifier and an evaluator is that an evaluator is not just a general attribute assigned to the input or to data retrieved from memory, but an assessment of a possible impact of the input or the memory materials on the self (e.g. whether the input endangers the self, can benefit the self, etc.).

Arousers:
Such operators *arouse* or *reduce* the level of specific drives or emotions associated with certain pieces of information.

Purpose setters:
The operators listed above, in particular the arousers, induce the internal processing to *set itself a purpose* to be attained by the output.

Predictors:
These operators *predict* the expected results of the output.

To illustrate, let us go back to Case 2.1 (Linda). Below is a formulation of Linda's share of the difficulties (ignoring Sam's) in the above information processing language. It will be noted that some of the clauses in this formulation are not available in the manifest data of the case, but are inferred or hypothesized. This technical formulation is a part of an idiographic theory about Linda's case. It instantiates some concepts and generalizations explicated and formalized in The Diamond Model (e.g. transference). Like every idiographic theory, its validity can be tested by its relative simplicity (see Chapters 1 and 3).

30 Theoretical and methodological foundations

Linda's program with respect to Sam

INPUT
Sam is not responding to my calls and comes home late from work.

RETRIEVAL FROM MEMORY
My father left home suddenly when I was ten *AND* preferred another woman over my mother *AND* didn't maintain contact with us for a full year *AND* died of a heart attack shortly after he returned.

INTERNAL PROCESSING
I *BOTH qualify* my memorized father image as "not trustworthy", "betraying", "not loving", "not caring" *AND evaluate* my father's behavior as unfavorable with respect to myself, due to his *attributed qualifiers.*

RETRIEVAL FROM MEMORY
My father had a fatal disease when he was absent.

My father preferred another woman over me and my mother.

INTERNAL PROCESSING
My father's return home was *necessarily caused* by his illness, by his needing care and attention he couldn't get from the other woman *AND NOT* because he missed me and my mother.

The RETRIEVED memories of my father *arouse* in me again the intense unpleasant emotions I felt as a child: worry (about his health), sadness (about his having abandoned us and about his death), anger (about his having abandoned us) and fear (of being abandoned).

IF my father had the bad *qualities* I attributed to him *AND evaluated* them as unfavorable to myself *THEN probably* all men in an intimate relationship have the same *qualities* and should be *evaluated* in the same way. Sam has *probably* to be *qualified* as "not trustworthy", "betraying", "not loving", "not caring".

Therefore (an effector) I attribute to the INPUT the same set of *qualifiers* and the same *pragmatic connoters* that I attributed to my father *AND* I evaluate the input as unfavorable with respect to myself.

I do not attribute to the INPUT any other *qualifiers* or *connoters AND* I do *NOT* attempt to *evaluate* it in any other way.

Therefore (an effector) *IF* Sam doesn't respond to my calls when he is absent *THEN probably* he is *EITHER* ill *OR* has abandoned me, *probably* for another woman.

Therefore (an effector) the same unpleasant emotions (worry, fear of abandonment, anger, sadness) are *aroused* in me toward the INPUT as have been *aroused* toward the memorized information concerning my father.

To reduce the level of arousal, I *set as purpose* to be informed about Sam's state of health when he is absent *AND* to make sure he hasn't abandoned me.

IF this purpose is not achieved I should try again and again until it is achieved

AND when Sam is back, to reduce the level of arousal I *set as purpose* to prevent Sam from abandoning me and from being unfavorable toward myself.

I *predict* that *IF* I openly express my turbulent emotions and explain to Sam that he should always be available *THEN* he will *probably* understand, empathize with me, reform and change.

IF this *prediction* is refuted *THEN* I should continue until my purpose is achieved.

OUTPUT

Obsessive, worried calls when Sam is absent *AND* scolding him *AND* lecturing him for hours, threatening to leave home, when he is back.

Obviously, such technical formulations are much less readable and flowing than natural language formulations. Their advantages have been explained above. Such technical formulations facilitate the task of locating the bugs. This is elaborated below.

As stated above, the possibility of using such technical formulations does not rule out using natural, informal, everyday language in clinical discourse. The formal sublanguages introduced here are available, if required, in more thorough discussions, training or research.

Bugs as manifestations of lack of simplicity

The criterion of *simplicity* applies to two different but related entities: to the patterns of information processing produced by the clients and to the idiographic theory about these patterns composed by a therapist (or, for that matter, by a researcher). The latter application of simplicity is illustrated in Chapter 1.

The notion of simplicity when applied to the clients' information processing programs has the same subnotions as when it is applied to the therapist' idiographic theory, namely comprehensiveness, parsimony, consistency and plausibility. The clients' programs are goal-oriented. Linda (Case 2.1), for instance, processed the information in the ways she did in order to achieve certain goals with respect to Sam. When these subnotions of simplicity are applied to the clients' programs, they serve as criteria of

32 Theoretical and methodological foundations

a subsystem's proper functioning, its ability to achieve the desired goals. Accordingly, these subnotions, when applied to the clients' programs, can be defined as follows:

Comprehensiveness: clients' programs are optimally comprehensive if they can take in, retrieve, process and produce as output all the information needed for the proper functioning of the subsystem they are part of (e.g. the family subsystem).

Parsimony: clients' programs are optimally parsimonious if they do not take in, retrieve, process or produce as output information not needed for the proper functioning of the subsystem they are part of.

Consistency: clients' programs are optimally consistent if they do not include self-contradictions in the internal processing or output. Let us assume, for instance, that Sam explained to Linda that he could not answer her calls because he was busy working and she both believed him and didn't believe him and said so. In such a case, her internal processing and output would be inconsistent. Consistency in this sense is needed for the proper functioning of the subsystem to which the programs in question belong.

It is important to distinguish between inconsistency in the above sense and ambivalence or indecision. The latter are not necessarily dysfunctional. A person who feels ambivalent or indecisive can mobilize corrective feedback that will enable him to decide between options. Inconsistency as an aspect of lack of simplicity is closer to the notions of *double message* and *double bind* (see Gibney, 2006). It chronically prevents the person from interpreting the data consistently and producing consistent output.

Plausibility: clients' programs are optimally plausible if they interpret input or retrieved data correctly and if they make reasonable inferences based on given information. For example, Linda's interpretation of Sam's failure to answer her calls when he was busy working was implausible. An exception is culture-prescribed beliefs that seem implausible to outsiders. For instance, if in a certain culture illness is believed to be caused by evil spirits, this wouldn't be considered implausible in this model. Plausibility, as defined here, is needed for the proper functioning of the subsystem to which the programs in questions belong.

A program that is less than optimally simple is *bugged*. The bugs are given mnemonic names.

When a program is less than optimally comprehensive, it is infected with a *horse blinder* bug.

Sublanguages   33

When a program is less than optimally parsimonious, it is infected with a *fifth wheel* bug.

When a program is less than optimally consistent, it is infected with a *flip-flop* bug.

When a program is less than optimally plausible, it is infected with a *non-sense* bug.

Bugs are kinds of emotional defenses. When a battered wife blames herself or her husband's mother or a demon for his violence against her, she defends herself emotionally against the intolerable thought and feeling that she has been a helpless victim of senseless, wicked violence from the side of the man who is supposed to love and protect her. Her blaming programs, including self-blaming, are infected with a non-sense bug. It follows that bugs cannot be softened or removed just by trying to persuade the client to see reason. This goal can be achieved only if a way is found to reduce the intensity of the emotional distress that energizes the bugs.

As explained in Chapter 1, not every program that fails to process all and only the relevant information in a consistent and plausible way is necessarily bugged. It is bugged only if it has lost the ability to mobilize corrective feedback.

Let me ferret out the bugs in the above technical formulations of Linda's programs (Case 2.1).

Bugs in the input:

Horse blinders (lack of comprehensiveness). Linda did not take into account any relevant data beyond the fact that Sam didn't answer her calls or text messages. She did not consider the possibility, for instance, that he was probably delayed in his workplace or too busy to answer.

Bugs in the retrieval from memory:

Fifth wheel (lack of parsimony). Her childhood memories, though very vivid, were irrelevant to the present situation she had to deal with.

Bugs in the internal processing:
The following clause in Linda's internal processing has a number of bugs:

IF I *evaluated* the bad qualities that I *attributed to my father* as *unfavorable* with *respect to myself THEN probably* all men in an intimate relationship have the same *qualities* and should be *evaluated* in the same way. Sam has *probably* to be *qualified* as "not trustworthy", "betraying", "not loving" and "not caring".

34 Theoretical and methodological foundations

This part of Linda's program is infected with non-sense, because the generalization from the particular case of Linda's father to all men in intimate relationships is implausible. This part of the program is also contaminated with horse blinders because it ignores all the cases in which men in intimate relationship are trustworthy, loyal, loving and caring. This clause is not based on direct evidence. It is hypothesized. An alternative hypothesis would replace *probably* all men, etc., with *necessarily* all men, etc., which would be even more strongly improbable. In therapy, Linda could be asked by the therapist, directly or indirectly, to confirm or refute this hypothesis. The very fact that a detailed formulation includes such a hypothesis is useful for the therapy, even if it would eventually be refuted.

The clause "I do *NOT* attribute to the INPUT any other *qualifiers* or *connoters AND* I do *NOT* attempt to *evaluate* it in any other way" is infected with horse blinders. It rules out any other possible explanations of Sam's behavior beyond the one Linda was fixated on.

Likewise, the clause "*Therefore* (an effector) *IF* Sam doesn't respond to my calls when he is absent *THEN probably* he is *EITHER* ill *OR* has abandoned me, *probably* for another woman" is infected with non-sense and horse blinders.

The clause "*Therefore* (an effector) the same unpleasant emotions (worry, fear of abandonment, anger, sadness) are *aroused* in me toward the INPUT as have been *aroused* toward the memorized information concerning my father" is infected with a fifth wheel.

The following clause is contaminated with non-sense: "I *predict* that *IF* I openly express my turbulent emotions and explain to Sam that he should always be available, *THEN* he will *probably* understand, empathize with me, reform and change. *IF* this *prediction* is refuted I should continue until my purpose is achieved." This is a wrong prediction (non-sense), which is also infected with horse blinders, because Linda didn't consider other, adverse effects that her output could have on Sam.

As stated above, such a detailed analysis enables the therapist to pinpoint the foci of dysfunction and design more accurate therapeutic moves.

The sublanguage of cybernetics

Cybernetics is the science of control mechanisms. The function of such mechanisms is to keep a certain system (a machine or another device, a living body, a social unit such as the family, etc.) in a balanced, homeostatic, more or less steady state. The stock example of a control mechanism is the thermostat. We expect a heating device (e.g. an air conditioner) to be in a steady, balanced state, a state of homeostasis, to keep the room not too hot and not too cold and to make us feel comfortable. When the heat in the room surpasses a certain level, the thermostat reads this information and switches the heat-producing device off. Then the thermostat reads again the new temperature data and, if they are below a certain point, it switches the device on again. The information received by the control mechanism is called *deviation-correcting feedback*, or more briefly *corrective feedback*. It happens that the thermostat does not function well. In such a case, when the heat goes up above a certain degree, the thermostat reads this by mistake as a sign that the heat went below that degree. Then, instead of switching the device off, the thermostat lets the device increase its heat. The result is an ever-mounting heat. This is termed *deviation-amplifying feed-forward*, or more briefly *feed-forward*. The thermostat fails to fulfill its function of preserving the homeostasis, the balanced, steady state of the room temperature. It leads to ever-growing deviation from the desired homeostatic, balanced state.

The human information processing systems act like cybernetic control systems. This applies to all the internal and external subsystems listed in Chapter 1. The body is a cybernetic system, monitoring functions such as body temperature and blood pressure, hunger, fatigue and so forth. In the emotional subsystem, the "heat" is the emotions or, more accurately, pieces of information associated with particular levels of arousal of certain emotions. When the level of arousal is too high or too low, corrective feedback is mobilized to restore the balanced, homeostatic state. An elevated level of fear, for instance, activates fight or flight. A low level of fear mobilizes a rational evaluation of the situation (see Chapter 4).

The cybernetic mechanisms and the information processing programs interact closely. The internal processing of the input and the retrieved memories arouse emotions. If the emotions get off-balance and the information processing programs are not bugged, then the internal processing mobilizes corrective feedback and the emotional balance is restored. If, however, the programs are bugged, then the internal processing, like an out-of-order thermostat, is unable to enlist corrective feedback. Instead, deviation-amplifying feedforward is set into operation. The level of emotional arousal gets uncontrollably higher and higher. The infected information processing programs not only cannot stop it from continuing to deviate from homeostasis, they actively amplify the deviation.

To illustrate, let us go back to Case 2.1 (Linda). Imagine that Linda's program was not bugged. Sam's being late home from work and not responding to her calls would perhaps worry her a little, but she would reassure herself that he was probably busy working and calm herself down (emotion-balancing corrective feedback). She wouldn't call into question Sam's explanation when he was back home. This would quieten her down completely. On a deeper level, her bug-free program would perhaps help her reduce the level of emotional arousal with respect to her childhood memories of her father. She would perhaps see her father's behavior in a different light or apply to these memories

36 Theoretical and methodological foundations

the statute of limitations. In any event, she wouldn't generalize her view of her father and the associated emotions to all men, including Sam.

The above-listed bugs in Linda's program, however, mobilized feed-forward, deviation-amplification processes. Her emotions of worry, sadness and fear grew more and more intense. Her program not only did not include any operations that could enlist corrective feedback and restore the balance, but also did include operations that were bound to actively fan the flames. Her output was apt to invite responses from Sam that would only throw the system of their relationship more and more off-balance. The dysfunction caused by bugged programs can grow and grow like a snowball and spread to more and more subsystems like cancer.

Debugging a program, fixing or weakening its bugs, can therefore renew its ability to mobilize corrective feedback and re-establish homeostasis. This would restore its simplicity, its ability to function properly, in accordance with the client's goals. The types of therapeutic interventions aimed at removing or weakening bugs are termed *bug-busters*.

The sublanguage of semiotics

Semiotics is the science of signs and symbols, their meanings and uses. This science includes linguistics and theories applying to other systems of expression and communication, such as kinesics (the science of non-verbal behavior), proxemics (the science of the meaningful uses of personal and interpersonal space) and animal languages.

A semiotic description of verbal and non-verbal behavior is arranged on three *levels of analysis*: the *raw material* level, the *semantic* level and the *pragmatic* level.

The raw material level, as can be discerned from its name, is the level on which the entities whose function is to signify contents and convey inter-personal messages are described and analyzed. The entities on this level are concrete, tangible. They can be directly perceived by the senses. In spoken language, the raw material level is phonetics.

Raw material entities can be classified into *spatial, motional, vocal* and *tactile*.

Spatial. The manners in which behavior relates to the surrounding space have meanings and communicative functions. If in a play therapy session a child hides under a table, this means something. If he is running around the room, this means something else. If in couple therapy the partners face each other, this means something. If they face away from one another, this means something else.

Motional. Body and face motions and postures have significance. A girl in play therapy is running with spread arms. She is playing as if she is an airplane. A boy in play therapy stands still, erect. He is playing as if he is a robot. A man in couple therapy makes a threatening gesture toward his partner.

Vocal. The prosodic features of speech (stress, intonation, pauses, etc.), non-speech vocals and sounds have meanings and communicative functions. A boy in play therapy produces high-pitched voices. For him, this signifies a hungry chick. A girl in play therapy makes scratching sounds with a pencil. For her, it means a crow.

Tactile. The manners in which a person is touching himself, other people or objects have significance. If in therapy a client suddenly begins pinching her own cheeks, it can mean that she is angry at herself. If in couple therapy one of the partners is plucking a crumb out of her partner's shirt, this can mean that she still cares about him. A boy in play therapy is squeezing the head of a rubber doll representing a woman. This can signify that he is angry at his mother.

The semantic level is the level on which the *thematic and emotive meanings* of raw material signs are specified. Some such meanings have been mentioned above (e.g. running with spread arms on the raw material level signifies a flying airplane on the semantic level [thematic meaning]; pinching one's own cheeks signifies anger at oneself [thematic and emotive meanings]).

The pragmatic level is the level on which the uses of semantically interpreted raw materials are described. Their uses are the ways they are employed in verbal and non-verbal contexts in general and in interpersonal communication in particular. Some examples have been mentioned above. For instance, if in play therapy a boy is hiding under a table, this can mean, on the semantic level, "I'm hiding in a shelter." On the pragmatic level, it can have a message directed at the therapist, something like, "I'm protecting myself against your attempts to invade my personal space." Plucking a crumb from a partner's shirt can serve, on the pragmatic level, as a message implying, "Although we fight so often, I still care about you."

Key concepts in analyzing behavior on the pragmatic level are *presuppositions* about the addressee's intentions and aims and the *purposes* of the responder's messages, that take into account his or her presuppositions. In the picking the crumb example, for instance, the responder presupposes that her partner believes she does not care about him anymore. Her purpose is to reassure him that she still cares about him.

A *microscopic* semiotic analysis of behavior means dividing the behavior continuum on each of the three levels into units and combinations of units. A *macroscopic* analysis means revealing and formulating general recurring patterns behind the series of units. The patterns are constraints on the choice and combinations of types of units on each level and on the relations between the levels. Such patterns are analogous to the grammatical and syntactic rules of a natural language. Techniques of microscopic and macroscopic semiotic

38 Theoretical and methodological foundations

analysis of behavior in general and of play behavior in particular are proposed in Chapter 6 and in Ariel (1992, 1999 and 2002).

Here is an episode from the imaginative play of two six-year-old boys.

Observation 2.1 Liam and Andrew

Liam is making a stack of big pillows. He collects a large number of dolls representing "bad" animals and monsters. He is sitting down behind the stack of pillows, placing the collection of toys by his side. Andrew is standing at the other side of the room, holding a toy gun that can make flickering lights. Andrew is advancing slowly toward Liam, "shooting" his toy gun and making shooting sounds with his lips. Liam remains hiding behind the stack of pillows. He cannot be seen by Andrew. He places some toy animals and monsters on the upper part of the pillows so that they can be viewed by Andrew. He makes hoarse "monstrous" voices, whispering, "If he comes close, catch him and bite him!" Andrew is hollering, "Come out, you coward, and fight like a man!" He reaches Liam's pillows and starts pulling them. Liam is crying, "Don't!" Andrew obeys and stops. The same episode is repeated several times, with little variations.

A microscopic analysis of this play will identify various raw material units that carry meaning on the semantic level.

In Liam's play: stacking pillows (tactile), meaning "erecting a wall"; sitting behind the pillows (motional, spatial), meaning "hiding behind a protective wall, a fortress"; placing the toy animals and monsters on the upper part of the pillows (tactile, spatial), meaning "fortifying the wall with protective, threatening creatures"; making hoarse voices (vocal), meaning "the animals and monsters make menacing voices".

In Andrew's play: advancing toward Liam (spatial, motional), meaning "preparing to raid the fortress"; holding a toy gun and making noises (tactile, vocal), meaning "shooting"; pulling the pillows (tactile, motional), meaning "destroying the fortress".

On the pragmatic level, Liam's presupposition is that Andrew, as "the enemy", is preparing to invade the fortress. His purpose is to prevent him from achieving this. Andrew's presupposition is that the character played by Liam is afraid to confront him directly. His purpose is to persuade him to do so.

A macroscopic analysis on the raw material level will identify some general features of the types of raw material units employed by Liam and Andrew (e.g. close space vs. open space; mobility vs. immobility; an erect vs. a crouching posture; loudness of voice vs. low volume). General constraints on the co-occurrence of these general features will be, for instance, "close space, immobility, crouching and low voice go together, but these features do not go together with open space, mobility, erectness and loudness".

These general features on the raw material level signify general features on the semantic level. For example, the raw material features of Liam's play signify on the semantic level general features like "introversion", "passivity" and "low energy". The raw material features of Liam's play signify on the semantic level general features like "extroversion", "being active" and "high energy".

On the pragmatic level, Liam's play exhibits some features of interpersonal communication, such as "avoiding exposure", "preferring isolation and withdrawal", "avoiding confrontation" and "reliance on others for protection". Andrew's play manifests on the pragmatic level features of interpersonal relations, such as "not avoiding exposure", "seeking confrontation" and "relying on my own power".

Central pragmatic concepts are *proximity and control goals* and *plans to achieve these goals* (see Chapters 5 and 6). A macroscopic generalization on the pragmatic level is, for instance, "Liam's goals are to avoid proximity with Andrew and not to let Andrew control me". His plan to achieve these goals includes creating a territorial boundary, hiding, avoiding contact and warning the trespasser. Andrew's goals are "to seek Liam's proximity and control Liam". His plan to achieve these goals includes approaching, attacking, challenging and attempting to invade Liam's territory.

The language of semiotics and the language of information processing are at least partly inter-translatable. One may say that the language of semiotics refers to the structures of systems of expression and communication, whereas the language of information processing refers to the question of how such semiotic structures are set into operation in a person's cognition. In other words, the language of semiotics and the language of information processing refer to the same entities, but the former looks at them as static entities, whereas the latter looks as them as dynamic processes.

In semiotic terms, the output of a program belongs to the raw material level. The operators: connoters, denoters, effectors, qualifiers, evaluators and arousers belong to the semantic level as well as to the pragmatic level, because they expose the thematic and emotive meanings of the input and are also analogous to the person's presuppositions. Purpose setters and predictors belong to the pragmatic level. Connectors are equivalent to the syntactic relations among the various units on all three levels.

Returning to Case 2.1, Linda's program can be partly translated to the semiotic language as follows: her output (obsessive, worried calls when Sam is absent, scolding him, lecturing at him for hours and threatening to leave home when he is back) belongs to the raw material level. If described in more detail, it would include spatial, motional, vocal and tactile manifestations. These, plus the contents of her diatribe, would partly reveal the thematic and

40 Theoretical and methodological foundations

emotive meanings of her behavior on the semantic level. On the pragmatic level, her connoters, denoters, effectors, qualifiers and evaluators specify her presuppositions about Sam's input. Her purpose setters and predictors expose her proximity and control goals with respect to Sam and her plan to achieve her goal.

Summary of Chapter 2

This chapter presents the semi-formal theoretical language into which all the concepts and generalizations of all the internal and external subsystems can be translated. By being translated into this language, the concepts and generalizations are explicated, formalized and systematized. This theoretical language includes three sublanguages: information processing, cybernetics and semiotics. The information processing sublanguage reformulates all the subsystems as sets of goal-oriented information processing programs. These programs interpret and manipulate input information or data retrieved from memory, associate the processed information with emotions and produce output. Programs are optimally simple if they can process all and only the information needed for proper functioning in consistent and plausible ways. Loss of simplicity causes bugs to invade the programs: horse blinders (loss of comprehensiveness), fifth wheel (loss of parsimony), flip-flop (loss of consistency) or non-sense (loss of plausibility). The cybernetic sublanguage formulates the control mechanisms regulating and maintaining the subsystems' homeostatic, balanced state. Small deviations from homeostasis are kept within tolerable limits by corrective feedback. When programs are bugged, corrective feedback cannot be mobilized. Instead, uncontrolled deviation-amplifying feed-forward processes are set into operation. This causes multi-systemic dysfunction. The purpose of therapy is to restore the system's simplicity and therefore its homeostasis. This can be achieved by softening or removing the bugs so that corrective feedback can be remobilized. Since, however, the bugs are energized by unbalanced emotions, this goal cannot be achieved unless the relevant emotions are rebalanced. In the semiotic language, behavior is analyzed on three levels of analysis. On the raw material level are specified the observable spatial, motional, vocal and tactile features that signify themes and emotions on the semantic level. On the pragmatic level are analyzed the contextual and communicational functions of semantically interpreted raw material units. Microscopic semiotic analysis describes the units on each level. Macroscopic semiotic analysis describes the syntactic patterns of relations among groups of units. The semiotic language and the information processing language are partly inter-translatable.

Assignments

(a) Go back to Case 1.1 (Nonny). Reformulate a part of this case in information processing terms. Pinpoint those parts of the information processing programs that are bugged. Name the bugs. Analyze the adverse effects of these bugs in cybernetic terms (i.e. show how the bugs prevent mobilizing corrective feedback and initiate feed-forward, deviation-amplifying processes). Debug the program (i.e. suggest ways, based on your current knowledge and experience, to remove the bugs and rewrite the programs to allow them to mobilize corrective feedback in order to restore homeostasis).

(b) Do a microscopic and macroscopic semiotic analysis of the following observation. Use the analysis of Observation 2.1 (Liam and Andrew) above as an example of how to do it.

Observation 2.2 Dan and Ann

Six-year-old Dan and Ann play "forest animals". Dan is "the bear". He is standing on the floor. Ann is "the monkey". She is standing on a table signifying "a tree". She is hopping, making "monkey voices". Dan is saying, "Let's pretend the bear told the monkey, 'You should climb off this tree.'" Ann refuses. She says, "The monkey cannot climb down, because the tree is very tall and the bear can't help him because bears can't climb trees."

A classified list of publications

Human information processing

Ariel, S. (1987). An information processing theory of family dysfunction. *Psychotherapy, Theory, Research, Practice, Training*, 24(3S), pp.477–494.

Gibney, P. (2006). The double bind theory: Still crazy-making after all these years. *Psychotherapy in Australia*, 12(3), pp.48–55.

Lindsay, P.H. and Norman, D.A. (2013). *Human information-processing: An introduction to psychology*. New York, NY: Academic Press.

Peterfreund, E. and Schwartz, J.T. (1971). *Information, systems, and psychoanalysis: An evolutionary biological approach to psychoanalytic theory*. New York, NY: International Universities Press.

Cybernetics

Cliffe, M.J. (1984). The contribution of cybernetics to the science of psychopathology. *Kybernetes*, 13(2), pp.93–98.

Maltz, M. (2015). *Psycho-Cybernetics*. New York, NY: TarcherPerigee.

Semiotics

Ariel, S. (1992). *Strategic family play therapy*. Chichester, UK: Wiley.
Ariel, S. (1999). *Culturally competent family therapy*. Westport, CT: Praeger.
Ariel, S. (2002). *Children's imaginative play: A visit to Wonderland*. Westport, CT: Praeger.
Cobley, P. and Jansz, L. (2014). *Introducing semiotics: A graphic guide*. London, UK: Icon Books.

Simplicity

Richmond, S.A. (1996). A simplification of the theory of simplicity. *Synthese*, 107(3), pp.373–393.

Chapter 3

The synchronic and diachronic perspectives and the concept of simplicity

Loss of simplicity in periods of change or crisis

The multi-system and its subsystems can be looked at from a synchronic perspective (i.e. a cross-section at a particular point of time, usually the time of the onset of therapy) or from a diachronic perspective (i.e. from the past to the present). From a diachronic perspective, the history of the case is surveyed, its development, the changes it has gone through.

Bugs often invade the multi-system's programs in times of transition and crisis, such as passage from kindergarten to school, first child birth, death or serious illness, immigration, urbanization of a rural environment or loss of a job.

The simplest, well-functioning sets of information processing programs are at their best in familiar environments and in times of stability, when the rules of the game are clear to everybody. At such times and in such environments, people know how to read and interpret correctly the information they are exposed to and can respond to it in appropriate, functional ways. This applies not just to information of which the source is the external environment, but also to data that emerge from inside the person's mind and body (e.g. previously repressed memories or unfamiliar body sensations).

The external and internal reality of each of us keeps changing all the time. Every person is required from time to time to change and revise his or her goal-oriented information processing systems in order to preserve their simplicity – their comprehensiveness, parsimony, consistency and plausibility. If a person does not change his programs to adapt them to the changing reality, to the new, unfamiliar information he or she encounters, his or her programs lose their simplicity and bugs set in. Consequently, the programs lose their ability to enlist corrective feedback. Amplifying feedforward deviation from homeostasis escalates unabated, spreading to all the subsystems like a wildfire, like a snowball, like cancer. The main task of therapy is therefore to help clients adapt their information processing programs to the changing reality and restore their lost simplicity, or endow them with a new simplicity.

Restoring simplicity partially

The emergence of psychopathological symptoms and other problems presented to therapy are at least partly explained in The Diamond Model by the concept of *dysfunctional attempts to restore the lost simplicity of a set of information processing programs*. In periods of change and crisis, people face a new, unfamiliar, complex reality that cannot be fully and easily digested by the set of information processing programs previously available to them. Some of their information processing programs have therefore lost their comprehensiveness. The people are exposed to stimuli that cannot be assigned a reasonable explanation by the programs available to them. These programs have therefore lost their plausibility. A new experience is given contradictory interpretations, which call for incompatible responses by different sets of programs. Their previous sets of programs have therefore lost their consistency. New, unfamiliar information that previously was not available to their programs at all comes in. Their programs have therefore lost their parsimony.

Some people adapt themselves to such new circumstances in an adequate, appropriate manner. They vary their previous set of programs to fit them to the new situation. They add new programs or subprograms, so that the relevant novel information can be more easily digested. In this way, they restore the lost comprehensiveness of their information processing system. They get rid of previous programs that are no longer relevant to their new reality in order to make their new programs more parsimonious. They change programs to make them more plausible with respect to the new information. They remove contradictory or self-contradictory programs or modify them to settle the contradictions and in this way restore the system's consistency.

There are people, however, who are unable, in certain situations of transition or crisis, to introduce such adaptational changes to their information processing systems. They cannot fully restore their simplicity. Such failure of adjustment can be caused by programs that reside in the person's internal subsystems, in the nature of the external circumstances or in both.

Programs that make it difficult to create new simplicity can be found in any of the internal or external subsystems. In Chapter 4, it is stated that development along each of the developmental lines, in any of the internal or external subsystems, advances through the following dimensions: growth; internalization; complexity; coordination and integration; differentiation; depth of processing; concreteness vs. abstraction; constancy and stability; objectivity; and monitoring and control. A person who has not been able to reach an age-adequate level of development in any of these parameters in certain relevant developmental lines is likely to find it difficult to adapt to new situations. A youngster who has failed to attain an age-appropriate level of internalization of constant, stable parental figures and self-differentiation is apt to find it difficult to leave home and start an independent adult life. A person who has not reached a mature level of objective, as opposed to egocentric, thinking

Synchronic and diachronic perspectives 45

and is still unable to monitor and control his or her own thought processes and emotions will also find it difficult to adjust to unfamiliar situations.

Chapter 5 includes a discussion of cultural programs. Some cultures are more conservative and rigid in various respects than other, more flexible ones. Members of communities that belong to the former are likely to have a tough time trying to adapt to culture change or to encounters with unfamiliar cultures.

In Chapter 7, there is a general reference to *lacunae*, referring to an inherited or acquired lack of programs that are capable of processing data in an optimally simple manner required for adequate functioning. Lacunae stand in the way of adapting to new situations. A child who lacks basic social skills will not easily adapt to school.

External situations that make adaptation difficult are:

(a) The new information the person is faced with being of an extremely painful, stressful nature (e.g. in events such as sudden death in the family, war or exposure to extreme violence)
(b) The new data being totally incompatible with the information processing programs available to the person (e.g. when a person from a closed, isolated, extremely religious community has emigrated to a secular, open, modern urban environment)
(c) The person being flooded with a great amount of unfamiliar, extremely confusing and bewildering data

Often, when people are unable to restore the lost simplicity of their information processing system by changing it in the above-mentioned ways, they are reduced to making dysfunctional attempts to regain simplicity. The most common dysfunctional move is a desperate effort to maintain some semblance of simplicity by restoring only one or two of the four subcomponents of simplicity – only comprehensiveness, only parsimony, only consistency or only plausibility – while abandoning any attempt to re-establish the other two components. For instance, they restore only comprehensiveness and consistency but not plausibility, only plausibility but not consistency and comprehensiveness, and so forth.

Case 3.1 Daniel

Until the eighth year of Daniel's life, his family affairs had been carried on in fairly normal, smooth, congenial ways. Some of the information processing programs that regulated patterns of parental discipline were optimally simple and therefore well-functioning. These programs, internalized by both Daniel and his parents, were comprehensive (no horse blinders). They included rules covering almost all the characteristic

46 Theoretical and methodological foundations

situations in which exercising parental discipline was requires (e.g. when Daniel played ball in the living room, when he refused to go to sleep on time, etc.). The programs were plausible (no non-sense). Daniel's minor transgressions and their causes were correctly interpreted by his parents. Their disciplinary responses were correctly understood by Daniel as appropriate responses to his misbehavior. The programs were consistent (no flip-flop). His parents' disciplinary measures were more or less the same for similar transgressions. The programs were parsimonious (no fifth wheel). They did not include any irrelevant rules (e.g. rules related to behaviors of Daniel that had nothing to do with transgressions or rules applying to parental responses that were not direct reactions to Daniel's transgressions).

This optimally simple set of programs included also good cybernetic control mechanisms (i.e. clauses that made it possible to mobilize corrective feedback in cases of minor deviations from the balanced, homeostatic, steady state of relationships between Daniel and his parents). For instance, if Daniel's mother saw a broken vase in the living room and blamed Daniel for having played ball there, she would listen to his explanation and if he said that it was the cat that did it, she would believe him and would refrain from punishing him.

But then, when Daniel was eight, crisis befell his family. His mother discovered that his father had an extra-marital affair. His parents began going through extremely painful and aggressive divorce procedures. His mother projected her anger at her husband onto Daniel, whom she saw as "an exact copy of his father." She would scold Daniel and punish him for no reason whatsoever. But then she would be tormented by feelings of guilt and would refrain from scolding or punishing him even when he deserved it. His father took the opposite position. He identified with Daniel, formed a coalition with him against his wife and abandoned any attempt to set any appropriate parental limits, even when Daniel badly needed such limits.

Obviously, in these new circumstances, the previous parental discipline programs were no longer valid. These programs lost their simplicity. They were not comprehensive anymore, because various kinds of unfamiliar information could not be recognized by their various clauses (e.g. Daniel's mother's arbitrary penalties and his father's failure to set any limits). The same programs were not plausible anymore. It would no longer seem reasonable to interpret Daniel's mother's angry accusations and unjustified penalties as benevolent attempts to edify him. The programs were not consistent anymore, because Daniel had no way to assign any consistent interpretations to his mother's fluctuating between scolding and punishing him for no wrongdoing on his side and her fits of repentance.

What would Daniel do in this scenario? In all probability, in this critical, traumatic, disoriented time, he would be unable to fully restore simplicity by revising his previous programs and adapting them to the new family situation. In all likelihood, he would attempt one of the following among other dysfunctional solutions:

(a) Restoring comprehensiveness and consistency while forgoing plausibility. He would convince himself, for instance, that his mother was all bad, a witch, whereas his father was all good, an angel. He would interpret all evidence to the contrary as attempts to deceive and mislead him. Or, Daniel would persuade himself that both his parents were all good, angels. He would justify his mother's unfair treatment by leading himself to believe that he himself was bad, deserving to be punished and mistreated. His programs would then process all and only the relevant information in a consistent way, but they would be infected with the bug non-sense.

(b) Restoring plausibility and consistency, while giving up comprehensiveness. Daniel would ignore, for instance, all evidence that his parents' disciplinary policy had become inconsistent and unrelated to his own behavior. He would process only information bespeaking of a direct, sensible correlation between the nature of his own actions and his parents' reactions. Thus, Daniel's programs would become infected with the bug horse blinders.

Such partial attempts to restore simplicity would damage the previous cybernetic control mechanisms. Instead of mobilizing corrective feedback that makes it possible to create a new balance, a new homeostasis, the bugged programs would kindle feed-forward, deviation-amplifying processes that put the emotional responses off-balance. For example, if Daniel adopted the non-sense tactic of seeing his mother as a devil, a witch, and his father as an angel, this could reinforce his coalition with his father and his mother's image of him as "an exact copy of his father." This in turn would redouble her aggressive attacks on him. If he adopted the non-sense tactic of seeing his parents as angels and himself as bad, this could reinforce his father's overprotective coalition with him. This would make his mother feel even more guilty and therefore more unstable emotionally. Alternatively, Daniel could start misbehaving to prove that he deserved to be punished. Similar feed-forward, deviation-amplifying processes would occur if he ignored all evidence to the fact that he did not deserve to be punished.

These bugged programs could cause Daniel serious emotional and developmental difficulties. Seeing his mother as all bad could cause severe damage to his healthy attachment abilities. Seeing himself as all bad could injure his self-image and induce intolerable guilt feelings in him that would lower his self-image and make him prone to anxiety and depression. Disregarding

48 Theoretical and methodological foundations

his parent's fault could hamper his internalization of realistic identification objects.

The therapeutic strategy that should be adopted in such a case will attempt to remove or weaken the bugs in both Daniel's and his parents' programs and help them create a new simplicity by revising or replacing their previous programs, so that new homeostatic balance-preserving cybernetic control mechanisms are created. Since, however, the bugs are defenses against acute emotional distress, it would be impossible to soften or remove them unless a way is found to help the clients rebalance their bug-related emotions.

As mentioned above, simplicity can be lost not only when external reality has changed. In the following example, the simplicity of internal programs was lost as a result of an unexpected outbreak of serious illness.

Example 3.1 The Death of Ivan Ilyich

In this masterpiece by Lev Tolstoy, just as the official Ivan Ilyich had been promoted to an executive position and expected to enjoy a rewarding career, he suddenly contracted a fatal disease and had to quit his job. His attempts to cope with this crisis (loss of simplicity) included denial (horse blinders), blaming his family (fifth wheel) and believing that he did not deserve to suffer because he was a good man (fifth wheel and non-sense).

Summary of Chapter 3

This chapter deals with the etiology of dysfunction from a diachronic perspective.

The emergence of psychopathological symptoms and other problems presented to therapy is explained in The Diamond Model by the concept of dysfunctional attempts to restore the lost simplicity of a set of information processing programs. In periods of change and crisis, programs lose their simplicity and are unable to mobilize corrective feedback. If the previous programs are flooded with a great amount of unfamiliar, stressful information, the people involved, who are in deep emotional distress, are unable to adapt themselves to the new reality by changing the previous programs or developing new ones. They make dysfunctional attempts to regain simplicity by keeping or restoring only some of the four subcomponents of simplicity – only comprehensiveness, only parsimony, only consistency or only plausibility – while abandoning any attempt to re-establish the other components. Their partially simple programs are therefore bugged, infected with horse blinders, fifth wheel, flip-flop or non-sense. The bugs prevent the programs from mobilizing corrective feedback. Dysfunctional deviation-amplifying feed-forward processes are activated, spreading and infecting other programs in other subsystems like cancer. Various psychopathological syndromes and symptoms are generated in this way.

Assignments

Go back to Case 1.2 (Joyce). Show how in times of transition and crisis previous programs lost their simplicity and the people involved attempted to restore simplicity partially. Demonstrate how this dysfunctional strategy infected the programs with deviation-amplifying bugs. Consider the contributions of these bugs to the development of psychopathology. Use the analysis of Case 3.1 (Daniel) above as an example of how to do this assignment.

A classified list of publications

The concept of simplicity in the philosophy and methodology of science

Forster, M. (2001). The new science of simplicity. In: Zellner, A., Keuzenkamp, H. and McAleer, M., eds. *Simplicity, inference and modeling.* Cambridge, UK: Cambridge University Press, pp.83–117.

Ladyman, J. (2002). *Understanding philosophy of science.* London, UK: Routledge.

Part 2

The internal and external subsystems

Chapter 4

The internal subsystems

As stated in Chapter 1, every case brought to therapy, whatever the presenting difficulties, is multi-determined, a product of a dynamic interaction between programs belonging to different internal and external subsystems. In designing and carrying out the therapy, all these programs have to be considered. This is required not just in order to understand the case and know how to approach it therapeutically; it is also needed for creating a common ground between therapist and client and achieving good therapeutic rapport. Programs in each of the subsystems can be explicated, formalized and systematized in terms of the sublanguages of information processing, cybernetics and semiotics. The same languages can be used also to describe the dynamic interactions among the subsystems.

Many psychotherapy professionals would doubt the possibility of explicating concepts from such heterogeneous worlds into a single unified theoretical language. Can concepts of all the internal and external subsystems be translated into the same language? Constructs developed in the framework of various theories of personality and in disparate models of psychotherapy seem to be derived from assumptions about learning and development, the mind, human relations and the influence of the environment that are so incompatible that it is hard to imagine how they can be formulated in the same language. Still, the proof of the pudding is in the eating. Although full-fledged reformulations are not attempted below, the possibility of explicating programs of all the subsystems in information processing, semiotic and cybernetic terms is demonstrated to a sufficient degree.

Dysfunction in a subsystem occurs if bugs (horse blinders, fifth wheel, nonsense or flip-flop) have invaded one or more of its programs. The bugs interfere with the program's ability to fulfill its goals or tasks. Instead of mobilizing corrective feedback, the programs bring about deviation-amplifying feedforward that throws the program and other programs off-balance.

Each of the subsystems can be looked at diachronically, examining its development through the lifespan, from conception to death, and synchronically,

54 The internal and external subsystems

portraying the current developmental profile of each person in all the subsystems. Genetic processes work in combination with the organism's environment and experiences to influence the development of each of the subsystems.

Here is a brief description of some of the internal subsystems and their developmental stages. A full-blown presentation of all the subsystems is beyond the scope of this book. The descriptions presented here are unavoidably sketchy, an attempt to recap whole worlds in few words.

Developmental lines and dimensions

The concept of a *developmental profile* refers to the question of which stage of development a person has reached on each of the subsystems relative to age norms in the population he or she belongs to.

Development in each of the internal subsystems moves along *developmental lines*. The main developmental lines belong to the following categories:

(a) The body and its various structures and functions (see Mckinley and O'Loughlin, 2015)
(b) Cognitive and psychomotor development (the senses, attention, perception, memory, language, reasoning, creative thinking and psychomotor action)
(c) The emotions and their development
(d) Personality and social development (self and body image and concept; gender identity; object relations; attachment; basic trust; body and self boundaries; egocentrism vs. empathy and ability to see things from someone else's perspective; self-control; psychosexual development; and moral development)

The culture subsystem is both external and internal because it is shared by groups of people, but also internalized by each individual.

Development on all these lines in any of the internal or external subsystems advances through the following dimensions: growth; internalization; complexity; coordination and integration; differentiation; depth of processing; concreteness vs. abstraction; constancy and stability; objectivity; and monitoring and control. Not all the dimensions are relevant to every line, however.

Constancy and stability should not be confused with rigidity. For example, a person has acquired a constant and stable internalized self-concept. His or her self-concept is, however, complex. It has manifold differentiated, but coordinated and integrated, aspects. This person has reached a high level of self-development. He or she can, however, flexibly bring to the fore aspects of his or her self that are appropriate to particular situations, such as job tasks, family duties, recreation and dealing with difficulties.

A fairly accurate developmental profile can be obtained by formal standardized tests. A therapist who lacks expertise in administering such tests can still estimate clients' developmental profiles by observations and interviews.

Characteristically, the rate and pace of development is not uniform across the lines. A three-year-old baby can be very advanced in sensorimotor development but way behind in language development. A thirty-year-old woman can have a highly developed reasoning capacity but still be very dependent emotionally. A typical developmental profile has disparity in levels of development across the lines.

Space limitation prevents me from diving here into the depths of the ocean of learning and development theories, which seek to explain how and why development is happening in each of these internal and external subsystems. I will only refer to the fact that the various theories locate themselves on different places along the continuum between the poles of nature vs. nurture. Discussions about the extent to which knowledge is inherited or acquired from the environment are as old as Western philosophy. They are related to controversies concerning empiricism, pragmatism and phenomenology vs. rationalism and metaphysics. These controversies still nourish scientific efforts to understand learning and development in humans and animals. There are learning and development theories that are closer to the nurture pole (e.g. radical behaviorism; see, for instance, Johnson, 2013). Other theories are closer to the nature pole (e.g. Chomsky's theory of language and mind [2006]). Still other theories are placed somewhere between the two extremes (e.g. Piaget's genetic epistemology [1971], social learning theory [Bandura, 1976] and post-Freudian personality theories – ego psychology [see Blanck and Blanck, 1974], self-psychology [see Lessem, 2012] and object relations theory [see Scharff, 1995]).

One of the reasons for the skepticism of proponents of psychotherapy integration with respect to the possibility of achieving theoretical integration in the full sense of the word is the great difficulty in reconciling epistemologies that appear to be incompatible. I am not so skeptical. I believe that each of the theories of learning and development covers only a part of the puzzle. The various theories complement each other and, taken together, address the whole puzzle.

In my view, the process of learning and development and its outcomes are the products of dynamic interactions between all the external and internal subsystems. It would therefore be wrong to postulate a deterministic causal relation between any set of independent variables (e.g. a genetic imperfection, poor parenting, a vulnerable self or a traumatic event) and a set of dependent variables such as developmental fixation or regression, an unstable self, an inability to adapt to changing situations, etc. In order to understand the causes of normal or abnormal development or of considerable gaps in one's developmental profile, the mutual influences, case by case, of programs belonging to all these subsystems should be taken into consideration. In my clinical practice, I have met people whose life histories were full of deprivations, miseries and traumatic events, such as being abandoned as babies by their mothers and staying temporarily with various foster parents and institution where they had been neglected and abused. And yet, despite all these unbearable conditions, they eventually managed to develop an intact self and to lead a rewarding, self-fulfilling social, professional and creative life. Among the causes of these unbelievable developmental achievements were elements of various internal and external subsystems that compensated for their privations, such as inborn talents and skills, being charming, cunning and quick-witted, having qualities that helped them enlist the guidance and support of benevolent adults and having strong willpower. Such compensations can be reinforced in a gratifying therapeutic process.

It is important for a therapist to have at least rough knowledge of the developmental profile of each client involved in the therapy. Such knowledge is needed for deciding on suitable therapeutic interventions. Suppose, for instance, that a client is low on the lines of language and reasoning development, but high on the lines of sensorimotor, emotional responsiveness and non-verbal creativity. With such a client, a therapist will opt for non-verbal physical and expressive therapeutic techniques rather than for cognitive and verbal techniques. Or assume that a client is low on the line of basic trust, but high on the line of rational thinking and reasoning development. With such a client, the therapist will prefer to use techniques that appeal to the client's logic and self-interest over techniques that require intimacy and emotional openness such as psychodynamic or expressive techniques.

In the following sample of internal subsystems and their developmental stages, it will be briefly shown how each subsystem can be explicated, formalized and systematized in terms of the languages of information processing, cybernetics and semiotics.

The cognitive and psychomotor subsystems

These subsystems include the so-called higher mental functions: sensory reception, attention, perception, memory, conceptualization, language, rational and irrational reasoning, creative imagination, motivation and drives to act. All these can be expressed in information processing and cybernetic terms. Here is a sample.

Perception

The perceptual system of the brain is an information processing cybernetic system. It organizes and interprets sensory information. It enables individuals to see the world around them as stable, even though the sensory information

The internal subsystems 57

is typically incomplete and rapidly varying. It is cybernetic in the sense that it has an innate ability to correct errors in the ways sensory information is construed by internal processing. Imagine, for instance, that you happened to meet on the street a friend you had not seen for a long time. For a moment, you did not recognize him because he has grown a beard. But after a while you did recognize him. Your perceptual mechanism adjusted itself to his new look.

Corrective feedback doesn't work properly when a person is under the influence of fatigue, drugs, alcohol or other toxic substances or is in a psychotic state, a delirium or other such conditions.

The main information processing operators activated in perception are, according to Gestalt theory (Koffka, 2014), *grouping, closure, constancy* and *contrast effects*. Grouping is the tendency to perceive different sensory data as parts of the same configuration if the data are similar, close to each other in space or time, behave in the same way, are similar or overlap. Closure is the ability to finish up missing details to a complete configuration (e.g. given some details of a human face in a drawing, one can perceive the whole face). Constancy is the capacity to perceive various occurrences of the same configuration in different contexts as the same configuration (e.g. recognizing a familiar face as the same if seen from different angles or under different lighting conditions or identifying a tune as the same even if it is performed by different instruments). Contrast effects represent the influence of a perceived configuration on the way a contrasting configuration is perceived (e.g. a short person is perceived as shorter than she really is if standing by a tall person).

Failures to activate these operators can lead to ignoring information relevant to correct perceptions (horse blinders), to an inability to distinguish between relevant and irrelevant data (fifth wheel), to misperceptions (nonsense) and to confusion and inconsistent processing (flip-flop). Such failures can hamper learning, social development and many other functions. In some situations (e.g. driving), such failures can be dangerous.

These capabilities are innate, but they can be elaborated and refined by learning, experience and special training. There are also cultural and ecological differences in the ways these capacities are realized. In field work I conducted with Bedouin children in the Sinai Desert, I found that the children could not perceive patterns in simple drawings of stick figures. These children had no access to books, paper or writing tools. After some training, they identified a drawing of a triangle as "a woman". It is not impossible to see a Bedouin woman in a traditional attire as a triangular figure (Ariel, Sever and Kam, 1978).

Individual and cultural differences in perceptual capabilities have to be taken into account in choosing diagnostic and therapeutic techniques such as Rorschach, drawing and play with toys.

58 The internal and external subsystems

Perception capabilities develop along the following dimensions:

Growth and complexity. The ability to perceive more and more complex configurations of input stimuli, such as multi-dimensional figures or a complex musical harmony.

Coordination and integration. The ability to apply grouping capacities to input stimuli that are not obviously interrelated. For example, perceiving a show in which dancing, sound and lighting effects are harmoniously coordinated as a single whole.

Differentiation. The capacity to differentiate between configurations that are not easily perceived as distinct (e.g. figure from background).

Depth of processing. A higher level of development on the above dimensions requires deeper processing in the brain.

Concreteness vs. abstraction; constancy and stability; objectivity. A higher level of development on these dimensions is involved in the ability to achieve grouping and closure.

Monitoring and control. The ability to self-correct errors of perception.

Internalization. Perceived configurations become internalized as mental images. One of the reasons that preschool children need toys is that they haven't yet fully acquired this internalization capacity.

As stated above, therapists are advised to fit their therapeutic techniques to the client's level of development on each line, including the line of perception. For instance, if the client is low on the above-mentioned dimension of internalization of perception, the therapist is advised to apply techniques using concrete images that are directly available to the senses (e.g. pictures), rather than techniques that require the client to visualize such images.

Language

Language is the main instrument of thought, inner experience, expression and communication. There are other non-verbal systems with the same functions (e.g. visual – thinking and feeling in visual images, visual expression and communication; auditory – thinking and feeling in non-linguistic sounds, expression and communication through sounds and music; and movement – body language, touching, dancing). All of these are major tools in different genres of psychotherapy.

Verbal language (as well as the above-mentioned non-verbal languages) is a semiotic, information processing and cybernetic system. As a semiotic system, it organizes, categorizes and labels the chaotic jumble of human internal and external experience in conventional, rule-governed ways that are flexible enough to allow for productivity and creativity. Even the least structured uses of language, such as free associations, are rule-governed. The associated expressions share conceptual features.

The internal subsystems 59

Like every semiotic system, language is stratified on three level of analysis: raw material, semantic and pragmatic. As an information processing system, it takes in perceived information from the outer and inner worlds, processes it (puts it into words), classifies it, structures it, interprets it and sends it out (output) to one's inner self or to other people. As a cybernetic system, it is governed by rules and procedures that secure proper functioning, not letting bugs come in the way of achieving one's personal or interpersonal goals, such as understanding oneself or organizing one's thoughts in ways that enable the planning of effective actions (personal goals) or making oneself understood and approved by others (interpersonal goals). The grammatical, semantic, syntactic and pragmatic rules of language are very elastic and allow for endless variations. Minor deviations, such as the wrong choice of words and sentences that makes it difficult to be understood, can be put right by corrective feedback, provided by the user of the language or by the audience. This cybernetic mechanism does not work when the ability to think and talk in conformity with the rules is lost (e.g. in schizophrenic gibberish).

Although language is a conventional system, each cultural group has its own dialect, each small group such as a family has its own jargon and each individual has his or her own *idiolect*, his or her private language. A good therapeutic rapport depends, among other things, on having a common language between therapist and client.

The therapist is advised to at least partly learn and try to use the peculiarities of the client's dialect and idiolect. To achieve this, it is necessary to pay attention to the following things, among other:

(a) On the raw material level, the therapist should notice characteristics and peculiarities of speech performance that are either coded or not coded in the conventional linguistic rules (e.g. speed, volume, pitch, hesitations, stress and intonation, monotony vs. melodious speech, flat vs. effusive affect).

(b) On the semantic level, a therapist should pay attention to preferences for concrete vs. abstract concepts, detailed descriptions vs. generalizations, words, idioms and phrases that are used frequently, emotional expressions, dryness vs. florid images, metaphors and similes, register (everyday vs. literary speech), symbols, clarity and accuracy of expression, richness of semantic nuances, originality, correct use of words and slang. Some people, especially little children, use words not in their conventional meanings or invent words and give them their own idiosyncratic meanings.

(c) On the pragmatic level, a therapist is advised to ask him or herself the extent to which the messages conveyed by expressions are explicit or insinuated, expressed directly or indirectly. For example, a client can respond to a therapist's interpretation by saying, "Interesting," but what she implies is, "Rubbish!" A therapist should be attuned to the use of irony, ambiguity and double talk.

60 The internal and external subsystems

Other questions pertaining to the pragmatic level are: is the choice of words and sentences appropriate to the verbal and situational context? What are the presuppositions on which the clients base their expressions and what are their communicative purposes? For example, the client is telling the therapist, "I'm sorry I was late for the meeting. I'll make it up to you, I'll invite you to dinner." This expression is not appropriate to the situational context and is based on the wrong presuppositions about the therapeutic relationship and about who really missed something because of the client having been late.

What kind of non-linguistic knowledge is needed to really understand what the client is trying to say? For example, the client is saying, "The good old days are over." The therapist cannot guess what the client has referred to, unless he or she knows that the client is a fan of a certain soccer team that lost an important game the day before the therapeutic meeting.

Do the clients talk in a way they are not accustomed to just because they are speaking with a therapist (e.g. with exaggerated politeness and respect)?

The same semiotic aspects of the use of language can be reformulated in information processing terms. The task of the therapist is to detect bugs in the linguistic information processing programs that can lead to dysfunctional feed-forward instead of corrective feedback in various subsystems. Bugs in input and output that belong, in the semiotic language, to the raw material level can be the following:

(a) Failing to consider or wrongly predicting the impact on oneself and others of using certain modes of speech (horse blinders; non-sense); for instance, wrongly believing that talking in a loud voice with powerful accentuation can decrease one's own or the addressee's anger and distress (corrective feedback) rather than increase them (feed-forward).
(b) The way the message is transmitted on the raw material level does not reflect what the person really feels (horse blinders; e.g. a flat affect on the surface and a storm inside).
(c) Using superfluous modes of speech that reduce rather than enhance its effectiveness (fifth wheel; e.g. too many pauses to examine the impact on one's speech on the addressee).

Bugs in the internal processing of materials that belong, in a semiotic language, to the semantic level include:

(a) Generalizations instead of descriptions (horse blinders; e.g. saying, "Life is shit," instead of, "I had a terrible fight with my husband today").
(b) Not expressing what one wants to express (horse blinders; e.g. saying, "Everything is OK," instead of, "Nothing is OK").
(c) Florid images, metaphors or similes that are not suitable to transmitting the message (fifth wheel; e.g. saying, "I am drowned in a sea of grief,"

instead of saying, "I feel bad because I accidentally dropped my smart-phone into a toilet").

(d) Inability to distinguish between nuances (horse blinders; e.g. saying, "I sometimes act idiotically," instead of, "I sometimes act silly").

(e) Failure to be clear or accurate (non-sense; e.g. saying, "I am manic-depressive," instead of saying, "I am moody").

(f) Inconsistencies of meanings (flip-flop; e.g. saying, "My husband is a devil" once in the sense of "he is evil" and sometimes in the sense of "he is extremely talented").

Bugs on the pragmatic level include:

(a) Understanding ironic, sarcastic or other indirect expressions literally (non-sense, horse blinders).

(b) Double message or double-bind (flip-flop; e.g. a woman is saying to her lover, "I want you to love me and prove it by doing things for me, but I don't want you to do it because I told you. I want you to do it spontaneously").

(c) Assumed shared knowledge that the addressee doesn't possess (horse blinders; e.g. saying, "You know what Hamlet's dilemma was." The addressee doesn't know who Hamlet was nor what his dilemma was).

(d) Failure to take into account the status of the addressee or the personal distance between the participants (horse blinders, non-sense; e.g. a subject says to the King, "What's up, pal?").

Language, like most of the other subsystems, develops along the following dimensions:

> *Growth.* In the course of development, the vocabulary and the reper-toire of means of expression and rules on the raw material, semantic and pragmatic levels steadily grow. In the first five years, they grow dramatically.
>
> *Complexity and integration.* As the child's age advances, he or she can understand and produce more and more complex linguistic structures on the raw material, semantic and pragmatic levels. During develop-ment, the child's ability to create and understand rule-governed struc-tural and content relations among linguistic expressions on all three levels and between levels steadily grows. The developing person can decipher and produce connections among linguistic units that are not adjacent in a text and see and create relations between linguistic expressions and their non-verbal contexts.
>
> *Differentiation.* The child can produce and understand more and more distinctions between modes of expression on the raw material level, meanings on the semantic level and uses on the pragmatic level.

Concreteness vs. abstraction. The ability to express abstract ideas grows with the child's age.

Depth of processing. More fully developed capabilities on the above dimensions require deeper processing in the brain.

Objectivity, constancy and stability. In the first years of life, the child's use of language tends to be shifting, associative, private and egocentric. Piaget (2001) documented many such uses. As the child grows, his or her language becomes more governed by stable social conventions and rules, more in line with the physical and social reality.

Monitoring and control. With development, the child becomes more aware of his or her own linguistic productions and more able to monitor them and correct errors in the choice of words and sentences.

Internalization. The ability to generate inner speech, verbal self-reflection and soliloquy grows with the child's age.

As stated above, one of the considerations that should guide the choice of therapeutic techniques is the level of development of the client on each line. For example, the therapist must avoid using abstract ideas and subtle linguistic nuances with a client who is low on the dimensions of linguistic differentiation and abstraction.

The subsystem of emotions

Emotions are innate and therefore a part of the body system. The physiology of emotions is closely linked to arousal of the nervous system and to various body functions. This is confirmed by ample research evidence. Studies have shown that a baby is born with the following emotional repertoire: fear, anger, joy, surprise, sadness and disgust. With development, the emotions become more manifold, complex and refined and get associated with various cognitions, partly prescribed by culture and language.

In The Diamond Model, the subsystem of emotions is explicated, formalized and systematized as a cybernetic information processing system. Central to this representation is the concept of an *emotive*. An emotive is a person's central emotional concern; in other words, an emotion associated with a specific theme (e.g. sadness about the loss of a loved one, anger about being mistreated, joy about finding love). Some emotives are very common, perhaps universal (e.g. fear of death). Some are culture-specific (e.g. guilt for the violation of a religious commandment). Some last for a lifetime and some are temporary.

A more elaborate definition of the concept of an *emotive* is "a specific emotion correlated with a potentially infinite field of associations". Some associations in such a field are closer to the emotive's core and some are more and more peripheral or marginal. Associations closer to the core arouse more intense emotional responses. The farther the association from the core, the

The internal subsystems   63

less intense the arousal of the emotion. For instance, in the emotive "sadness about the death of a loved one", the acutest sadness is aroused by vivid memories of the death (the core). A fainter feeling of sadness is aroused by the loss of a cherished object.

Most of the higher mental functions – sensory reception, attention, perception, memory, rational and irrational thinking, creative imagination, motivation and drives to act – are sensitized to our emotives. In information processing terms, our brain gives the highest priority to processing data associated with the core of the field of associations of specific emotives, a lower priority to processing more peripheral data of such a field of associations and the lowest priority to data outside that field of associations.

In semiotic terms, emotives belong to the semantic level of analysis.

The cybernetic mechanism that controls and regulates the levels of emotional arousal works as follows: prioritized data belonging to the core of an emotive are processed by all the higher mental functions. In the internal processing, the operator *arouser* (see Chapter 2) amplifies the intensity of the emotion until it reaches an intolerable peak. Corrective feedback is mobilized to lower the emotional flames. This can be achieved in various ways. One way is shifting from the core of the emotive to its periphery. If the emotive is, for instance, "fear of being abandoned by a loved one", this is replaced by "fear of being ignored by the loved one when the latter is busy". If this doesn't cool the fear down to a sufficient degree, the mind is distracted to data outside the emotive's field of associations (e.g. to thinking about a soccer game). Various other soothing tactics are often employed (e.g. imagining that the loved one will never leave, thinking about reasons why he or she would prefer to stay or planning various measures [output] to be taken for making him or her stay). In more extreme cases, defense mechanisms such as repression or denial are activated. The level of emotional arousal is kept down for a while and then goes up again, and the cycle of arousal and cooling down repeats itself.

Case 4.1 Emma

Five-year-old Emma developed an emotive "sadness and anger with respect to the thought that her mother doesn't love her" after her mother had given birth to her sister. Her mind was focused on any sign of inattention on the part of her mother, especially when her mother was taking care of her sister (senses alertness, attention and perception). She would do everything to draw her mother's attention to herself when her mother was busy. When her mother was looking after her sister, she would pretend that something happened to herself to draw her mother's attention away from her sister toward herself. In her make-believe play, she repeatedly chose human-like or animal-like dolls that represented a mother, a daughter and a baby daughter. She would make the mother doll nurse the baby doll and abuse or neglect the older sister doll in various ways: ignoring her, refusing to give her food, throwing her away or locking her in a box. After bringing these acts of cruelty to an extreme peak, Emma would reverse the trend. First, she would make the older sister doll physically assault the mother and baby dolls. Then she would replace the mother doll by another mother doll that nursed the sister doll and refused to nurse the baby doll. After that she would get rid of the baby doll and make the mother doll hug the older sister doll and tell her how much she loves her. Later she would turn herself into a mother who takes good care of the baby. Having fulfilled her wishes in these ways and calmed herself down, she would go back to play moves expressing the core of her emotive.

These corrective feedback mechanisms do not work if the emotion dysregulation is too acute. Instead of corrective feedback, uncontrolled feed-forward takes place, an escalating deviation from homeostasis. Manifestations are a panic attack that cannot be stopped, tantrums, uncontrolled aggression, depression or the like. Such reactions can eventuate in extremely stressing situations, post-trauma, psychoses or disorders of the neurological and physiological mechanisms in charge of emotion regulation. Restoring homeostasis in such cases requires therapeutic interventions using emotion-balancing techniques (see Chapters 9 and 10) coupled, if necessary, with medication.

The above-listed developmental parameters apply to the system of emotions too.

Growth. With developmental progress, more and more emotives are created that relate to more and more thoughts and situations.

Complexity and integration. With the progress of development, more complex configurations of emotions, semantic contents and pragmatic functions are formed. A six-year-old child can already say, "When Mom is angry at me I become sad, but only a little, because I feel guilty. It is my fault." An adolescent might say, "I feel excitement mixed with anxiety."

Differentiation. With development, more and more emotional nuances are experienced, which can also be expressed verbally with various shades of meaning. A five-year-old girl can already say, "I don't love this boy, I just like him a little bit."

Concreteness vs. abstraction. The ability to be aware of and express abstruse emotions related to abstract concepts grows with development. Consider, for instance, this sentence: "When I feel connected to my spirituality, I am filled with a kind of serene elation."

The internal subsystems 65

Objectivity, constancy and stability. Over the years, children have fewer and fewer mood swings and less emotional lability. Their emotional responses are more stable and consistent, more related to clearly defined situations.

Monitoring and control. Children learn gradually to identify their own emotions and control them.

Internalization. Children gradually learn not to express their feelings in tears, tantrums and other kinds of emotional outbursts, but to hold the feelings inside.

Again, the choice of therapeutic techniques should take into account the level the client's development on each dimension. The therapist will avoid referring to subtle nuances of emotions with a client who is low on the dimension of emotion differentiation. With a client whose development on the dimensions of internalization of emotions and self-control is low, the therapist will opt for techniques requiring concentration and reflection rather than explosive expressive techniques.

Personality and social development

As stated above, the subsystems in this category are self and body images and concept; gender identity; object relations; self and body boundaries; basic trust; attachment; egocentricity and narcissism vs. empathy and prosocial attitude; reality testing; psychosexual development; self-control; and moral development. Below, only some of these subsystems are discussed.

I must note that each of the following concepts has been taken from very complex theories, most of which belonging to the psychoanalytic tradition. My purpose is not to propose a full explication of any of these concepts. The goal is only to demonstrate the possibility of reformulating them in the languages of information processing, cybernetics and semiotics.

Self and body images and concepts, self and body boundaries and object relations

Body image is the way a person imagines or visualizes his or her physical appearance. One's body image can be realistic or erroneous. It can be positive or negative. It has a significant impact on one's self-esteem.

Self-image is one's mental picture of oneself, not just of one's physical appearance, but also of the impression one makes on oneself and others (e.g. whether one is attractive or not so attractive).

Body and self-concepts are more abstract than body and self-images. They are not just mental images, but ideas and beliefs about the characteristics of one's body and one's personality.

The concept of *body boundaries* refers to subjective experience of the limits of one's own body in relation to other animate or inanimate objects. Where

66 The internal and external subsystems

does one's body end and another body begin? Is the limit of a body drawn at the skin or does it extend beyond its epidermis? The subjective experience of body boundaries affects the question of how far a person keeps away from bodies outside him or herself or how close he or she lets them get to his or her own body. It also affects the extent to which a person can distinguish between external stimuli and stimuli emerging from inside his or her own body.

The concept of *self-boundaries* refers not just to one's subjective experience of the limits of one's body, but also to the question of the extent to which one sees oneself as a differentiated entity, as an individual with an identity of his or her own. This has implications with respect to the question of how much a person is influenced by others and allows them to penetrate his or her own inner self.

The theory of *object relations* is based on the hypothesis that during life and especially in early childhood, a person internalizes parts of prominent figures in his or her life ("objects"), which become parts of his or her own inner experience and personality.

The notion of *self-object* (Kohut, 1971; Kohut and Wolf, 1978) refers to experiencing other people (objects) as integral parts of the self, from which the person derives narcissistic satisfaction.

The notion of *part-object* (Klein, 1935) refers to experiencing other people not as whole persons, but as partial entities whose function is to satisfy one's needs. According to Klein, an infant in the initial stages of his or her development sees his or her mother as a part-object (e.g. as "a feeding breast").

There are considerable cultural differences in the ways these phenomena manifest themselves in the life of the individual (see Chapter 5).

These notions are interrelated. It will be emphasized that these are not fixed monolithic entities. Every person has more than one self and body image and concept, some more dominant than the other. Some of these images and concepts are internalized objects. Each comes to the fore in different contexts. A man can feel powerful, competent and confident in business, but inferior and incompetent in intimate relationships. These notions can be explicated, formalized and systematized in semiotic, information processing and cybernetic terms.

In semiotic terms, patterns of a person's external vocal and verbal, spatial, motional and tactile behavior on the raw material level express semantic patterns constituting the distinctive features of his or her self and body images and concepts, of his or her self and body boundaries and of his or her internalized objects. On the pragmatic level, regularities in the ways the latter are used in verbal and non-verbal contexts are described.

In information processing terms, these subsystems can be explicated as patterns of internal processing of input data and data retrieved from memory, leading to characteristic patterns of output. Such patterns can be formalized in the vocabulary, grammar and syntax of the information processing language presented in Chapter 2.

The internal subsystems   67

Example 4.1 Jack's body image

A part of Jack's program:

I RETREVE FROM MEMORY an image of myself that I *qualify* as being fat.

INPUT people tell me that I am slim.

INTERNAL PROCESSING

They say this *because* they don't want to offend me (*effector*).

IF I am fat *THEN* I am *necessarily* repulsive (*logical connoter* and *qualifier*).

IF I see myself as repulsive *THEN necessarily* all people find me repulsive (evaluator).

I can't be *BOTH* repulsive in some respects *AND* attractive in other respects.

Arouser: mounting feelings of shame and self-hate.

OUTPUT

Avoiding the company of people.

In cybernetic terms, the information processing in this example is bugged and therefore unable to enlist corrective feedback. Jack cannot use the input as corrective feedback because his interpretation of the input is infected with horse blinders and non-sense. He believes people do not tell him the truth and therefore he filters out the input. He does this to preserve partial simplicity (avoiding flip-flop, inconsistency between the input and the way he qualifies the image he retrieves from memory). Maybe he was considered fat as a child. The clause, "*IF* I am fat *THEN* I am *necessarily* repulsive," and the following two clauses are also infected with horse blinders and non-sense. The output is infected with horse blinders, because Jack fails to take into account the results of his being aloof. People will stay away from him. He will see this as a confirmation of his erroneous belief that they find him repulsive. This will augment his shame and self-hate – escalating feed-forward.

The following case illustrates how the internalized self, part-objects and a lack of self-boundaries can be explicated in information processing term.

Case 4.2 Matthew and Olivia

Twenty-five-year-old Matthew met twenty-two-year-old Olivia at a party. She went home with him. Immediately after she had slept with him, he clung to her physically, refused to let her go home, claiming that he and she were twin flames, that they were one, that she was his other

68 The internal and external subsystems

half. Afterwards, he stalked her for days, until she was forced to file a complaint with the police. Matthew had the same pattern of behavior with other girls too. When he was six months old, his mother stopped breastfeeding him abruptly and placed him in a nursery school.

Here is an analysis of Matthew's information processing program:

INPUT
Olivia let me have physical contact with her willingly, without me having to work for it.

RETRIEVAL FROM MEMORY (unconsciously)
I am recalling my mother nursing and breastfeeding me.

INTERNAL PROCESSING
Olivia behaved this way *because* she wanted to nurture me (*effector, evaluator*).

In my unconscious memory: *IF* my mother was nursing and breastfeeding me *THEN* me and my mother were *necessarily* one unit, consisting of two complementary parts, the nursing and the nursed.

In my unconscious memory: my mother had *NO* other existence or role beyond being the nursing part of our unity.

IF my mother and I were the two sides of such a unity *THEN necessarily* my mother couldn't and wasn't allowed to separate from me and tear our unity apart.

Olivia having physical contact with me *denotes* my mother nursing me.

Arouser: bliss and peace of mind.

Purpose setter: continue the union with Olivia and not letting it fall apart.

INPUT
Olivia wants to go away.

RETRIEVAL FROM MEMERY (unconsciously)
In my unconscious memory: my mother tore me off her abruptly, stopped breastfeeding me and put me in a nursery school. She wasn't allowed to break our unity apart and have an existence or a role of her own (*evaluator*).

IF Olivia having physical contact with me *denotes* my mother nursing me *THEN necessarily* she isn't allowed to break our unity apart and have an existence or a role of her own.

Arouser: mounting frustration and anger.

Purpose setter: not letting Olivia go away.

Predictors: IF I cling to Olivia and explain to her that we are twin souls, she will stay and continue to be a part of our unity.

OUTPUT
Clinging, lecturing, stalking.

In cybernetic terms, this program is infested with many bugs that prevented Matthew from mobilizing corrective feedback and achieving his goal of developing a lasting relationship with Olivia. Instead, the bugs activated a deviation-amplifying feed-forward process that led Olivia to seek police protection against Matthew's stalking.

Some parts of this program and the bugs that invaded them explicate and formalize some concepts of ego psychology, self psychology and object relations theory. For instance, the clauses in which Matthew projected on Olivia his infantile memory of an inseparable unity with his nursing mother were a partial instantiation of the concepts *self-object* and *lack of body and self-boundaries*, the developmental stage preceding *separation-individuation* and *development of autonomy*. The clauses in which he projected on Olivia his babyish conception of his mother as having no existence or role beyond nursing him may be viewed as an instantiation of the concept *part-object*.

Attachment

The subsystem of attachment is closely related to the above-mentioned subsystems of object relations, self and body boundaries, basic trust, ego-centricity and narcissism vs. empathy and prosocial attitude and moral development. This subsystem, like the other subsystems, can be explicated and formalized in information processing, semiotic and cybernetic terms.

In information processing terms, in the earliest and later stages of life, a person takes in data from another person or from other persons (input) and evaluates them as more or less favorable with respect to his or her self. The data arouse in the person pleasant, positive emotions or negative, unpleasant emotions, according to the question of whether the input data are considered favorable or unfavorable with respect to the self. Input data that are evaluated as favorable with respect to one's self include reading one's needs and responding to them adequately, feeding and nurturing, protecting, assisting, enjoying one's company and one's achievements, providing pleasant holding and physical warmth, sexual satisfaction (later in adulthood) and more. The pleasant emotions aroused by input considered

70 The internal and external subsystems

favorable with respect to one's self cause one to set him or herself a purpose to seek proximity with the person or persons (or, for that matter, the animal or animals) who satisfy at least some of these needs (proximity goal). If these needs are met consistently over a long time, the person who enjoys them internalizes and stores in memory the images of the person or persons who have satisfied these needs, as well as the associated pleasant emotions (internalized objects). This facilitates the development of basic trust and self and body boundaries. The person feels the proximity of the persons he or she is attached to even if the latter are physically distant. With development, the person feels an urge to reciprocate with his or her attachment figures, to give and not just to take. The positive associations related to the attachment figure get generalized to other people. This assists the development from egocentricity and narcissism to empathy and prosocial attitude. It also promotes moral development.

If, however, the input is not considered favorable with respect to the self, it arouses unpleasant emotions and the person develops programs with protective proximity and control goals. Unfavorable input can be of various kinds: inability to read one's needs and respond to them adequately and consistently; neglect and failure to meet one's needs and to provide assistance and protection; aggression, abuse and exploitation; rejection and hostility; lack of appreciation of one's positive traits and behaviors; and more.

The research literature abounds with typologies of faulty attachment patterns, manifested in the person's inner experience and behavior (e.g. insecure attachment, ambivalent attachment, anxious-avoidant attachment, disorganized-disoriented attachment and so on) (see Wallin, 2015). I do not find these typologies particularly useful for clinical practice because attachment-related dysfunctional programs in each case rarely fit into any clear-cut type. In each multi-systemic idiographic theory, such attachment-related programs are the products of the mutual influences of many life events and of other programs and have their own idiosyncratic peculiarities.

Faulty attachment-related programs can be infected with bugs as manifested in the relationships not just with people who are the primary attachment figures. Such bugs are found, for instance, in Cases 1.2 (Joyce), 2.1 (Linda) and 4.2 (Matthew and Olivia), discussed above.

The attachment subsystem is cybernetic in the sense that it is flexible, allowing for considerable fluctuations within a basically stable relationship. For instance, the normal, positive attachment between a child and his or her main attachment figure (e.g. the mother) can survive situations in which the mother temporarily cannot be available and meet the child's needs. Corrective feedback will restore the basically healthy attachment. Faulty attachment, however, can start deviation-amplifying feed-forward that damages the relationship.

The self and body images and concepts, object relations, self and body boundaries and attachment develop along the same parameters as the other subsystems.

Growth. Over time, more and more components are added to the self and object images and concepts. Little children define themselves and others by few simple attributes, usually things they like to do or accidental properties: "I'm a boy"; "I like playing soccer"; "I have long hair"; "My dad has brown shoes." Older children already have richer definitions: "I am tall"; "I am Catholic"; "My mom is Catholic too. She was born in Ireland. She is very close to her sisters"; "I believe in God"; "I have a good musical ear"; "I have lots of friends."

With development, the person becomes attached to more people and the attachment is based on more and more types of mutual input. A baby is attached to a parental figure that mainly provides him or her with his or her basic physical needs. An older person can become attached to a person who gives gratifying intellectual stimulation, shares interests and engages in similar activities.

Complexity and integration. With the progress of development, more complex configurations of the components of self and others emerge: "I usually trust people, but if they betray my trust, I don't give them another chance"; "My dad loves my mom, but he is too immersed in his own affairs and doesn't give her enough attention." Attachment becomes multi-dimensional.

Differentiation. Over time, the self and body boundaries become more clearly delineated. Differentiation between various parts of the self and of objects develops: "I have my mom's temperament and my dad's spirituality." When a baby grows, he or she doesn't clings to his or her mother so much as earlier in his or her development. The person becomes more selective with respect to touching other people or being touched by them. Even identical twins can point out the differences between them. People can differentiate between other people they are attached to and know which traits and types of behavior they are attached to in different people.

Concreteness vs. abstraction. The ingredients of the conceived self and other and of the self-boundaries become more abstract: "I don't associate with people whose values are not humanistic." Attachment can be based on sharing abstract ideas such as a belief in goals that transcend one's self-interests.

Objectivity, constancy and stability. Self and object constancy develop. The child identifies him or herself and the significant others as the same over various times and situations. The self and object concepts become less shifting, more stable and permanent. The self and objects are defined by essential rather than by accidental properties. Permanent, life-long attachments develop.

Monitoring and control. As development progresses, the child knows who he or she is and who their significant others are. He or she understands his or

72 The internal and external subsystems

her autonomy and protects it. He or she is less influenced by other people's views of him or herself. One can consciously choose appropriate attachment figures and stay away from the wrong ones even if one finds them attractive.

Internalization. Over time, the self and object images and concepts become more internalized, experienced consciously or unconsciously inside the person. The attributes of others are assimilated by the person and become an inseparable part of his or her personality. One can remain attached to the internalized image of a person even if that person died many years before.

Again, the choice of therapeutic techniques should take into account the client's level of development on each dimension. For example, with a client whose level of development on the dimension of internalization of objects is low, the therapist will not use techniques that require the client to get in touch with his or her internalized objects by introspection. The therapist will prefer techniques that help the client internalize external objects.

Summary of Chapter 4

This chapter includes a brief synchronic and diachronic (developmental) survey of a sample of the internal subsystems that play roles in the etiology of cases brought to therapy and in the therapeutic process. Each subsystem can be explicated, formalized and systematized in the languages of information processing, cybernetics and semiotics, but such reformulations are not carried out fully in this chapter. The concept of a *developmental profile* refers to the question of which stage of development a person has reached on each of the subsystems relative to age norms in the population he or she belongs to. Development in each of the internal subsystems moves along developmental lines. Development on each line advances through the following dimensions: growth; internalization; complexity; coordination and integration; differentiation; depth of processing; concreteness vs abstraction; constancy and stability; objectivity; and monitoring and control. The subsystems surveyed in this chapter and their development along these dimensions are: perception and language of the cognitive and psychomotor subsystems; the subsystem of emotions; and the personality and social development subsystems – self and body images and concepts, object relations, self and body boundaries and attachment.

Assignments

(a) Try to show how the key features of the following cognitive subsystems can be explicated, systematized and formalized in the languages of information processing and cybernetics. (A deep knowledge of these subsystems is not required. You can base your answers on summaries found on the internet.) Show in what respects each of these subsystems develops along all the relevant dimensions. The subsystems relevant to this task are: sensory

The internal subsystems 73

reception, attention, memory, conceptualization and reasoning and creative thinking. You may use the analysis of the subsystem of perception above as an example of how to do this task.

(b) Try to show how the key features of the following personality development subsystems can be explicated, systematized and formalized in the languages of information processing and cybernetics. (Again, a deep knowledge of these subsystems is not required. You can get the essentials from summaries found on the internet.) Show in what respects each of these subsystems develops along all the relevant dimensions. The subsystems relevant to this task are: basic trust, egocentricity and narcissism, empathy and prosocial attitude, reality testing, psychosexual development, self-control and moral development. You may use the analysis of the subsystem of self and body images and concepts, object relations, self and body boundaries and attachment above as an example of how to do this task.

(c) Here is an excerpt of the play of a six-year-old boy in a play therapy session:

Example 4.2 Julian

Six-year-old Julian built a little house with two doors and two windows and said, "This is a secret house." Then he said he needed a cat. He only found a small toy dog in the room. He took the dog and put it inside the house. The therapist asked him who lived in the house and Julian said, "No one." Then he put the house on wheels and said that now it was a truck. The therapist asked him if anyone was driving it and he said, "No, it's a robot." He then took a toy helicopter and said, "The helicopter is the police and the robot car is the thief." The thief's truck picked up the dog. Julian said that the thief stole the dog. A minute later, he made the helicopter go down and said that the police were going to rescue the dog. But he did not make the police catch the thief and punish him. He then made the dog break down the sides of the house-truck and said, "Now it's a regular truck." He then went on to build a place for the dog to be.

Try to identify Julian's main emotives as reflected in this play session. Attempt to analyze the emotion regulation mechanism manifested in this play. You may use the analysis of Case 4.1 (Emma) above as an example of how to do this.

(d) Choose or create therapeutic techniques that would suit the levels of development on the developmental lines discussed or mentioned in this chapter to be used with the various cases described so far. Justify your choices.

74 The internal and external subsystems

A classified list of publications

Learning and development theories

Bandura, A. (1976). *Social learning theory*. Upper Saddle River, NJ: Prentice-Hall.
Chomsky, N. (2006). *Language and mind*. 3rd ed. Cambridge, UK: Cambridge University Press.
Johnson, J.M. (2013). *Radical behaviorism for ABA practitioners*. Cornwall-on-Hudson, NY: Sloan Educational Publishing
Piaget, J. (1971). *Genetic epistemology*. Translated from the French by E. Duckworth. New York, NY: Norton.

Developmental lines and dimensions

Sigelman, C.K. and Rider, E.A. (2014). *Life-span human development*. 8th ed. Boston, MA: Wadsworth Publishing.

Anatomy and physiology

Mckinley, M. and O'Loughlin, V. (2015). *Anatomy and physiology: An integrative approach*. 2nd ed. New York, NY: McGraw-Hill Education.

Cognitive development

Galotti, K.M. (2016). *Cognitive development: Infancy through adolescence*. 2nd ed. Los Angeles, CA: Sage Publications.
Piaget, J. (2001). *The language and thought of the child*. Translated from French by M. Gabain and R. Gabain. London, UK: Routledge.

Perception

Ariel, S., Sever, I. and Kam, M. (1978). Play in the desert and play in the town: On play activities of Bedouin Arab children. In: Schwartzman H.B., ed. *Play and culture*. New York, NY: Leisure Press, pp. 164–174.
Goldstein, B. (2009). *Sensation and perception*. 8th ed. Boston, MA: Cengage Learning.
Koffka, K. (2014). *Perception: An introduction to The Gestalt-theorie* [online] (first published in 1922). Available at: http://library.manipaldubai.com/DL/Perception_an_introduction_to_the_gestalt.pdf

Language and its development

Akmajian, A. and Demers, R.A. (2010). *Lingistics: An introduction to language and communication*. 6th ed. Cambridge, MA: MIT Press.
Hoff, E, (2013). *Language development*. 5th ed. Belmont, CA: Wodsworth.
Watzlawick, P. and Helmick Beavin, J. (1967). *Pragmatics of human communication: A study of interactional patterns, pathologies and paradoxes*. New York, NY: Norton.

The internal subsystems   75

Emotions

Ariel, S. (2002). *Children's imaginative lay: A visit to Wonderland.* Westport, CT: Praeger.

Ekman, P. (2012). *Emotions revealed: Understanding faces and feelings.* London, UK: Weidenfeld & Nicolson.

Feldman B.L. (2017). *How emotions are made: The secret life of the brain.* Boston, MA: Houghton Mifflin Harcourt.

Gross, J.J., ed. (2015). *Handbook of emotion regulation.* 2nd ed. New York, NY: Guilford.

Self and body image and concept and gender identity

Bracken, B. (1995). *Handbook of self-concept: Developmental, social and clinical considerations.* Hoboken, NJ: Wiley.

Cullari, S., Vosburgh, M., Shotwell, A., Inzodda, J. and Davenport, W. (2002). Body-image assessment: A review and evaluation of a new computer-aided measurement technique. *North American Journal of Psychology,* 4(2), pp.221–232.

Owen Blackmore, J.E. and Berenbaum, S.A. (2008). *Gender development.* Hove, UK: Psychology Press.

Object relations, ego and self-development

Blanck, G. and Blanck, R. (1974). *Ego psychology: Theory and practice.* New York, NY: Columbia University Press.

Greenspan, S.I. (1989). *Development of the ego: Implications for personality theory, psychopathology and the psychotherapeutic process.* Madison, CT: International Universities Press.

Klein, M. (1935). *The psychoanalysis of children.* London, UK: Hogarth Press.

Kohut, H. (1971). *The analysis of the self.* New York, NY: International Universities Press.

Kohut, H. and Wolf, E.S. (1978). The disorders of the self and their treatment: An outline. *The International Journal of Psychoanalysis,* 59, pp.413–425.

Lessem, P.A. (2012). *Self psychology: An introduction.* New York, NY: Jason Aronson.

Scharff, D.E. (1995). *Object relations theory and practice: An introduction.* New York, NY: Jason Aronson.

St. Clair, M. and Wigren, J. (2003). *Object relations and self-psychology: An introduction.* 4th ed. Boston, MA: Brooks Cole.

Body and self-boundaries

Mahler, M.S., Fine, F. and Bergman, A. (1975). *The psychological birth of the human infant: Symbiosis and individuation.* Reprint. New York, NY: Basic Books.

Attachment

Wallin, D.J. (2015). *Attachment in psychotherapy.* New York, NY: Guilford.

Empathy

Coplan, A. and Goldie, P., eds. (2011). *Empathy: Philosophical and psychological perspectives*. Oxford, UK: Oxford University Press.

Psychosexual development

Moll, A. (2016). *The sexual life of the child: A study into psychosexual development and the stages of puberty*. Charleston, SC: CreateSpace Independent Publishing Platform.

Moral development

Killen, M. and Smetana, J.G., eds. *Handbook of moral development*. 2nd ed. Hove, UK: Psychology Press.

Chapter 5

The external subsystems

Important life events

Important life events are events that cause loss of simplicity of information processing programs that belong to any of the subsystems. Such life events expose the information processing programs to new, unfamiliar input information. Important life events are not necessarily traumatic. They can be passage stages such as the transition from childhood to adolescence or from adulthood to old age, relocation, a new job, non-malignant diseases and so forth.

The external and internalized culture

In The Diamond Model, the concept of *culture* is explicated, formalized and systematized as a set of interactive semiotic, cybernetic, information processing programs shared by a particular social group and internalized by its individual members in the course of socialization. Since culture is both a social and a psychological entity, it may be viewed both as an external subsystem and as an internal subsystem. The size of the social groups whose members share their own culture ranges between whole nations or believers of the same religion and much smaller groups such as employees of a workplace, a tribe, an extended family or a nuclear family. In the current period, there are very few social groups whose culture belongs only to them exclusively. Most societies share cultural programs with other societies. Some cultural programs, however, are unique and exclusive to a particular social group.

Most therapists are not experts at cultural anthropology or sociology. They do not possess in-depth knowledge of any specific culture. Yet, they are usually required to treat clients of various cultures. Therefore, the way to become culturally sophisticated proposed in The Diamond Model is to acquire basic concepts and tools for analyzing any culture and to apply them in the therapeutic work, while trying to learn the relevant aspects of the client's culture from the clients themselves. Furthermore, to become culturally sophisticated, therapists should first be aware of their own culture. They can apply the

78 The internal and external subsystems

concepts and tools proposed below to achieve this. They should also beware of the following common errors:

(a) Ignoring the fact that most of the existing therapeutic models are ethnocentric, applicable mainly to some mainstream modern Western cultures in specific periods and locations. Some models (e.g. Bowen's [see Gilbert, 2011] and Boszormenyi-Nagy's contextual psychotherapy [2014]) explain mental problems as resulting from failure to achieve personal independence, individuation, autonomy and differentiation from parents or other figures. But such concepts are culture-specific, true only of Western liberal individualistic societies. In many traditional collectivistic societies, the opposite is true. Emotional difficulties result from physical and mental separation from the family and the community. Or, let us look at structural family therapy. The basic assumption behind this approach is that dysfunction is the result of an inability of the family structure to adapt itself to external or internal tasks and stresses or to developmental challenges. One should have no quarrel with either of these assumptions or with the techniques based upon them. Both, however, fail to take into account the following consideration: the same structural properties (e.g. *enmeshment, disengagement, triangulation*) can be normative and functional in one culture and non-normative and dysfunctional in another culture (see Minuchin, 1974; Falicov and Brunder-White, 1983). The same applies to *parentification, hierarchical reversal* or *incongruity* (see Nichols and Davis, 2016).
(b) Adhering to ethnocentrically biased generalizations and stereotypes (e.g. "Scandinavians are cold and Italians are warm").
(c) Confusing the diachronic and the synchronic perspectives. We tend to attribute to other cultures patterns of thinking and behavior that may have existed in the past but are no longer valid today. It is especially easy to make such a mistake when it comes to behavior patterns of a culture that appear to be identical to the past, but today have different meanings and roles. For instance, Halloween in many countries no longer has the role of commemorating the saints and martyrs. It has become a fun holiday for children and families.

Here are two cases in which the cultural naivety of the therapist led the therapy astray.

Case 5.1 Adelina

Adelina, a student from a traditional minority community in the USA, lived in student dormitories at the university in a big city. She became depressed and had trouble concentrating on her studies. Laura, a specialist in the university's counseling services, tried to strengthen her spirit and help her "find her own voice" by looking for her personal uniqueness, her strengths and abilities. She also encouraged her to participate in the student union's activities, go to parties and meet boys. For the next session, Adelina did not show up. After a while, she dropped out of the university and returned home.

Laura's approach to Adelina's case was ethnocentric. Adelina belonged to a collectivistic community in which the individual's identity and value were measured by his or her loyalty to the family and the community. Adelina's depression stemmed from her having felt lost when she was cut off from her family and community. Her newly acquired autonomy and independence were not empowering in the cultural world she had grown up in. She also felt guilty that she, as it were, betrayed her family and community by leaving them to acquire education that would put her above them. Partying and dating boys would be considered breaches of her society's cultural norms of modesty. Laura's therapeutic goals, derived from her modern Western cultural norms of individualism and free relationships between men and women, ran counter to Adelina's internalized culture.

Case 5.2 The Jaja family

A multi-problem family of an African origin, the Jaja family, lived in appalling conditions in an overcrowded apartment in a low-socioeconomic area of a big city. The family consisted of twenty people belonging to four generations. The difficulties included chronic diseases, psychiatric disorders, juvenile delinquency and drug addiction. Amanda, the social worker in charge of the case, attributed their difficulties to poverty and overcrowding. She recommended a rehabilitation program that included the following components: dividing the family into single-generation nuclear families; settling each nuclear family in a small, subsidized housing apartment; transferring elderly and diseased family members to rehabilitation institutions; placing some of the children in therapeutic boarding schools; delivering psychiatric treatment for mentally disturbed family members; and providing family therapy to each nuclear family separately.

The family refused the housing plan and agreed only when they learned that the neighborhood in which they lived was destined for demolition. All the children fled from the therapeutic boarding schools and returned home. The nuclear families who were housed in small apartments did not live in the apartments they received. All the family members returned to live in one of the small apartments where Adeesa,

80 The internal and external subsystems

the oldest woman in the family, a widow, lived with two of her unmarried daughters. Collaboration with the family therapists was just paid lip service. The family went back to the way it had been before the social and therapeutic intervention.

Amanda's rehabilitation plan was benevolent but ethnocentric. It was based on her own internalized Western cultural programs. She was not aware of the following cultural programs the Jaja family's life had been regulated by: first, the family belonged to a matriarchal society. The head of the family and its ruler was Adeesa, the oldest female. If Amanda had known that, she would have consulted with Adeesa before taking any steps. The basic family unit in that culture was the extended family, not the nuclear family. The natural habitat in that community was collective residence. They didn't consider overcrowding a problem. Physical and mental disorders were treated within the family by the elders, who were presided over by Adeesa, using traditional methods. The attitude toward institutions such as psychological and social services, which were perceived as part of the white establishment, was suspicious and hostile. The attitude toward juvenile delinquency was tolerant.

A central conceptual distinction in The Diamond Model is between *intra-culture dysfunction* and *inter-culture dysfunction*. The former refers to difficulties originating not from cultural change, crisis or an encounter with unfamiliar cultures, but due to difficulties resulting from internal pressures within a closed culture. People who grow up in a particular cultural group learn, in the course of their socialization, culture-specific ways to manifest their emotional distress. They also learn ways, dictated by their culture, to get help, recover, get rid of their symptoms and return to normalcy. The culture defines what are considered disturbances of thought, emotion or behavior, when and how such disturbances appear and how to treat them. Such disturbances and the ways they are dealt with constitute a cybernetic mechanism that allows for fluctuations within the balanced homeostasis, but also supplies corrective feedback that restores the status quo ante. The culture creates both order and disorder. An intra-culture disorder serves as a kind of pressure-relief safety valve. The social group allows for some flexibility in functioning according to the norms it dictates. Such flexibility guards these norms against shocks that can damage or destroy them.

A stock example of such cultural cybernetic mechanisms are the so-called *culture-bound syndromes.*

Example 5.1 Grisli Siknis

A syndrome called *Grisli Siknis* was documented in the Misikito society lining the Atlantic coast of Nicaragua and Honduras. In this social group, men are held to be unreliable and promiscuous. Young women are

The external subsystems   81

strictly chaperoned. The syndrome appears in young girls. The victim is running amok through the village into the bush, seducing young men on the way. The girl is cured by a group of men who catch her, tie her with ropes and perform various exorcism rituals (Dennis, 1985).

It would be wrong to assume that culture-bound syndromes exist only in "exotic" societies. Various phenomena in modern Western cultures seem to fulfill such cybernetic functions (e.g. violent behavior, not limitless, in soccer games, bars or dance clubs; reactive depression as a way of escaping pressures to compete and be successful, a "winner", and so forth).

We, as professional psychotherapists, are not usually required to treat symptoms of intra-culture dysfunction. Most cultures have the necessary and sufficient tools for dealing with such syndromes. Our professional expertise is, however, needed for treating inter-cultures dysfunction.

Inter-culture dysfunction results from changes and crises in the cultural programs of a community, as for instance in immigration, urbanization and industrialization or exposure to electronic media. In such transitions, the culture loses its simplicity. It is faced with unfamiliar information. Its previous programs cannot process all the data needed for achieving adequate functioning in the unfamiliar environment (loss of comprehensiveness). Some of its previous programs have become superfluous with respect to proper functioning in the new reality (loss of parsimony). Some of its previous programs do not include means for interpreting the new information correctly or in a consistent manner (loss of plausibility and consistency). The culture shock and the need to adapt to the new circumstances engenders considerable emotional distress in people who are equipped only with cultural programs that can no longer serve them well. As explained in Chapter 3, a characteristic coping mechanism in such circumstances is restoring simplicity partially. This causes bugs to invade the programs: horse blinders, fifth wheel, flip flop or non-sense. The bugs prevent the programs from mobilizing the corrective feedback needed to preserve homeostasis and to secure effective functioning. Instead of corrective feedback, feed-forward processes take effect.

The tasks of the therapist in such situations of inter-culture dysfunction is to mediate between the client's original culture and the new culture they should adapt to. They will be helped to get rid of the bugs and create a new, well-functioning simplicity. To achieve these goals, the therapist should be culturally sophisticated to a sufficient degree.

Case 5.3 Giorgi

When Giogri was thirteen, his family immigrated from a rural area in a non-Russian country in the former Soviet Union to a big city in the USA. They lived in a neighborhood inhabited predominantly by residents of their own community of origin.

When Giorgi was twenty-one, he was married off by his mother to Elene, a fifteen-year-old girl of the same extended family. Although Elene was below the legal age of marriage according to the law of the state, the marriage was an internal arrangement within the community.

On the marriage night, Elene refused to do her matrimonial duty. This was considered by Giorgi a violation of his honor. He beat her up. She complained about him to her mother, but the latter told her to go back to her husband and obey him. She did what her mother told her. When she was back, Giorgi cried and asked her to forgive him. That night, he was physically unable to have intercourse with her. But the next night he tried again to force her to have sex with him. She refused and he beat her up again. She decided to file a complaint about him with the police, but on her way there she changed her mind and went back to him.

After two years of marriage, Giorgi found out that Elene was cheating on him. He consulted with his co-workers in a shoe factory. His foreman advised him to talk to a social worker and try couple therapy. A colleague, not a member of his community, told him to divorce her. Another worker, a member of his community, told him to kill her to save his own and the family's honor. Giorgi began to oscillate obsessively between these three options. His internal conflict was so distressing that it developed into full-blown OCD.

Giorgi's is a case of inter-culture dysfunction. In the pre-immigration culture of his community, the rules, however cruel, were clear and usually obeyed by all sides. The programs were comprehensive, parsimonious, consistent and, from the viewpoint of the members of the culture, plausible. After immigration, the original culture lost its simplicity. In the Western urban culture, marrying a minor is, as a rule, forbidden. A mother does not choose a bride for her son who has reached the age of majority. Forcing a wife to have sex, especially if she is a minor, and beating her up if she refuses are considered punishable offenses. The mother of an abused wife does not usually force her daughter to go back to her abusive husband. A wife's refusal to obey her husband is not considered a violation of his masculine dignity or family honor. Family disputes are often settled by external agencies, such as social workers and family therapists. For a man who had used violence on his wife, it is considered normative to cry and beg her to forgive him in the new culture, but not in the old culture. A man whose wife cheated on him is not supposed to kill her in order to protect his own honor and the honor of his family. These unbridgeable disparities between the old and the new norms were extremely distressing for both Giorgi and Elene. His previous culture norms had lost their simplicity. To deal with these enormous disparities and preserve partial simplicity, both chose, in the terms of The Diamond Model, to preserve comprehensiveness, parsimony and plausibility at the cost of consistency. They didn't filter out any information, nor process any superfluous information nor misinterpret any information. But Giorgi was behaving inconsistently, fluctuating between the norms of the old culture and the new culture. The same applied to Elene. She disobeyed him, wanted to go the police and cheated on him, but remained his wife. Their programs were bugged with flip-flop. They could not mobilize any corrective feedback and engendered escalating deviation-amplifying feed-forward.

A therapist who tries to understand this case must be wary of ethnocentric interpretations based on the norms of his or her own culture rather than on those of the clients. For instance, the fact that Giorgi let his mother marry him off does not attest to his having a dependent personality, fixated on an early stage of attachment. In Giorgi's culture of origin, this was the norm – a man's mother choosing a bride for him even after he had passed the age of majority.

Types of cultural programs

The following types can help the therapist learn and interpret the client's culture in the framework of the diagnostic evaluation and the therapeutic process. Due to space limitations, only the category headings, subheadings and a few examples will be presented here, without attempting to translate them into the languages of semiotics, information processing and cybernetics. For a fuller, much more detailed presentation, the reader is referred to Ariel (1999).

Cultural programs are cross-classified below by their roles and by their contents, as displayed in Table 5.1.

Table 5.1 A typology of culture programs

Roles Contents	Axioms	Categories and relations	Explanations	Rules
Existential (ontological and epistemological)				
Ecological				
Identity				
Structural				
Functional				
Communication	.	.		
Coping and problem-solving				

84 The internal and external subsystems

The types of roles are:

Axioms. Basic tenets and beliefs, whose truth from the standpoint of the members of the culture is absolute, undisputable. An obvious example of such an axiom is the belief in the existence of God in the monotheistic religions.

Categories and relations. These are the ways in which the members of a culture divide and sort out the external and internal world and relate to these classifications. Examples of categories are: purity vs. impurity; the secular vs. the holy; belonging to us vs. aliens; and consanguinity (blood relationship) vs. affinity through marriage. Examples of relations are: crime and punishment; ruler vs. subjects; and teachers and pupils.

Explanations. How the members of the culture explain intra-psychic and external phenomena. For example, "Calamities are punishments from heaven for violations of religious precepts"; "The first woman was created from Adam's rib".

Rules. Laws that the members of the culture must abide by (e.g. incest taboos and kosher food laws in the Jewish religion). Values such as honesty and norms of behavior such as politeness are also rules.

The types of content are:

(a) *Existential programs*

These are programs that specify axioms, categories and relations, explanations and rules about the nature, meaning and purpose of reality. In terms of Western philosophy, such programs would be considered *ontological* (pertaining to the nature of existence) and *epistemological* (related to the nature and acquisition of knowledge).

Ontological existential axioms are, for instance:

God exists (axiom).

Reality doesn't exist as a separate objective entity. It exists only in our subjective mind (axiom).

There are two worlds: this world (our earthly existence) and the next world, the world to come (axiom, category).

Existence has no reason or purpose beyond existence itself (axiom, explanation).

Man has to justify his existence by his deeds (rule).

Epistemological existential programs are, for instance:

Knowledge exists independently of any human mind (axiom).

There is such a thing as a universal mind, which should be distinguished from particular minds (category).

The external subsystems 85

At birth, the mind is a tabula rasa. All knowledge is acquired by learning (explanation).

Man is forbidden from knowing the true nature of God (rule).

Human life has supreme value (axiom, rule).

Human life has no purpose or meaning beyond the subjective self. Each individual is responsible for his or her own life and is free to choose his or her own purposes (axiom, explanation).

It should be emphasized that ontological and epistemological tenets are not of interest just to philosophers and theologians. They are directly relevant to the mundane difficulties we as therapists need to diagnose and treat. Although the writings of philosophers and theologians express the most complex and profound, often obscure, thoughts, simplified versions of these have seeped into the minds of laymen and have become inalienable assets of cultural traditions. Every culture chooses its values and beliefs and develops programs that determine how they should be manifested in its members' lives, in what contexts and under what conditions. People born into a culture internalize these programs whether they are aware of it or not. The programs influence the ways they experience things, understand them and act upon them, as well as the ways in which they deal with difficulties and problems. There is a strong connection between the culture-bound ontological and epistemological axioms, categories, explanations and rules, the style of life of the members of a community and their emotional world. Psychopathological phenomena are highly influenced by such tenets. For instance, a person who believes in life after death is likely to cope with death, loss and bereavement better than a person who believes in the finality of death.

Cultures vary in in terms of their tolerance of open expressions of deviant beliefs and opinions.

(b) *Ecological programs*

This term applies to the relations between a community and its physical and human environment. For example:

Everything belongs to God (axiom).

Strangers are not allowed to trespass in a territory that belongs to a member of the culture (rules).

Foreigners are welcome to stay or even settle in a territory that belongs to members of the culture (categories and rules).

Shepherds and tillers of the soil are forbidden to share the same territory (categories and rules).

Sins cause rains to stop (explanation).

Natural calamities are caused by evil spirits (explanation).

86 The internal and external subsystems

Example 5.2 Malgri

In one of the tribes in Australia, there is a culture-bound syndrome called Malgri, manifested by headaches and a swollen abdomen. This happens to a person who has entered the sea after handling land food without washing his hands.

The locals attribute the syndrome to intrusion of a spirit considered to be a guardian of the sea. The victim's failure to wash his or her hands is taken to be an "insult to the sea". Offending the sea can also lead to disasters such as floods or attacks by dangerous sea creatures (Cawte, 1976).

Researchers attributed this syndrome to a violation of laws governing relations between residents of different territories: land workers and seafarers. The treatment involves tying a rope to the victim's foot with the other end of the rope dipping in the sea for the spirit to return to the sea through the rope.

This syndrome is clearly related to a violation of ecological rules forbidding the infringement of territorial rights.

(c) *Identity programs*

Such programs pertain to the distinctive features of the identity of human beings at large, in social groups, in families and as individuals. For example:

"God created man in His own image" (Genesis, 1:28) (axiom).
Buddhist vs. Hinduist (category).
A member of the community must not leave the community or convert to another religion (rule).
The identity of our cultural groups was created by our ancestors and must never be changed (explanation and rule).

There are conservative cultures of which the identity, as perceived by its members, is stable throughout generations. Usually, such cultures zealously protect their distinctive identity and prohibit their members from changing its manifestations (functional rules). There are cultures, however, in which the subjective identity keeps changing within a relatively brief period. Some ultra-Orthodox Jewish sects have preserved their self-perceived identity for many generations. In 1939, a group of Jews who lived in what was to become The State of Israel preferred to identify themselves as Canaanites (the pre-Jewish inhabitants of The Land of Israel), rather than as Jews.

In many cultures, identity perception is supported by constitutive myths, traditions and rituals (e.g. the Jewish Passover, the myth of the foundation

The external subsystems 87

of Rome [the tale of Romulus and Remus] and St. Patrick's Day, which commemorates the arrival of Christianity to Ireland and celebrates the heritage and culture of the Irish in general).

In most cultures, identity is externalized by dress style, symbols and patterns of verbal and non-verbal behavior. For example, many Muslim women wear a *hijab*, a head and chest cover, which in recent years has come to serve not just the purpose of declaring modesty, but also the purpose of demonstrating religious and cultural identity.

In culturally sensitive therapeutic work, we must be careful not to relate to the clients our own preconceived notions about their cultural identity. We must find out how they themselves define their own cultural identity. For example, it is considered politically correct to refer to black Americans as African Americans. But some black Americans who were interviewed said that they found the title "African American" offensive and preferred to call themselves blacks or just Americans.

(d) *Structural programs*
Programs of this type pertain to the structure of the individual, the family and the community.

Here are some types of structural programs found in various cultures.

Chakras. In Hinduism, Jainism and Buddhism, *chakras* are believed to be the meeting points of non-physical energy in various parts of the body (categories, relations).

In some polytheistic societies, the family structure in humans is considered a mirror image of the family structure of deities (axioms, explanations).

In some societies, slaves and even domestic animals are viewed as members of the family that enjoy various rights (categories, relations, rules).

Collectivism vs. individualism. Is the structure of the family and the tribe considered an aggregate of individual identities or one unit, a whole in which individuals are integral parts (categories, relations, rules)?

Homogeneity vs. heterogeneity. Is the family or the social group diverse in terms of race, ethnicity and religion or homogeneous (categories, rules)?

Endogamous vs. exogamous marriage. Is marriage limited to spouses from the extended family or the community? Is it acceptable to find partners outside the community (categories, relations and rules)?

Patrilocal, matrilocal or neolocal habitation. Is a married couple expected to reside with the husband's family of origin, the wife's family of origin or in a new location (categories, relations, rules)?

Patrilineal descent (through the father's line) vs. matrilineal descent (through the mother's line). Is the family membership of an individual derived from and is recorded through his or her father's lineage or through his or her mother's lineage? In many societies, the line of descent prescribes various

88 The internal and external subsystems

rights, such as inheritance, ownership of property and mutual obligations of family members (categories and relations, rules).

Hierarchy, proximity, division of labor and roles (categories, relations, rules). The nuclear family, the extended family and the tribe (categories). Professional guilds (categories).

Monogamy vs. polygyny (one male has more than one female mate). Polygyny is attributed to scarcity of adult males, to preference for males with a better genetic makeup or better resources (categories and explanations). Polyandry, in which one female has more than one male mate, also exists in various parts of the world.

Structural rigidity vs. flexibility. In some cultures, the roles, functions and proximity-hierarchal relations between members of the family and of larger social groups are determined by strict, unbending rules. Other cultures allow for a great deal of flexibility in all these respects.

(e) *Functional programs*

These are programs that regulate the general and everyday functioning of members of a particular social group.

Here is a sample of the areas of life that are guided by functional programs.

Physical and spiritual purity vs. impurity. Various customs of ritual purification are practiced in many cultures. The aim is to purify the body and the soul prior to a particular type of activity, especially prior to the worship of a deity (categories, rules).

Mutual responsibility. In various cultures, certain types of people are supposed to be responsible for the life and wellbeing of other types of people. The obvious examples are parents and children, armies, police, social services and members of the nuclear or extended family or the clan. A less familiar example was the responsibility of seniors to their vassals in feudal societies (categories, rules).

Vendettas or blood vengeance in various traditional societies. This custom is related to the concepts *the honor of the family* and *the sanctity of marriage.* In some societies, it is the duty of specific males to take revenge on anyone who has harmed or insulted the family. Unacceptable sexual behavior of women in the family, such as a prenuptial sexual relationship or sexual infidelity, is also considered in some societies as a violation of family honor to be redeemed by the execution of the transgressor, usually by male members of the family (rules).

Tolerance of premarital or extramarital sexual behavior of women or even of Platonic relationships with men varies considerably across societies. The same applies to behavior or clothing considered provocative or immodest (rules).

The external subsystems   89

- Cultures differ in terms of the degree of tolerance of what is viewed by mainstream Western cultures as deviant, unacceptable behavior (e.g. physical, verbal and sexual aggression) (rules).
- Cultures vary with respect to what is considered acceptable and appropriate in interpersonal relations (e.g. openness, intimacy and physical touch even between spouses, parents and children and all the more so between friends, acquaintances and strangers) (rules).
- Cultures are diverse in attitudes toward respect for personal space and other individual rights (rules).
- There are culture-specific programs that regulate everyday family and social life: daily agendas and daily rituals, division of labor and duties, household chores and decision-making in financial and other matters. Other programs regulate the year's calendar – holidays, ceremonies, rituals and days of rest (rules).
- Cultures vary in terms of the rigidity in which functional rules are imposed. In the early days of the Israeli Kibbutz, all the members were expected to conform to self-imposed uniform daily routines. The present-day kibbutzim allow much greater flexibility and free personal choice in this respect.
- There are societies that explain some of their functional programs by attributing them to binding world orders prescribed by deities (axioms, explanations, rules). In the book of Genesis, Chapter 3, The Lord God said to Eve, "…Your desire shall be to your husband, and he shall rule over you…"

(f) *Communication programs*

The programs that regulate the patterns of verbal and non-verbal interpersonal communication vary from culture to culture. Communication programs differ in various respects, such as the typical roles of communication (sharing concerns, expressing feeling and emotions, exchange of ideas, achieving interpersonal proximity or control and managing daily affairs); amount of communication; the ratio of verbal vs. non-verbal communication; directness vs. indirectness of messages transmitted; candor vs. falsity of messages; and formality vs. informality according to interpersonal distance and social status.

The communication rules in certain cultures are uniform and standardized. They are not subject to free choice. There are acceptable and unacceptable modes of communication with parents, siblings, superiors and subordinates. Other cultures are more flexible in this respect.

(g) *Coping and problem-solving programs*

People of diverse cultures do not conceive of their problems and difficulties and do not attempt to solve them in the same ways. Cultural groups differ in what they identify as symptoms or problems, in how

90 The internal and external subsystems

they define and explain the difficulties and in their modes of coping and help-seeking. Psychopathological phenomena, personal and interpersonal crises and other difficulties are culturally relative both in their root causes and in their outward manifestations. In culturally competent psychotherapy, it is crucial for the therapist to learn the culture-specific tenets of the clients in these respects and take them into account in designing and carrying out the therapy by choosing the right therapeutic techniques and communicating with the client in their own terms.

Here are some examples of cultural differences in these respects:

(a) What are considered problems that need to be treated? Therapists and clients can differ in what they see as psychological symptoms or situations of stress and crisis. What therapists regard as psychopathological symptoms (e.g. hallucinations and delusions) are not necessarily seen as such by members of the culture, who view such phenomena as normal or as manifestations of spirituality.

Violence against children can be viewed as a family problem by the therapist and as normative behavior by the family.

Conflicts between a teenage girl and her parents, however, can be seen as normal by the therapist and as a serious family problem by the family.

(b) Attribution of meaning and functions to psychopathology.

Traditional Chinese medicine is based on the concept of two opposing elements in cosmic forces – *yin* and *yang* – which must remain in harmony to produce health. Mental and physical troubles are explained as manifestations of disharmony between these two forces.

In different societies, traditional explanations offered for psychopathological symptoms include, for instance, possession by spirits, insects or animals, soul loss and religious transgressions.

(c) Indigenous helpers.

It is important for a therapist to know which people and social bodies the clients are accustomed to consult with: elders of the family, religious leaders, shamans, etc. It is advisable to cooperate with these traditional figures.

(d) Coping strategies.

People of diverse cultures employ different strategies for coping with life's difficulties and situations of emergency and crisis. In some cultures, the main strategies are resourcefulness, active search for solutions and thinking "outside of the box". In other cultures, the strategy is resignation, fatalism, religious and cultural conservatism, family and community solidarity and messianic beliefs in future redemption.

(e) Methods of healing.

Every culture has its own procedures for curing mental illness, deviant behavior and personal and interpersonal problems. Native therapeutic methods are organic to the culture, systematically interrelated with other aspects of the culture.

According to Lutz (1985, p.70), feelings in some Chinese subcultures are private and embarrassing events that are best not to be explored. Therapy cannot use insight and analysis of feelings with these clients. Therapy should concentrate on improving the client's social functioning and instructing him or her not to neglect his or her duties toward family and society.

In working with Giorgi (Case 5.3), the therapist found that insight and interpretations simply did not work. She had to use concrete images and physical means such as talismans, amulets, suggestion and physical action. For example, she told Giorgi to cover the left part of his forehead and temple with the palm of his left hand and the right part of his forehead and temple with the palm of his right hand. She told him that the right side of his head was the traditional side and the left side was the modern one. She asked him to feel which palm was getting warmer. He said the left one. She said, "OK, your brain chose the modern side, so listen to it and behave toward your wife according to the advice you get from your 'modern' friends who do not belong to your community."

(f) What works.

Cultures differ in the ways they explain the causes of therapeutically mediated recovery. Some cultures attribute recovery to divine intervention. Some other cultures attribute improvement in one's mental condition to understanding the causes of the difficulty. Other cultures ascribe the recovery to social support. The way a therapist understands the change mechanisms that have brought about the improvement can be very different from the ways the clients understand them. The therapist is advised not to argue with the clients and not to reject their own explanations.

It is important to emphasize again that all aspects of culture discussed above are crucial with respect to our understanding and treatment of the difficulties we are supposed to deal with. This applies even to the most abstract concepts of culture; for instance, ontological axioms such as "existence has no reason or purpose beyond existence itself". Such an axiom can affect the ways a client deals with life crises (e.g. reacting with fatalistic resignation).

Case 5.4 Avner

Avner, twenty-five, grew up in an Orthodox Jewish family in a village populated by a closely knit, ethnically homogeneous religious community in Israel. During his adolescence, he attended a religious boarding school, where the daily agenda was organized around religious studies and routine religious services. Avner was a pensive person with a tendency to delve into philosophical questions. Toward the end of his high school studies, he began to doubt the existence of God and the obligation to observe His commandments. After he had completed his compulsory army service, he moved to Tel Aviv and completely abandoned religion. He enrolled in the university to study sociology and anthropology. In Tel Aviv, a big city in Israeli terms, he felt lonely and lost. He couldn't concentrate on his studies. He would walk along the streets, feeling that the world was empty and pointless and that words no longer had any meaning. He felt that he had lost his identity and was unable to form a new identity. He was seized by obsessive suicidal thoughts. He suffered from strange physical pains and sensations without a medical basis. He began to look for answers in philosophy books, Buddhist writings and New Age texts, but was disappointed that he did not find answers to questions he could not even formulate.

Avner began therapy with me after his mother had urged him to do so. During the meetings, he spoke, among other things, about life in the yeshiva high school. The rigid daily agenda, independent of his free will, demanded obedience, but was in a way convenient and reassuring. He admired the authoritative headmaster, an imposing figure, who was very different from his own father, whom he saw as weak and indifferent. He was wrapped in the warm collective social life of his peers. The spiritual world on which he was brought up included the following ontological axioms and explanations: G-d is all knowing. He knows and controls every minute detail of each individual's inner and external life. Life has reasons, meaning and purpose, determined by G-d, even if humans do not always understand them. Jewish people must observe G-d's commandments, as written in the Torah and in later religious scriptures.

In terms of The Diamond Model, Avner's social, ecological and cultural programs had been optimally simple before he lost his religious faith and moved to Tel Aviv. After these transitions, their former simplicity got lost. The previous programs were no longer comprehensive. They did not cover the isolated social life in the city, the lack of daily routines and clear rules, the absence of parental authority figures and the lack of religious belief. In Avner's new life, these previous programs became infected with horse blinders.

The previous programs lost their parsimony. They were not relevant to Avner's new life. Continuing to adhere to them would infect Avner's current programs with fifth wheel.

His previous religious beliefs were not valid anymore. They became infected with non-sense.

The loss of simplicity caused Avner severe emotional distress. The loss was so massive and pervasive that he was almost totally deprived of his cultural and personal identity, hence his feelings of emptiness, meaninglessness and loneliness that explain his suicidal thoughts. His pains and physical sensations were the results of somatization of his emotional distress. He attempted to overcome his suffering by trying to connect and regain faith in other ways. This was doomed to failure. No philosophy books, Buddhist writings or New Age texts and practices could replace his lost religious faith and the style of life derived from it. Believing they would was implausible (non-sense) and irrelevant to his new situation (fifth wheel). But he didn't attempt to re-evaluate and change his lifestyle to make it fit into the new cultural environment (lack of comprehensiveness, horse blinders).

My therapeutic strategy included the following steps, among others:

(a) Practicing emotion-balancing techniques (see Chapters 9 and 10).
(b) Helping Avner realize that, at least for the time being, his religious faith with all its implications and ramifications could not be revived or replaced by a substitute and to mourn its loss (weakening his fifth wheel, non-sense and horse blinders bugs).
(c) Encouraging him to recognize that secular life without absolute faith can be meaningful and satisfying if a person sets himself worthy goals in this world.
(d) Assisting him to get acquainted with and understand his new ecological and cultural environment and enjoy its advantages.
(e) Helping him find and create for himself new structured social, study and work environments (weakening his horse blinders bug that does not let him develop programs that process the current information).

The family and other social systems

Although social systems such as peer groups, work teams, etc., are different from the family, similar concepts can be applied in their description and analysis. The family and other social systems can be explicated and formalized, synchronically, as information processing systems, as cybernetic systems and as semiotic systems.

In the language of information processing, an interpersonal system such as a family or other social organizations can be represented as a group of inter-communicating information processing programs. Each of the members is

94 The internal and external subsystems

like a kind of "human computer" that receives input from the other members and from sources outside the family or the group. Such a human computer can retrieve from memory information related to the other family or group members or to outside sources. The human computer interprets and processes this information according to given programs and produces output; that is to say, transmits parts of the interpreted and processed information to the other family or group members or to targets outside the family or the group. The interpreted and processed information can also be stored in memory and retrieved when wanted or necessary. The information stored in memory by each such human computer, retrieved from it and processed constitutes the social system's *narratives*. Some narratives are shared by the members of the family or the social group and some are not. There are genuine memories and false memories (see Bjorklund, 2014).

Some readers are likely to find the use of the expression "human computers" to denote human beings objectionable, even though it is no more than a metaphor. The answer to this is that studying the operation of human-made machines as a means of investigating humanity has always been widely accepted in the various sciences. Sigmund Freud studied the mind as a hydraulic system whose substance is not liquids but mental energy. Brain simulations in brain research refer to the brain as a computational system, an inordinately complex and elaborate computer.

The routine, stable rules by which such interpersonal information is processed have been called in the family therapy literature names such as family rules, family interaction patterns and family communication cycles. In The Diamond Model, they are termed *family or social information processing programs* or, more briefly, *family and social programs.* Some such programs are bugged and therefore dysfunctional. Bugged family or social programs cannot mobilize corrective feedback. They start deviation-amplifying processes that take the family or the social group increasingly far away from a balanced, homeostatic state.

Family and social programs are goal-oriented. They are directed toward two kinds of goals: proximity and control. Numerous observations and investigations of humans and animals have attested to the fact that proximity and control are the main regulatory forces of interpersonal and inter-group relations. Control relations hold, for instance, between rulers and subjects, leaders and followers, privileged and deprived. Both among animals and among humans, there are various degrees of closeness between individuals and groups, from highly intimate relationships to total rejection and distancing, alienation, hostility and enmity.

Here are some examples of control goals:

> A husband wants his wife to free him of the burden of making decisions concerning the home and the family. He wants her to make such decisions instead and instruct him on what to do.

The external subsystems   95

A brother wants his little sister to serve him.
A fifth-grade schoolgirl wants to oust another girl from her position as "the class queen" and become the "queen" herself.

Here are some examples of proximity goals:

A husband wants his wife to always be with him and give up all her independent connections and occupations.
A wife is not interested in her husband's approaches and wants him to leave her alone.
A boy is clinging physically to his mother and does not let her go.
In a workplace, one of the employees wants to have an intimate relationship with the boss (this is a proximity goal but also a control goal).

Often, the proximity and control goals of family or group members with respect to each other are incompatible or diametrically opposed. For example, the husband wants his wife to make all decisions, but she wants him to make such decisions or at least participate in making the decisions. The boy clings to his mother, but she wants him to let her be by herself. His sister wants to get him away from his mother and take his place by her. The schoolgirl wants to oust "the queen of the class" from her position and take her place, but "the queen" mobilizes her friends to prevent the competitor from achieving her goal.

Such interpersonal conflicts can take place within the framework of the common culture of the family or the group or between family members whose internalized cultures are different (e.g. the husband is religious and the wife is secular).

To overcome these obstacles, family or group members develop strategic plans to get over them. For instance, the husband whose wife demands of him to be a partner in making decisions concerning the home and family evades talks concerning such issues by various excuses or "forgets" decisions he himself has made. The boy whose sister competes with him about their mother's attention stages some "accident" (e.g. falls from a chair and cries) whenever his sister tries to draw his mother's attention away from him.

Each such tactical plan includes the input received by another family member (e.g. the input "My sister is demanding my mother's attention" received by the boy), the internal processing and interpretation of the input (e.g. "My sister wants to take Mommy away from me and have her all to herself"), the internal planning of the output (e.g. deciding to stage an accident and cry to draw the mother's attention and prevent the sister from taking her away from him) and the production of the output.

Some plans to achieve the goals are rather complex. They can be formalized in the vocabulary and grammar of the information processing language introduced in Chapter 2. A partial formalization, skipping some of

96 The internal and external subsystems

the thoughts and emotions of the participants, is presented in the following example.

Example 5.3 Gabriel and Ella

Gabriel and Ella were young, childless married couple.

Ella's proximity and control goals: to keep Gabriel close to her and to control all his independent activities.

Gabriel's proximity and control goals: to keep a reasonable distance from Ella and not let her control his independent activities.

Ella's plan:

IF INPUT is Gabriel being at home busy with things that are not related to me, such as computer games or correspondence with his friends by his smartphone, *THEN* I *set myself a purpose* of making him pay attention to me and show his love.

I predict that *IF* I touch him in a way that expresses affection and attraction, *THEN* he will probably pay attention to me and return my affection.

OUTPUT

I hug Gabriel from behind *OR* sit on his lap.

IF he ignores the output and continues doing his thing *THEN* I *set as purpose* to make him aware of how much he offends me *AND* to force him to see me and my feelings.

I *predict* that *IF* I tell him off loudly and blame him *THEN* probably he will understand, stop doing his thing, pay attention to me and return my affection.

OUPUT

Yelling that he doesn't see me and doesn't love me.

IF he responds by reassuring me that he loves me and showing affection *THEN* I calm down. *BUT* if he responds by demanding angrily that I stop bothering him and blaming him *THEN* I *predict* that *IF* I act miserably *THEN* he will understand and mellow down.

OUTPUT

I lie on the sofa and weep loudly.

IF Gabriel is out of the home, busy with his own independent activities, such as playing basketball with his friends *THEN necessarily* he enjoys himself, forgets about my existence and prefers his friends.

THEN I *set as purpose* to make him come back home and reassure me.

I *predict* that if I call him and tell him that some emergency occurred *THEN* he will necessarily come back home.

OUTPUT

Call him and tell him that I feel terribly ill *OR* that I fell and injured my arm *OR* that a water pipe burst *OR* that some other emergency I cannot deal with happened.

When he comes back home I *set as purpose* to know everything related to his life out of the home. I *predict* that if I show interest in everything he does or is going through out of the home *THEN* he will understand that I am really interested in him and this will draw us closer together.

OUTPUT

When he is back home I ask him to tell me everything he did or went through out of the home in great detail.

Gabriel's plan:

At home, *IF* Ella is calm, nice and doesn't bother me *THEN* this *arouses* affection in me *AND* I come and hug her and tell her pleasant things.

BUT IF Ella touches me in an affectionate or sexual way when I'm busy doing my own thing *THEN* this *arouses* in me feelings of annoyance and resentment.

I *predict* that *IF* I do not reciprocate and do not show her signs that she disturbs and bothers me *THEN* she will leave me alone.

IF she responds by blaming me that I don't love her and that I'm blind to her and her needs *THEN*, to get her off my back, I tell her, as lip service, that I do love her and care for her *AND* I return to my own activity. *BUT* if she continues yelling and blaming me *THEN* I tell her to stop *AND* I return to my own activity.

IF she is crying loudly *THEN* I come and hug her and try to calm her down.

IF she continues *THEN* I give up and go back to my activity.

Out of the home, *IF* she calls me and tells me that there is an emergency *THEN* I leave and go back home.

IF I see that there was no emergency that she couldn't deal with *THEN* I tell her that she is like the boy who cried wolf in Aesop's fable *AND* that next time *IF* she calls me I will not come.

OUTPUT

I go back to my activities out of the home.

IF when I'm back home she questions me about every little detail of my life out of the home *THEN* I just give her a little information and keep the rest to myself.

Gabriel's and Ella's plans are laden with bugs, which will not be listed here.

98　The internal and external subsystems

Dysfunction in the family or group programs is considered a central concept in most schools of systemic family therapy. Many family therapists believe that the difficulties presented to therapy are at least partly the external manifestations of dysfunction in the family system. Repairing the dysfunction will cure the difficulties experienced by its individual members.

In order to pinpoint the targets of change and to fix the dysfunction, a therapist should be equipped with exact information, enabling him or her to identify precisely the location of dysfunction or, in the terms used here, the bugs in the family programs. In the systemic family therapy literature, many concepts and terms referring to specific types of dysfunction have been defined; for example, *double bind* (Watzlawick, 1968), *detouring* (Minuchin, 1974), *hierarchical incongruity* (Madanes, 1982), *strange loops* (Cronen, Johnson and Lannamann, 1982), etc. All of these and other such types of dysfunction can be explicated as bugs in family programs.

From a cybernetic viewpoint, bugs prevent the programs from mobilizing homeostasis-maintaining corrective feedback. Feed-forward processes increasingly amplify the deviation from the homeostatic, balanced state. In the above example of Gabriel and Ella, their mutual programs are infested with many bugs that prevent them from mobilizing corrective feedback and achieving their mutual goals. For example, Ella thought that if Gabriel was at home and busy with things that are not related to her, then necessarily he was not interested in her and probably did not love her. This thought was infected with horse blinders and non-sense. She did not recall his manifestations of love and affection toward her when she was calm and let him be. She erroneously misinterpreted his normal temporary preference for doing his own thing as proof that he did not care about her. She was unable to procure corrective feedback, such as telling herself that this is an irrational misinterpretation or accepting Gabriel's reassurance. Gabriel's program is also infected with bugs. For example, the following thought, included in his program, was bugged with horse blinders and non-sense: "If Ella touches me in affectionate or sexual way when I'm busy doing my own thing, I predict that if I do not reciprocate and show her signs that she disturbs and bother me then she will leave me alone." He did not use corrective feedback (e.g. recalling that on previous occasions his failure to reciprocate caused Ella to double her pressure rather than leaving him alone).

Case 5.5 Ethan

Ethan, a nine-year-old boy, was referred to therapy because of his violent behavior directed mainly toward his mother. The therapist asked his mother to give him a detailed description of episodes in which her son presented such behavior. She described the following episode that occurred one afternoon that week:

She told Ethan to do his homework. From the way she described it, the therapist could understand that her order was said in a begging tone, betraying weakness. Ethan ignored her. He did not show any sign that he heard what she said to him at all. Then she let her body sink into an armchair and sat there prostrate with a tortured expression on her face. At that point, Ethan lost control of himself, attacked her physically and threw objects at her until she pressed her temple and cried in a weeping voice, "Stop it! Stop it!"

After the therapist interviewed the parents and observed the family in free play, he believed he had enough data to formulate, at least tentatively, the dysfunctional, bugged programs underlying Ethan's behavior. He hypothesized that Ethan and his mother had the same control goals. She wanted to have appropriate parental control over him and he wanted her to succeed in achieving this goal. But his plan for achieving this goal – provocatively ignoring her – prevented this goal from being achieved. The therapist's investigation led him to form hypotheses concerning hidden bugged internal information processing operations applying to the interactions between Ethan and his mother. For example, Ethan's output of ignoring his mother provocatively was influenced by unverbalized presuppositions such as, "My mother knows that I want her to control me. My mother does not want to control me. If I cause my mother to get angry, she will control me." These presuppositions were bugged with horse blinders, because Ethan took their truth for granted and did not use any information that could corroborate them. They were also bugged with non-sense, because they assigned a wrong interpretation to his mother's input. (I must explain that I do not claim that the child consciously puts these things to himself. The formulations are the therapist's attempt to explain the child's behavior as part of his own idiographic theory.)

The therapist also found that the mother's plan included the following presuppositions: "My son ignores me because he doesn't love me. If I apply pressure to control him he will love me less." Both presuppositions were bugged with horse blinders (no information used to corroborate them) and non-sense.

It should be stressed again that, in most cases, the presence of bugs doesn't attest to cognitive limitations. Bugs are kinds of defenses against arousal of unpleasant emotions related to the emotives of family or group members. In Gabriel and Ella's case, for instance, Ella's over-involvement with Gabriel's life was motivated by her fear that if she did not know everything about him, she could lose him, or by a fear that he was hiding things from her. Therefore, purely cognitive therapeutic interventions, exposing the irrationality of the bugged communication, will rarely achieve the desired results. They will work only if the unbalanced emotions energizing the bugs are rebalanced.

100 The internal and external subsystems

Bugs can also invade programs regulating the relations between a family and external people or bodies, as well as the relations between members of non-family organizations. The following case refers to bugged communication between a family and a school.

Case 5.6 Kye

Kye, a fifth-grade pupil, complained to his parents that all the boys in his class were harassing him for no fault of his own and the teachers were not doing anything about it. His parents believed him. They complained to the teacher. She said that the real bully was Kye. The other boys had just been defending themselves. Kye's parents were angry and claimed she was lying, discriminating against Kye and prejudiced against him. Kye told them that the teacher hated him. They believed him. They refused to consider any refuting evidence.

And here is an example of a bugged program in a non-family organization:

In a shoe factory, the general manager decided to delegate authority to some of his subordinate managers. He required a daily report on their activities and would very often give them advice on how to improve their functioning. He claimed that his interventions were temporary, as part of their training, but in fact he did not rely on them and continued to over-supervise them. This impaired the functioning of the management team.

The family and other social groups can also be explicated, formalized and systematized in the language of semiotics. These organizations can be described, as with every semiotic system, on three levels of analysis: the raw material level, the semantic level and the pragmatic level. A macroscopic semiotic analysis will yield recurring patterns that can be formulated as syntactic generalizations governing each level of analysis and the relations between the levels. Some of the generalizations are shared by all the family members, some are not. The family system and other social systems may then be represented as the sum of the raw material, semantic and pragmatic generalizations that are shared and those that are not shared by their members. Techniques for doing semiotic analyses of interpersonal relations in families and other groups are proposed in Chapter 6 and in Ariel (1999, 2002).

Methods for creating a diachronic idiographic theory that describes and explains the development of the case, emphasizing how bugs set in within family or social programs in times of change and crisis, are proposed in Chapter 7.

Summary of Chapter 5

This chapter presents briefly the external subsystems: important life events, the culture, the family and other social systems. Important life events are not necessarily traumatic. They can be normal passage stages in a person's life. Such events cause loss of simplicity of previous programs.

The concept of *culture* is explicated, formalized and systematized as a set of interactive semiotic, cybernetic, information processing programs shared by a particular social group and internalized by its individual members during socialization. Taking into account the client's culture must be an integral part of any therapeutic model. Cultural naivety can lead to fatal errors in understanding and treating a case. A therapist, equipped with some basic concepts of culture and cultural change, can learn from the client themselves those aspects of their culture that are relevant to the therapy. A central conceptual distinction is offered between an *intra-culture dysfunction* and an *inter-culture dysfunction*. The former refers to culturally prescribed cybernetic mechanisms. Culture enables the release of pressure by deviating from norms, but also provides the tools for healing and restoring homeostasis by traditional methods. The latter refers to dysfunctions caused by the loss of the simplicity of previous cultural programs in times of cultural change, crisis or an encounter between distinct cultures. Expert professional interventions are required only to treat inter-culture dysfunction. A typology of cultural programs is proposed to assist the therapist in learning the relevant aspects of the client's culture. Cultural programs are cross-classified according to their roles (axioms, categories and relations, explanations and rules) and according to their contents (existential, ecological, cultural identity, structural, functional, communication and coping and problem-solving).

The family and other social systems can be formalized, synchronically, as sets of goal-oriented information processing programs. Each member has proximity and control goals with respect to each of the other members. Since the respective goals are often incompatible, each member develops a strategy or plan of how to achieve their goals. The plan can be formalized as patterns of internal processing. In cybernetic terms, the goals and plans of all the members can be together in a state of equilibrium or homeostasis, which enables the system to maintain maximum simplicity. Deviations from homeostasis are reversed by corrective feedback. However, especially in times of change and crisis, the programs can become bugged. The bugs cause irreversible deviations from homeostasis by feed-forward. In the language of semiotics, the family and other social systems can be described, synchronically, as a set of patterns or syntactic rules that are organized on the levels of analysis of raw material, semantics and pragmatics.

102 The internal and external subsystems

Assignments

(a) Go back to Case 1.1 (Nonny). Itemize the relevant programs in all of those internal and external subsystems that are discussed in Chapters 4 and 5. Try to formulate these programs in information processing and cybernetic terms. Ferret out the periods of transition and crisis. Show how the previous simplicity was lost in these periods and how attempts to restore simplicity partially infected the programs with deviation- amplifying bugs.

(b) Analyze your own internalized culture using all the relevant categories introduced above (types of roles and content areas). If you have internalized more than one culture, analyze these cultures using the same terms. Describe periods of culture change in your own life history. How did you deal with the loss of the previous simplicity in such periods?

(c) Try to formulate your own family as an information processing, cybernetic and semiotic system.

A classified list of publications

Transitional life events

Bridges, W. (2004). *Transitions: Making sense of life's changes*. Cambridge, MA: Da Capo Press.

Ecological systems

Steiner, F.R. (2016). *Human ecology: How nature and culture shape our world*. 2nd ed. Washington, DC: Island Press.

Culture, culture change and culturally sensitive psychotherapy

Ariel, S. (1999). *Culturally competent family therapy*. Westport, CT: Praeger.

Boszormenyi-Nagy, I. (2014). *Foundations of contextual therapy: Collected papers of Ivan Boszormenyi-Nagy*. London, UK: Routledge.

Cawte, J.E. (1976). Malgri: A culture-bound syndrome. In: Lebra, W.P., ed. *Culture-bound syndromes, ethnopsychiatry and alternative therapies*. Honolulu, HI: University of Hawaii Press, pp.22–31.

Dennis, P.A. (1985). Grisi Siknis in Misikito culture. In: Simons, R.C. and Hughes, C.C., eds. *The culture-bound syndromes: Folk illness of psychiatric and anthropological interest*. Dordrecht, The Netherlands: D. Reidel, pp.289–306.

Falicov, C.J. and Brunder-White, L. (1983). The shifting family triangle: The issue of cultural and contextual relativity. In: Falicon, C.J., ed. *Cultural perspectives in family therapy*. Rockville, MD: Aspen Systems, pp.51–67.

Gilbert, R.M. (2011). *The eight concepts of Bowen theory*. Lake Frederick, VA: Leading Systems Press.

Lutz, C. (1985). Depression and the translation of emotional worlds. In: Kleinman, A. and Good, B., eds. *Culture and depression: Studies in the anthropology of cross-cultural psychiatry of affect and disorder*. Berkeley: University of California Press, pp.63–99.

Sue, D.W. and Sue, D. (2007). *Counseling the culturally diverse: Theory and practice*. 5th ed. Hoboken, NJ: Wiley.

Welsch, R.L. and Vivanco, L.A. (2014). *Cultural anthropology: Asking questions about humanity*. Oxford, UK: Oxford University Press.

Family and social systems and family therapy

Ariel, S. (1992). *Strategic family play therapy*. Chichester, UK: Wiley.

Ariel, S. (2002). *Children's imaginative play: A visit to Wonderland*. Westport, CT: Praeger.

Bjorklund, D.F. (2014). *False memory creation in children and adults: Theory, research, and implications*. Hove, UK: Psychology Press.

Cronen, V.E., Johnson, K.M. and Lannamann, J.W. (1982). *Paradoxes, double binds and reflexive loops: An alternative theoretical perspective*. Family Process, 21(1), pp.91–112.

Madanes, C. (1982). *Strategic family therapy*. San Francisco, CA: Jossey-Bass.

Minuchin, S. (1974). *Families and family therapy*. Cambridge, MA: Harvard University Press.

Nichols, M.P. and Davis, S. (2016). *Family therapy: Concepts and methods*. 11th ed. Cambridge, UK: Pearson.

Smith-Acuna, S. (2010) *Systems theory in action: Applications to individual, couple and family therapy*. Hoboken, NJ: Wiley.

Stroh, D.P. (2015). *Systems thinking for social change: A practical guide to solving complex problems, avoiding unintended consequences and achieving lasting results*. White River Junction, VT: Chelsea Green Publishing.

Watzlawick, P., Beavin Davelas, J., Jackson, D.D. and O'Hanlon, B. (1968). *Pragmatics of human communication: A Study of interactional patterns, pathologies and paradoxes*. London, UK: Faber & Faber.

Part 3

Multi-systemic diagnosis

Chapter 6

Collecting and analyzing diagnostic data

The stages of therapy

The stages of therapy according to The Diamond Model include:

(a) A preliminary, multi-systemic diagnostic evaluation (collecting and analyzing diagnostic data, constructing alternative idiographic theories about the case and choosing the best one).
(b) Designing alternative therapeutic strategies based on the diagnostic evaluation and choosing the best one.
(c) Forming a therapeutic alliance and a therapeutic contract.
(d) Carrying out the strategy flexibly. Continuously monitoring the process and revising the strategy accordingly.
(e) Termination. Evaluating the outcomes of the therapy.

Even though this sequence of stages seems rigid and binding, the therapist is not always obliged to strictly adhere to this given order. The therapy must be carried out flexibly, taking into consideration what actually happens during the sessions.

Preliminary diagnostic evaluation

The purpose of the diagnostic evaluation is to get the information needed for constructing an idiographic theory that describes the development of the case and explains it. Alternative idiographic theories can be proposed and the best, the simplest one, will be preferred.

Relevant diagnostic data are collected in many ways. Here are some of these ways: presenting problems interview; case history interview; family interview; situations questionnaire; observation of free or structured play and non-play behaviors of individuals, groups and families; and other sources of diagnostic data such as medical reports and psychological tests.

108   Multi-systemic diagnosis

Presenting problems interview

When a person seeks therapy or a child is referred to therapy, there are usually external symptoms or problems presented that have external manifestations. An adult can have physical complaints such as pains with no medical explanation, phobias or uncontrolled anger. Children are referred because of behavior problems, tantrums, shyness, withdrawal or the like. Often the presenting problems are described to the therapist by the client or by the child's caretakers in vague, subjective, emotional terms, such as, "I've not been myself lately"; "I've stopped functioning"; "The boy's behavior is intolerable"; "I'm worried about her, she has been acting strange lately."

The first step toward better understanding the presenting problems is to get fuller, more exact and objective details about the presenting problems. Once these details have been elicited, the therapist can form a semiotic description, on the raw material level, of their verbal–vocal auditory features, their spatial and motional features and their tactile features. In addition, data will be collected about the contexts in which the presenting problems (symptoms) occur – the exact place and time, the antecedent behaviors of people in the vicinity and their following responses. The presenting problems may be viewed as expressions in a language that the therapist has to learn. Only if the therapist gets the full picture about the symptoms and their contexts can he or she decipher their meanings (on the semantic level) and communicative functions (on the pragmatic level).

Example 6.1 Nathan, a presenting problems interview

In an initial interview after referral, the parents of seven-year-old Nathan told the therapist, "Nathan suffers from fears."

THERAPIST: Can you give me some examples of such fears? Can you recall some of the last episodes?
MOTHER: Yes, yesterday he had such an attack.
THERAPIST: Where exactly did this happen and at what time (context: time and place)?
MOTHER: It was at home, about 4 pm.
FATHER: I was in my workroom, at the computer.
THERAPIST: Where was Nathan, in which part of the apartment?
MOTHER: He was in the living room, sitting on the armchair opposite the TV, playing PlayStation.
THERAPIST: And where were you?
MOTHER: I was taking a rest in the bedroom.
THERAPIST: And then what happened?
MOTHER: He had this panic attack.

Collecting and analyzing diagnostic data 109

THERAPIST: Was there something in the PlayStation game that frightened him?

FATHER: I don't think so. He plays the same game repeatedly, sometimes alone and sometimes with friends, and is always very excited and happy.

MOTHER: I saw the attack because I opened the door to my husband's mother.

THERAPIST: Did he have the attack immediately after you opened the door (context, antecedent stimuli)?

MOTHER: Almost immediately. My husband's mother came to hug him and then he had the attack.

THERAPIST: Can you describe the attack?

MOTHER: Yes, it's always the same, he is bellowing (vocal raw material), running to the bathroom (spatial, motional raw materials), banging the door behind him (sound, motional, tactile raw materials), and when I open the bathroom door I see him lying on the floor like a fetus, whimpering like a baby (motional, vocal, spatial raw materials).

The interview continues. The therapist is attempting to find clues to the thematic and emotional meanings of the symptoms (semantic level of analysis) and to its communicative functions (pragmatic level of analysis).

THERAPIST: Does the panic attack have the same features every time it happens?

MOTHER: More or less the same.

THERAPIST: And does it usually happen when your mother [addressing the father] comes to visit?

FATHER: [Hesitating] When I come to think of it, it often happens when she comes for a visit.

MOTHER: Yeah! That's right! I haven't thought about it, but that's right!

THERAPIST: And how do you respond when it happens (context, responses)?

MOTHER: I ask my husband to calm Nathan down.

FATHER: But he wouldn't let me approach him. He always wants his mom.

MOTHER: I take him in my arms and lie down with him in our bed until he calms down and becomes himself again.

THERAPIST: And what does his grandmother do until he calms down?

MOTHER: Nothing. She's learned that she shouldn't intervene.

Later in the interview, the therapist learned that often after the grandmother's visits the parents used to have heated arguments. The mother would claim that her husband's mother didn't like her, was criticizing her and was inciting her son against her. The husband would deny this and defend his mother. Nathan was often witness to these quarrels.

The therapist also found out that Nathan's lying on the bathroom floor in a fetal position, whimpering like a baby, reminded his mother of an event in which a burglar entered their apartment late at night. They hid in the bathroom and locked the door. Nathan was two years old then. That is how he reacted.

Having collected all this information, the therapist formed some hypotheses for herself concerning the semantic and pragmatic meanings of the symptoms. In information processing terms, the grandmother's visits were input that caused Nathan to retrieve from memory the burglar episode that had aroused in him intense fears. He identified the grandmother's visits with an invasion of a stranger that endangered his home and family (the fifth wheel bug, irrelevant information penetrates the program). His output was a regression to his babyish behavior during the burglar's episode. In semiotic terms, the thematic (semantic) meaning of the symptom was, "I am a baby under attack." The pragmatic meanings (communicative functions) of the symptoms were:

> *Presupposition*: Grandma invades our home to make trouble.
> *Purposes of the symptomatic behavior*: to divert attention from the grandmother to himself; to neutralize the grandmother; to separate the mother and father so that they do not start quarreling.

This analysis opens the road for the therapist to collect more information about Nathan and his family and to form more diagnostic hypotheses that can help her choose the right therapeutic strategy.

Case history interview

The purpose of the case history interview is to collect the data needed for constructing a multi-systemic diachronic idiographic theory, describing and explaining the development of the case. The elicited data should be such that they can give at least an initial picture of the development of all the internal and external subsystems that are relevant to the case. Special attention should be given to periods of change and crisis in which loss of simplicity occurred and bugs penetrated the programs, producing feed-forward, deviation-amplifying processes.

The interviewee can be the client himself or herself or, if the referred person is a child, the interviewee(s) can be parents, teachers and other people involved in the child's life. If the client is a child, the therapist collects information about genetics, history of pregnancy and birth, physical development, health and illness, psychomotor and neuro-psychological development, the main milestones in the child's cognitive and socio-emotional development, ecological conditions (e.g. the physical characteristics of the child's living environment), history of the family, including previous generations (grandparents and great-grandparents), history of socialization and education at home, schools and other educational agencies and the child's relations with other social institutions. It is important to collect information about major changes in the child's life and other major life events, especially situations of great stress and crisis, like death or serious illness in the family, immigration and exposure to violence or torture, war and terror.

Parents and other caretakers will be interviewed about their own life history according to the same parameters, with different emphases (e.g. less emphasis on early psychomotor development and more emphasis on·social, familial and cultural development).

The interview should be conducted with flexibility, sensitivity and cultural competence. The therapist may start by asking the interviewee(s) to tell their history in the way they would like to tell it. Then, listening to the clients' story, the therapist forms various hypotheses in his or her mind and asks direct or indirect question that can confirm or disconfirm the hypotheses. The therapist can also ask questions to get more information or further clarification of certain points. Often the therapist comes to the interview already informed about the interviewee and about the case, so he or she can start the interview with ready hypotheses and questions in mind.

Two points should be stressed:

The data collected by this and the other interviews should not be taken to be representations of objective reality, but of reality as perceived, conceived and recalled by the interviewee.

If the interview elicits just general and vague information and not detailed information, the diagnostic evaluation and the strategy will also be very general and vague and therefore not very useful.

Case 6.1 Moran

Here are some excerpts from a case history interview, with the interviewer's considerations in square brackets.

Identified client: Moran (a five-year-old girl, the youngest of eight siblings).

Moran was referred to therapy by the social services in her hometown in Israel following being a suspected victim of sexual abuse. The suspect was a thirteen-year-old boy who allegedly had abused some other little boys and girls in the neighborhood. The person who reported the event to the social services was the kindergarten teacher, not the parents. The same boy was alleged to have also abused Moran's eight-year-old brother.

The interviewees were Moran's parents: Tikva, forty-six, a housewife, and Mosheh, fifty-three, a civilian employee of the Israeli army.

The interviewer was Daliah, a clinical psychologist and family therapist.

The referring social worker told Daliah that Tikva had decided not to file a complaint with the police against the perpetrator because she said she didn't have the time or mental strength to deal with all the implications of filing a complaint, especially as the perpetrator was the son of neighbors with whom she has good relationships. Even her having to come to the mental health clinic and the need to bring the girl to therapy taxed her limited strengths. Her husband was too busy with his own affairs to be involved. Her expectation of therapy was that Moran would learn to say no. She was worried about Moran, afraid that because Moran needed touch, warmth and love so much, she could easily fall victim to people who wanted to harm her and give herself easily, being unable to judge the situations she was in correctly.

Daliah came to the interview ready with various questions and hypotheses implied by what she had heard from the social worker. She realized that Tikva seemed to be capable of loving her children, understanding them and being empathetic toward their difficulties. Developmentally, she was able to form adequate attachment. She was worried about Moran and understood her difficulties. At the same time, she did not assign the highest priority to protecting her children against the perpetrator. Preserving good relationships with the neighbors and other family tasks and duties seemed to have a higher priority. She wanted to lay on Moran's shoulders the responsibility for defending herself, oblivious to the developmental difficulty of a five-year-old girl who badly needs warmth, attention and touch to resist such temptations.

Daliah hoped to conduct the interview in such a way that she would understand better this contradiction (flip-flop) between Tikva's love, concern and empathy toward Moran and her avoiding the requirement to protect and defend her.

Daliah also asked herself why Moran needed love, warmth and attention so much. How deprived was she by her parents, who seemed to direct all their energies away from their children?

Daliah wanted to know what Mosheh was so busy with and why Tikva exempted him from the need to be involved with his children's difficulties.

Daliah hypothesized that Tikva felt very lonely with her husband and badly needed good relationships with her neighbors.

Culturally, the shame accrued by publicly exposing the sexual abuse would perhaps be more powerful than the wish to protect her children, Daliah thought.

Here are some parts of the case history interview, with Daliah's thoughts in square brackets:

DALIAH: Mosheh and Tikva, can you tell me your life history? I'd like to know you better before we work together. Mosheh?

MOSHEH: I studied for twelve years and then I went into the army and have remained there until today as a civilian worker.

[Daliah noticed that Mosheh started with talking about studies and work. He didn't say anything about his childhood or family. She knew that Mosheh came from a low-socioeconomic background, a family of immigrants from a Middle Eastern country. She paid attention to the fact that he had chosen economic stability over personal ambitions and that he seemed to be a responsible, stable working man. The question of culturally prescribed loyalty to Mosheh's family of origin versus his loyalty to his wife and children was high on Daliah's mind.]

DALIAH: Mosheh, are you the first-born?

[Is there a culturally prescribed duty of the first-born to support his family?]

MOSHEH: I am the second of nine children. The first-born was killed when he was in his army service. I was sixteen then.

[This was a major crisis. How did he and his family deal with this disaster? Did the crisis start bug-producing dysfunctional attempts to maintain simplicity? He devoted his professional life to the army. Was this related to the loss of his brother? Apparently, he had to replace the first-born. How devoted has he been to his family of origin?]

DALIAH: This must have been a big blow to you and your family.

MOSHEH: Of course, but after the period of mourning we stopped talking about it and behaved as if nothing had happened. Only my mother became kind of indifferent and shut herself within herself.

[Horse blinders. Much information about the loss kept out.]

DALIAH: How did you feel about that? What did you do?

MOSHEH: I was very worried about her, but I didn't show it. I just decided to be a good soldier and a good son.

TIKVA: He is very devoted and attached to his family. They live next to us. On Fridays he goes to his mother for supper and his brothers join in.

DALIAH: And you join him?

TIKVA: Sometimes. Most of the time I stay home with the children. I have eight children. The oldest one [sighing] is divorced. He is twenty-seven. Since the divorce he has lived with me.

[Daliah notices that Tikva said "I" and "me" and not "we" or "us". She seemed to be worried and hurt because of her oldest son's divorce. This supported the hypotheses that she was capable of feeling and caring for her children, but had a hard time carrying the burden of parenting eight children alone. Mosheh did seem to be devoted to his family of origin more than to his wife and children, a pattern that started after his pledge to compensate his family for the loss of his older brother. In the culture of the community to which this family belongs, it is customary for a husband and a wife to stay together for Friday supper. Either the husband, wife and children go together to have supper with the husband's or the wife's family of origin or they stay at home and have supper together. Daliah hypothesized that the son's divorce was a crisis situation, especially for Tikva. Daliah wanted to know more about the circumstances of the divorce. She wanted to find out whether that crisis gave rise to bug-producing attempts to maintain simplicity. Daliah registered in her memory all the information she had got up to that point, as well as all the questions and hypotheses formed in her mind. She decided to go back to some of these questions and hypotheses when the right moment in the interview occurred.]

DALIAH: Mosheh, I'll be back with you soon. Tikva, can you tell me more about your son's marriage and divorce? What's his name?

TIKVA: Shimon. He married his wife when he was very young, nineteen. Stupid, a child. After the birth of his second son he decided to divorce her. I encouraged him to send her away because I felt he was not happy at all. His wife made him miserable. She was too stubborn, too egotistic. Went to work and left Shimon to take care of the home and children. I don't understand how a young girl, eighteen, who commits herself to marriage, doesn't understand that this binds her for life. A married woman has to devote herself and give to her husband and children with no limits. There's no such thing as "I'm too tired, I have no strength, I can't." A mother is like an omnipotent God to her children. She should put the children's needs first and put her own needs last. I take responsibility for everything, carry everything on my own shoulders. When Shimon came to live with us, I told him, "Don't tell anybody that you are divorced and that you live in your mother's home." I told the neighbors that he was here just for some visits, to help us. I take care of his children who come here every weekend. He told me that he wanted to remarry and I told him, "God bless you! If you remarry, I'll take care of your children, to give you and your new wife a quiet life." Troubles. Only troubles. His younger brother who is now in the army also gives us trouble. He lives in Tel Aviv and he is not religious anymore. We are now very orthodox, very religious, much more than my parents and my husband's parents used to be. And he left religion altogether. We had so many fights about it and now we are not on speaking terms and he does not come to visit us, never.

[These words gave rise to various thoughts, hypotheses and questions in Daliah's mind. They confirmed the hypothesis that Tikva was capable of attachment, parental love and empathy toward her children. They also revealed Tikva's values concerning the roles of a mother and a wife. The question was to what extent these values were culturally prescribed and to what extent they reflected Tikva's own worldview, shaped by her own personal history. It could also be learned from these words that Tikva was taking an extremely dominant position with respect to her home and children and was over-involved with the life of her older boys, who were not minors anymore. She seemed to be more active and emotionally involved with their lives than with the lives of her youngest children, Moran and her eight-year-old brother. Her declarations concerning the duties of a married woman and a mother stood in diametric contradiction to her previous declaration that she didn't have the time and mental strength to file a complaint with the police about the abuse her two youngest children suffered and to the fact that she wanted her five-year-old daughter to learn how to protect herself. The question arises again: why did she fight for her oldest sons and not for her youngest children? By taking such a dominant position, Tikva seemed to exempt her husband from taking any marital, familial and parental role. She even seemed to push him to the margin. Why? Is she protecting him from something? Is she OK with his not being involved? Is she bitter but hides it?

Daliah had the feeling that underneath Tikva's criticism of her son Shimon's ex-wife there was a concealed envy and identification with her power and independence.

Tikva saw the fact that her son was divorced and living in his parents' home as something to be ashamed of and to hide from the neighbors. This seemed to be culturally prescribed and perhaps also related to Tikva's personal history. This confirmed Daliah's hypothesis that one of the reasons why Tikva avoided filing a complaint to the police about the sexual abuse was culturally prescribed shame and a great sensitivity to public opinion in the neighborhood.

Another question that formed in Daliah's mind was: why had Tikva and her husband become more religious than their families of origin? When did they shift to becoming more orthodox? Was that also a response to another crisis in the family?

At this point, Daliah decided not to confront Tikva and Mosheh with their neglect of their duty to protect their youngest children, but to get more information about Mosheh's and Tikva's present and past lives and then about the life history of Moran. She decided to start with their having become more orthodox.]

116 Multi-systemic diagnosis

DALIAH: Mosheh, when did you decide to strengthen your religious devotion?

MOSHEH: I can't tell you exactly when. Maybe in my work in the army I saw and heard so many terrible things, so many dangers that our country and our people were going through, that I thought, "God is punishing us because of all our transgressions."

[Daliah thought that this was one of Mosheh's ways of dealing with the loss of his brother in the army, which had never been worked through in his family. She thought that maybe his withdrawal from his current family was a defense against being too attached to his wife and children lest he lose them. She decided not to share these thoughts with Mosheh at this stage.]

TIKVA: I followed him. I thought, "So many families fall apart. So much corruption around. I thought yes, because we left God."

[Tikva's religious shift seems to be motivated more by her fear of losing control over her family, but perhaps also by her past, which should be explored.]

DALIAH: Mosheh, how is your strengthened religious devotion expressed in your life?

TIKVA: He works a long distance from home. He comes back from work at 7 pm and then he takes a shower, snatches something to eat and goes to study Torah (the Old Testament, Book of Genesis) and Talmud (Jewish post-biblical scriptures) for the rest of the evening. He will never miss his studies.

DALIAH: Mosheh, did you want to say something about this?

MOSHEH: It's OK, she can tell you.

TIKVA: He never participates in social gatherings of people from his work. For him, the studies are his sole social life, not to mention his parents and brothers, and a spiritual experience.

[Daliah feels subdued bitterness in Tikva's recounting of Mosheh's lifestyle.]

DALIAH: You seem to approve of his studies after work.

TIKVA: [Over-reacting] Yes! Of course! He needs it! It's OK, I can take care of everything. He relies on me. He tells me, "Whatever you decide."

I am also not at home in the evenings. After almost thirty years of staying at home and taking care of my family I started last year to work as an attendant in a *mikveh* (a ritual bath house for purifying women's bodies). I begin working at 5 pm. The place should be closed at 8 pm, but I sometimes stay till 10 pm because if a woman comes to purify herself in the *mikveh* after 8 pm I can't turn her away and tell her to go back home unpurified! This would be a transgression!

Collecting and analyzing diagnostic data   117

[All this information confirms Daliah's impression concerning an internal conflict, a dissonance in Tikva between her empathy and concern for her husband and children, her culturally prescribed values concerning any woman's and her own duties as a wife and mother on the one hand and her subdued, unexpressed bitterness and resistance to all the burdens that she has to carry alone on the other. She rebels against her role as a dutiful wife and mother, the "omnipotent mother", by leaving her youngest children at home every evening, apparently under the care of their older brothers and sisters, and refuses to deal with her children being victims of sexual abuse. Her religious duties provide her with a "justification".]

DALIAH: And when Mosheh is at his studies and you are at work, who takes care of the little children?

TIKVA: Their older brothers and sisters. They love them.

DALIAH: Tikva, can you tell me about your own childhood?

TIKVA: I am the sixth of seven children. My father died when I was eleven. My mother had to work very hard to maintain and support us.

DALIAH: Do you remember yourself when you were eleven?

TIKVA: My father was sick in bed for a whole year and then he died, but I was happy, you know, a girl, I didn't really understand what was going on. But I was a good girl, never gave any trouble to my mother and always helped her.

[Tikva saw the model of a woman who carries all the burden alone at home.]

Later in the interview:

DALIAH: Can you tell me Moran's life history?

TIKVA: Moran was born by a cesarean, with the umbilical cord tied around her neck. God saved her life.

When she was four months old, she was diagnosed with CDH [congenital dislocation of the hip]. She was treated by special belts in a hospital for four months. At two years and six months, she was treated in a child development clinic for delay in speech development. Later she was diagnosed with ADHD. In her early years, she was very sickly. Her immune system was weak. I used to run with her almost every day to hospitals and clinics and alternative treatments. She refused food, was asking for sweets all the time and I had to force-feed her. She is a kid that is always looking for touch, warmth, too much. I'm always worried about her.

[These details do not confirm the hypothesis that Moran's excessive need for touch, attention and warmth was due to early maternal deprivation, but they do confirm the hypothesis that Tikva got tired of many years of carrying the burden of raising eight children on her own shoulders. Moran's medical problems seemed to have exhausted Tikva, until she could not carry the burden anymore. Maybe at a certain point Moran felt abandoned by her mother and was looking for attention elsewhere.]

These have been only some excerpts from the full interview.

Family interviews

The purposes of such interviews is to get information about the family programs.

Daily life interview

One way to interview a family is to ask them to talk about their daily lives. I sometimes ask family members to tell me in great detail what each of them has done or gone through from the time he or she woke up in the morning until the time he or she fell asleep during each of the three or four days before the interview. From such stories one can learn quite a lot about the family life and the relationships between the family members.

Three requests

Another family interview technique is asking each family member to ask three requests from the other family members. I clarify to the family members that the requests should not refer to material things such as "I want you, Daddy, to buy me a computer game", but to relationships among the family members (e.g. "I want you, Daddy, to play with me when you come back from work").

These techniques can be added to the rich repertoire of family interviewing techniques found in the family therapy literature.

Other sources of diagnostic information

There are many other sources of diagnostic information: various kind of psychological tests, medical reports and products of the clients themselves (e.g. stories, poems, blogs, diaries, drawings and other creative products).

Observations of free or structured play and non-play behaviors of individuals, groups and families

Such observations can provide very rich diagnostic information about all the internal and external subsystems relevant to therapy: the family or group dynamics, culture, psychodynamics, developmental profiles, etc.

Collecting and analyzing diagnostic data 119

The family puppet show technique

When I do family play therapy, I conduct a family puppet show. I let the family have a choice of glove puppets representing different types of people, animals or fictional creatures. I ask each family member to choose one puppet. The very choice of the puppet is often significant. Almost always the puppet symbolizes something, exposes something about the person who chose it. After the choice, the participants are asked to give names to the puppets they chose. The choice of names is also usually not coincidental. Then I ask each of the family members, in turn, to make up a little story including all of these puppet characters and to enact it with all the family members.

The effects of this techniques are illustrated in the following case.

Case 6.2 Ron

Nine-year-old Ron was considered by everybody as an academic and social failure. He could not do homework even with the help of a private tutor. He was teased and ridiculed by his peers. While they attacked him, he would remain passive, suffering quietly.

Reading this description, you probably have imagined a rather dull boy. This is, however, a very wrong impression. Ron was a well-built, strikingly good-looking boy. Moreover, psychological tests have proved beyond doubt that his intellectual potential was very high.

Ron's seven-year-old brother, Oliver, was viewed by everybody as an academic and social success.

In an initial interview with the parents, the father, Anthony, a high-tech person, expressed concern over Ron's poor school performance. He was not so worried about his social and emotional difficulties. He described himself as an intelligent, rational person, a perfectionist who controlled both himself and other people. The mother, Edna, a big, strongly built woman, was anxious mainly about Ron's social and emotional difficulties. She gave the impression that she was afraid of her husband and wouldn't dare speak her mind in his presence. After some encouragement by the therapist, she said hesitantly that she disapproved of her husband's insensitive and harsh attitude toward both herself and Ron.

I conducted the family puppet show technique with this family. When I saw their choices of puppets, I was astonished. The characters they selected were sharply contrasted with the way they introduced themselves and their relationships in the initial interview. Anthony chose a cow puppet. Edna picked a lion puppet, which reminded one of her big and strong physique rather than of the weak and frightened facade she put on in the interview. Ron chose a puppet representing a devil. His brother, Oliver, chose a donkey.

Edna made the first move. "I am the king of the jungle," she declared.

120 Multi-systemic diagnosis

Anthony made his cow puppet walk toward her lion puppet and said in a funny, cow-like tone of voice, "Do you need a pet, King? I can be your pet."

"Thank you," said the lion. "I don't need a pet. By the way, your smell reminds me that I didn't have dinner today."

At this point, Ron made his devil puppet come close to his mother's lion puppet and said in a fiendish tone of voice, "Do you need a pet like me?" Edna looked at the devil puppet, hesitating. Then she smiled mischievously and said, "Yes, why not?"

The devil joined the lion and whispered in its ear, "Let's make fun of the silly cow."

At this moment, Oliver made his donkey puppet stand by his father's cow puppet and said in a braying manner, addressing Ron, "You yourself are silly."

Ron replied, "I am not, because I am a devil. Nobody can make the devil silly, not even the king himself."

Here is my attempt at analyzing, tentatively of course, this puppet show:

The show exposed she subconscious self-image of each member of the family and their covert interrelationships. This show then served as a debugging technique, removing the horse blinders and non-sense bugs with which the family programs had been infected. Anthony's hidden proximity goal was that his big, strong wife would pet him. Edna rejected him quite aggressively. She didn't want to pet him. She wanted a powerful, dominant man who would make her feel feminine and help her forget that she was so big and strong. Therefore, Anthony changed his plan to achieve his proximity goal. He attempted to get Edna's love and appreciation by pretending to be dominant and by emphasizing his intellectual strengths. Unfortunately, this plan also failed to win Edna's affection. She disapproved of and felt uneasy with what she took to be his rigidity and insensitivity.

Ron was caught in a paralyzing conflict. Like a normal nine-year-old boy, he wanted to be close to and identify with his father. However, he perceived with his keen senses that his mother "had been making his father silly". If he were too closely identified with his father, she would be likely to make him silly too.

One way out of this problem could be to join forces with his mother, forming a "fiendish" coalition with her. Together with his mother he could make a fool of his father. In this coalition, he would be quite safe ("Nobody can make the devil silly, not even the king himself"). However, this tactic would throw out the baby with the bath water. After all, Ron's main goal was to be close to and identify with his father, not to be his enemy.

Another way out might be to identify not with his father's submissive, dependent side, but with his pedantic and intellectual facade. This would

Collecting and analyzing diagnostic data   121

not work either, because his mother disapproved of this side of his father too. Ron's solution to this entanglement was to make *himself* silly. In this way, he could reach his goal of being like his father without becoming his mother's victim. He would be his own victim, not his mother's, hence the symptoms – underachievement in school and social passivity.

Oliver, the younger brother, had the same goal as Ron – to be close to and identify with his father. However, his plan had been to go all the way toward his goal. Therefore, he had embraced both his father's strong (intellectual, domineering) side and his weak ("donkey") side. Since he was only a child, there was no risk that he would be rejected by his mother.

Recording and transcribing the observations

Observations of the play or non-play behaviors of an individual adult or child, a family or a group are conducted before the therapy as a part of the pre-therapy diagnostic evaluation and continuously during all therapy sessions. When possible, an observation can be videotaped and, if impossible, hand-recorded.

It is not at all easy to see and hear what is going on and at the same time write a description of every detail on paper, especially when the activity includes a group of people. Here is a technique that can facilitate the task of writing a protocol in real time:

> The observer attempts to hear and see as many details of what is going on in the room. She holds a writing pad and a pen. She writes down what she hears and sees without looking at the writing pad, using a kind of shorthand. For example, in a group play session the observer sees one boy, Idan, in one corner of the room, holding a toy sword and shouting in a hoarse voice, "I am going to kill all the bad people!" And another boy, Gil, is hiding under a big pillow in the opposite corner of the room, shouting in a childish voice, "No! Don't!" The observer, without looking at the pad, is writing what she has observed in a kind of shorthand, "Idan corner, sword, I kill all bad people, hoarse Gil other corner under pillow yell No! Don't childish." After the termination of the observation, the observer can rewrite the observation based on the mnemonic "shorthand" and fill in the missing details.

Characteristic errors in observations

(a) Interpretations and generalizations instead of detailed, objective descriptions.

Instead of writing a detailed, objective description of observed behavior on the raw material level, such as, "Gil is lying on his back in the west corner of

122 Multi-systemic diagnosis

the room, his head covered with a big blue pillow, pressing the pillow hard to his head with the two palms of his hands and calling in a choking voice and a babyish intonation, 'No, Don't!'," the observer writes, "Gil is afraid of Idan and shouts to him to stop frightening him," which is a generalization and interpretation. The generalizations and interpretations should come after the observer has the details and not before.

(b) Ignoring non-verbal behavior.

For example, writing only, "Gil is shouting, 'No don't!'," and ignoring all the spatial, motional, tactile (e.g. the way the pillow is held) and vocal details (not just the words, but also the ways they were pronounced). Missing the non-verbal details can sometimes amount to missing or failing to understand the meaning of the observed behavior. As in language, some minute distinction can make the whole difference in meaning, as for instance the difference between "bad" and "bed". In non-verbal behavior, pressing a pillow to the head and not pressing it to the head can make a big difference in the meaning and emotional significance of the observed behavior. Non-verbal language is as important as verbal language.

Videotaping observations

In videotaping, especially if the videotaped observation is a family play therapy or a group play therapy session, we should try to get both a full picture of the whole activity as well as all the minute details. It is preferable not to use a fixed camera but a hand-manipulated camera. Of course, the presence of a cameraman in the room can divert the clients' attention, interfere with the natural flow of the activity and cause inhibitions. However, from my experience, especially with children playing, after a while they forget about the cameraman and behave more or less naturally.

The cameraman should move around the room, not stand in a fixed place, to get the best view of the activity. At the same time, the cameraman should attempt to remain as invisible and non-intrusive as possible. The zoom should be used often to switch between looking at the whole picture and observing the details (e.g. a child's hand playing with the toy, the child's facial expression).

Transcribing videotaped materials

Transcribing from video to writing is the first step in analyzing and interpreting the videotaped observation.

The next step is writing the recorded observation into a transcription form that can be prepared in a copybook with slots or on special sheets of paper.

The general structure of a transcription form is presented in Table 6.1.

Collecting and analyzing diagnostic data 123

Table 6.1 The general structure of the transcription page

Time units		*1*	*2*	*3*	*4*	*5*	*6*	*7*	*8*	...
Observed person X	*General* *Vocal–linguistic* *Spatial* *Motional* *Tactile*									
Observed person Y	*General* *Vocal–linguistic* *Spatial* *Motional* *Tactile*									
...										

The numbers on the horizontal plane represent time units. The size of each time unit will be determined according to the degree of precision required. The smaller the time unit, the greater the precision. The size of a time unit can be twenty seconds, thirty seconds or any other size decided on.

Five spaces are devoted to every participant in the activity. The first space will include an impressionistic description of the participant's activity in each time unit. The second space will include the words, speech and other sounds produced by the participant in each time unit and the characteristics of these voices and sounds. One can use more exact sign languages for this purpose, such as phonetic transcriptions or musical notes, but for our purposes we can make do with ordinary language, using impressionistic words such as "hoarse voice", "loud voice" and "nasal pronunciation". In describing the manners by which words, voices and sounds are produced, one should refer at least to the following parameters: intonation, tempo, rhythm and velocity, loudness (whispering, shouting), pitch, quality of voice (clear vs. hoarse, soft vs. hard, free-flowing vs. choked, etc.), accent (e.g. a Russian accent in a person whose mother tongue is not Russian) and so forth.

The third and fourth spaces will include descriptions of the spatial and motional characteristics of each participant in each time unit. For this description, one can also use formal transcribing techniques such as Noa Eshkol and Avraham Vachman's Movement Notation (Eshkol and Wachman, 1958) or Labanotation (Kipling Brown, 2008), but for our purposes we can use an impressionistic verbal description. The spatial description will refer to the location of the movement or posture, distance, direction and height (e.g. when someone is standing on a chair). The motional description will refer to the movements and postures of the body and facial expressions. There is also a formal transcribing method for facial expressions, Paul Ekman's Facial Action Coding System (Ekman, 2015). One should refer to which body parts are involved in the movement or postures, how they move (e.g. angular vs. round movement) and the manner of movement: tempo, muscle tension, force, precision of movement, rhythm, repetitiveness, easiness, etc. In facial expressions, one should describe which parts of the face move (eyebrows, eyes, jaws, etc.) and how they move (e.g. dropping the jaw, chewing movements, wide smile, staring eyes, wandering eyes), and also the degree of tension and intensity of the facial movements.

The fifth space will refer to touch between people, between a person and himself or herself or between people and objects (e.g. a child playing with toys). I developed a coding system for exact transcription called Touchnotation (unpublished). One should describe which part of the body touches which part of one's own body, of another person's body or of an object (e.g. a child's nose tip touches his own palm or the cheek of a teddy bear). The manner of touch will be described too: groping, caressing, knocking and so forth. The description will also include the purpose of the touch (e.g., getting something that fell on the floor, throwing something at somebody; not the psychological or social purpose, but the physical target). Other touch characteristics that should be described are the degree of pressure applied, muscle tension, repetition, etc.

The transcription of the characteristics of the verbal–vocal and sound, spatial, motional and tactile behavior constitutes a description of the behavior through time on the raw material level. What one gets after filling the transcription pages is a kind of score sheet, like the musical score of a chamber orchestra piece that tells the conductor what each instrument should play at any given moment. It shows the organization of all the elements of the observed behavior on the axis of time, which elements are simultaneous within and across the individual participants and which follow one another.

This transcribing helps one understand the relations between the various components of the behavior's raw material in space and time. Before one does such a transcription, one's view of the activity, even if it does not include interpretations and generalizations, is not objective. Our perception and imagination can distort the reality of the observed. For instance, a father laughed and his little son threw a doll at him. The boy threw the doll at his father after his father laughed, maybe as a response to the fact that the father laughed and the boy thought that he was making fun of him and was hurt. The observer, providing he paid attention to the fact that the father laughed at all, was under the impression that the father laughed only after the boy threw the doll at him, because we do not always perceive the time relations in an activity as they really happened. We do not really grasp what happened first and what happened after or what happened simultaneously. When we write the activity as in the transcription page, we can see what really happened first and what really happened later or at the same time.

Analyzing and interpreting the observed behavior

The next steps in the semiotic analysis of observations consist of:

(a) Dividing the transcribed behavior into *activity units*.

Activity units are the basic building blocks of the observed behavior.

An activity unit is a minimal raw material feature or combination of raw material features (spatial, movement, vocal–linguistic and tactile) that has a thematic or emotive meaning on the semantic level and possibly has use and communicative functions on the pragmatic level. It cannot be broken down into smaller units without losing its meaning. For example, a boy is holding a wheel, turning it, making a clattering sound with his lips and moving forward toward his playmate. On the semantic level, this combination of raw material features means "driving a car." On the pragmatic level, the boy wants to let his friend know that he wants to come close to him. Suppose that each of these features, taken separately, does not have any meaning or communicative function for the boy. Then the minimal activity unit will include all of these features taken together.

(b) Interpreting activity units on the semantic level; that is, finding their thematic and emotive meanings.

(c) Describing syntactic rules that apply to combinations of semantically interpreted activity units.

(d) Parsing series of semantically interpreted activity units into *structures* (i.e. combinations of activity units that have communicative functions; proximity and control presuppositions and purposes). For a combination of units to be considered a structure, the signified, semantic contents of the units must be interrelated, adding up together to a significant whole.

(e) Specifying the presuppositions and the *proximity and control purposes* of each structure produced by each participant. The series of presuppositions and purposes can bring to light the *proximity and control goals* of each of the participants with respect to one another and their plans to achieve the goals. Note the difference: the purposes of each structure and final goals of the producers of these structures (see Chapter 5).

(f) Formulating the pragmatic rules applying to the structures.

(g) Formulating information processing programs underlying the observed behavior.

Let me illustrate these procedures on the basis of an observation of a spontaneous imaginative play of a family.

126 Multi-systemic diagnosis

Observation 6.1 Aaron

Background: The family included forty-year-old Alan, his thirty-five-year-old wife Sofia and their six-year-old adopted son Aaron. For both parents this was their second marriage. Aaron was adopted by Sofia when she was still married to her first husband. Alan, who divorced his wife to marry Sofia, left three children with his first wife. He found it difficult to accept Aaron and treat him like his own son. Sofia, too, had difficulties realizing her acquired motherhood. Aaron's behavior was no help. He was aggressive, babyish and uncooperative.

Here is a transcript of an observation of a conjoint play session with the three of them:

> Aaron kneels by Alan, who sits on an armchair. Sofia sits on a chair a few yards away from Alan and Aaron.
> Aaron holds a squeaking toy shark in his right hand. Alan wears a hand puppet representing a fish on his right hand. Sofia also wears a hand puppet representing a fish.
> Aaron gets up. He makes his toy shark attack Alan's toy fish with sharp thrusts, squeaking violently. Alan evades the attacks. He winces. He says in a quiet, though somewhat anxious voice, "Oh no, no, no! You are not going to get me!"
> Aaron makes his shark bite Alan's arm.

> ALAN: [Shocked] You bit my arm!
> AARON: I did not.
> ALAN: You did!
> AARON: That's impossible. Mine is not a real shark.

> Aaron leaves Alan and approaches Sofia, making his shark attack her fish in the same manner. She smiles and evades him, saying pleadingly, "Please, Shark, don't eat me up! I don't want you to eat me up!"
> Aaron makes his shark bite her arm.
> Sofia pulls her arm away with a sharp movement. Her face becomes serious and wears an amazed expression. She says in a somewhat childish tone, "What a frightening shark!"

> AARON: I ate you up. Now I want to eat more fish.
> SOFIA: What an enormous belly he has! There's room there for so many fish. [To Alan] Maybe we can speak nicely to him, and then he won't eat us up.

> Aaron stands between his parents. He moves the shark in the air with wavy movements, apparently pretending it is swimming in water.

Collecting and analyzing diagnostic data   127

ALAN: If you don't eat us up, I'll give you another fish to eat, OK?

AARON: No, he is not hungry anymore [squeaking].

SOFIA: [Gratefully] So you will not eat us up.

AARON: It is not a shark now, it is an ordinary fish [his tone is now mild and childish, his movements limp].

SOFIA: [In disbelief] You don't want to eat us up anymore?

AARON: No, a fish doesn't eat up. A fish swims.

ALAN: Can we swim with him?

AARON: No, only he swims.

Sofia attempts to caress Aaron's toy shark.

SOFIA: You are a cute shark. Do you want to be my friend? You are a special shark. All the other sharks in the sea eat fish, and you don't.

Aaron makes his toy shark squeak violently. He evades Sofia's caresses. He sits on the carpet.

ALAN: Are you not a shark? May I join you?

AARON: He is not outside. He is at home. He is waiting for another fish to visit him, not you.

SOFIA: We are alright, we are still alive. [Nervously] Where does the shark live? Where does he live?

AARON: The other fish followed him from a distance.

Aaron walks slowly away from Alan and Sofia with the toy shark held in front of him.

Alan and Sofia follow him slowly.

SOFIA: [Anxiously] Aaron, Aaron, where are you going with that shark?

A full formal semiotic analysis of this play session will not be attempted here. The method of semiotic analysis is simply illustrated below.

In the following list, the stages of analysis are not separated but bound together. Since this observation is too short to generalize and formulate rules, only which meaningful activity units go together and form structures are shown, as well as what the presuppositions and proximity and control purposes of each structure are.

Aaron's structures

Structure 1: shark attacking. Moving forward toward Alan's fish, sharp thrusts, violent squeaking and biting ("an aggressive, angry, attacking shark").

Aaron's presuppositions: Alan doesn't want me to attack him. He doesn't accept me when I'm aggressive. He doesn't know how to defend himself against my aggression.

Aaron's purposes: To force Alan to tolerate my aggression. To test his tolerance. The same structure is directed against Sofia's fish.

128 Multi-systemic diagnosis

Structure 2: denial of aggression. After Aaron had made his toy shark bite Alan's arm and Alan, shocked, said, "You bit my arm," Aaron said, "I did not…That's impossible. Mine is not a real shark."

Aaron's presupposition: Alan is angry and can retaliate.

Aaron's control purpose: To appease Alan by denying the seriousness of my own aggression.

Structure 3: satisfied. Aaron says to Alan and Sofia, "I ate you up. Now I want to eat more fish."

Aaron's presuppositions with respect to Alan and Sofia: They didn't accept me when I was aggressive. They were too weak to defend themselves against my aggression.

Aaron's purposes: To show them that I've accomplished my purpose of *structure 1* and I don't need them anymore.

Structure 4: a lone fish. Moving away with wave-like, limp movements and speaking with mild, childish voice ("a lone, mild, child-like fish").

Aaron's presuppositions with respect to Alan and Sofia: They couldn't cope with my aggression and they don't know how to accept me and let me get close to them.

Aaron's purpose with respect to Alan and Sofia: To tell them that I don't need to be aggressive anymore. I can be my childish self, keep distance from them and show them that I don't need them.

Structure 5: don't touch me. Evading Sofia's touch and squeaking violently form together a structure ("Aaron doesn't want to be touched affectionately. He is angry").

Aaron's presupposition: Sofia wants to pet me just to please and appease me and abate my anger.

Aaron's purpose: To let Sofia know that I still don't trust her and am not ready to be touched in an affectionate way.

Structure 6: alone at home. Sitting alone and holding a toy shark, saying, "He is not outside. He is at home. He is waiting for another fish to visit him, not you" ("being at home, looking for the company of peers").

Aaron's presupposition: Alan and Sofia want to get close to me.

Aaron's purpose: To show them that I prefer being alone and looking for other friends.

Structure 7: invitation to follow. Aaron says, "The other fish follow him from a distance." He walks slowly away from Alan and Sofia with the toy shark held in front of him in both hands.

Aaron's presupposition: Alan and Sofia do want to get close to me.

Aaron's purpose: To let them know that they can join me without getting too close.

Alan's structures

Structure 1: evading attack. Holding a toy fish; evading Aaron's shark attacks; wincing; saying in a quiet, somewhat anxious voice, "Oh, no, no, no, you are not going to get me."

Alan's presupposition: Aaron really wants to attack me.

Alan's purpose: To let Aaron know that I'm not going to let him attack me.

Structure 2: buying off. Alan says to Aaron, "If you don't eat us up, I'll give you another fish to eat, OK?"

Alan's presupposition: Aaron wants to use me as an object of his anger and aggression.

Alan's purpose: To persuade Aaron to direct his anger and aggression elsewhere.

Structure 3: begging to join. Alan says to Aaron, "Can we swim with him?" And later, "Are you not a shark? May I join you?" ("not being attacked or threatened, wanting to join and be a friend").

Alan's presupposition: Aaron no longer wants to attack me.

Alan's purpose: To join Aaron.

Structure 4: following. Walking after Aaron slowly ("not being attacked or threatened, wanting to join and be a friend").

Alan's presupposition: Aaron gave up attacking me. He has given me the green light to join him.

Alan's purpose: To follow Aaron cautiously, without getting too close and possibly being rejected.

Sofia's structures

Structure 1: begging not to be attacked. Wearing a hand puppet representing a fish; when Aaron's shark attacks her fish, evading him, smiling, saying pleadingly, "Please Shark, don't eat me up, I don't want you to eat me up."

Sofia's presupposition: Aaron want to attack me.

Sofia's purpose: Persuading Aaron not to attack me by begging.

Structure 2: fear of the attacker. When Aaron makes his shark bite her arm, her face becomes serious, wearing an amazed expression. She says in a somewhat childish tone, "What a frightening shark!" ("fear, alarm").

Sofia's presupposition: Aaron really wants to show me his anger and aggression.

Sofia's purpose: To let Aaron know that he has succeeded in achieving his purpose.

130 Multi-systemic diagnosis

Structure 3: appeasing. Sofia says to Alan, "Maybe we can speak nicely with him, and then he will not eat us up."

Sofia's presupposition with respect to both Alan and Aaron: Aaron has attacked us because he feels that we haven't treated him well.

Sofia's purpose: To allay Aaron's anger and aggression by promising to treat him well.

Structure 4: grateful. Sofia smiles gratefully, telling Aaron, "So you will not eat us up."

Sofia's presupposition with respect to Aaron: He has given up being angry at us and aggressive.

Sofia's purpose: To express her gratitude.

Structure 5: petting. Sofia attempts to caress Aaron's toy shark (which now signifies a fish).

Sofia's presupposition with respect to Aaron: He is now ready to accept my affection.

Sofia's purpose: To express my affection.

Structure 6: praising good behavior. Sofia says, "You are a cute shark. Do you want to be my friend? You are a special shark. All the other sharks in the sea eat fish, and you don't."

Sofia's presupposition: Aaron wants us to know that he is good and has given up attacking us.

Sofia's purpose: To acknowledge Aaron's presumed purpose.

Structure 7: uncertainty. Sofia says (nervously), "Where does the shark live? Where does he live?"

Sofia's presupposition: Aaron lets me know that he doesn't want to share a home with me. He prefers sharing a home with someone else ("another fish").

Sofia's purpose: Finding out whether my presupposition is correct.

Structure 8: following. She follows Aaron's slowly.

Sofia's presupposition: Aaron lets me join him now.

Sofia's purpose: Follow Aaron cautiously so as not to spoil his temporary good will.

Formulating the information processing programs underlying the observed behavior

As stressed in Chapter 1, a fully mechanical procedure for discovering these programs cannot possibly be developed. What can be proposed is a set of heuristic procedures for facilitating the process of generalization and reasoning that eventually lead to the formulation of programs. Macroscopic analysis is basically not mechanical but creative. It yields a partial idiographic theory whose validity is tested by its relative simplicity.

Applying such heuristic procedures can be facilitated if the following considerations are taken into account:

(a) Look for features shared by activity units and structures.
(b) Pay attention to changes and turning points in the stream of consecutive structures.
(c) Consider the contexts in which such turning points occur. In such contexts, the person's presuppositions and purposes change or even seem to be incompatible with his or her previous presuppositions and purposes.
(d) The plan to achieve the proximity and control goals often includes alternative courses of action being adopted if certain courses of action have failed to attain the desired goals. The person interprets the input and produces a certain kind of output in one set of circumstances. He or she interprets the input in another way and produces a different kind of output in another set of circumstances.
(e) The plan is needed in order to achieve one's ultimate proximity and control goals. The various purposes are subordinated to this goal. Some purposes serve as means to achieving other purposes, which in turn lead to other purposes, until the final goals are attained.

Such considerations have been taken into account in attempting to formulate the following partial programs, which are supposed to recapitulate the observed play of Aaron, Alan and Sofia. These programs can be formulated in the vocabulary and grammar of the information processing language (see Chapter 2), but here, abbreviated, informal formulation will be presented.

The information processing programs underlying the observation of Aaron, Alan and Sofia:

Aaron's proximity goal: To be accepted by Alan and Sofia as their beloved son, even if I am "a bad boy".

Aaron's plan:

(a) *IF* I can judge from Alan or Sofia that they do not accept me as their beloved son because I am aggressive, "a bad boy", *AND* they don't like it and are afraid of it *THEN* I step up my aggression to test the limits of their fear and resistance and make them understand my anger.
(b) *IF* I can't reach my goal by step (a) because Alan rejects my anger and becomes angry himself *OR* tries to buy me off *AND* if I can't reach my goal because Sofia is afraid of my aggression and tries to appease me *THEN* I deny my aggression, distance myself from them and assume the role of a lonely little boy who doesn't need them but looks for other friends.

132   Multi-systemic diagnosis

(c) *IF* step (b) helps them understand the reasons for my anger and aggression *AND* makes them conclude that they should be really nice to me to make me less angry *AND* share their home with me, *THEN* I let them get closer to me, but not too close.
(d) Go back to step (a) and go again through all the steps until my goal is reached.

Alan's proximity goal: To be close to Aaron on the condition that he is not "a bad boy", an aggressive boy.

Control goal: To make Aaron stop being aggressive.

Alan's plan:

(a) *IF* Aaron attacks me *THEN* I let him understand that I won't allow it. *IF* he doesn't comply *THEN* I try to buy him off by trying to direct his aggression elsewhere.
(b) *IF* he denies his aggression, stops being aggressive and distances himself *THEN* I ask to join him.
(c) *IF* he refuses and prefers another's company *THEN* I respect his choice to be alone.
(d) *IF* he explicitly invites me to join him *THEN* I follow him cautiously.

Sofia's proximity goal: To get close to Aaron and make him trust me and accept my love.

Sofia's plan:

(a) *IF* Aaron attacks me *THEN* I let him know that he is the powerful winner.
(b) *IF* he stops attacking me and stops being aggressive *THEN* I praise him for being nice *AND* suggest being nice to him *AND* trying to pet him.
(c) *IF* he doesn't let me *THEN* I don't try to impose this on him.
(d) *IF* he prefers to be alone at home *THEN* I will anxiously try to find out whether he wants to be in the same home with me and Alan.
(e) *IF* he invites me to join in *THEN* I follow him cautiously.

These programs, although based only on a short observation of family play, are clearly related to the family situation described above: Aaron's being an adopted boy in a second marriage, Sofia's and Alan's difficulties in realizing their parenthood and Aaron's aggressive and oppositional behavior.

I must emphasize that I do not claim that clients are aware of the complex programs underlying their behavior. The explicit wording of the programs is a part of the therapist's idiographic theory, which attempts to expose the generative rules according to which the overt behavior is conducted, the permanent underlying the shifting. Even a language speaker is not necessarily aware of the rules by which he or she speaks, and this is true of all human behavior.

Context-Dependent Componential Analysis

Componential analysis is a heuristic technique developed by anthropological linguists as a method for revealing and describing semantic systems (i.e. covert interrelations among meaning dimensions of words in various "exotic" languages) (Hammel, 1965). *Context-Dependent Componential Analysis* (CDCA) is my own elaboration of this technique. It can be applied to any sample of observed behavior, especially individual or interpersonal play behavior, or to any text such as a verbal interview. The need to contextualize the original technique was motivated by the necessity to perform macroscopic analyses of unconventional behaviors. In analyzing the underlying dimensions of such behaviors, we rely less on the conventional knowledge we have about language and culture and more on attempting to learn the private verbal and non-verbal behaviors of the people we observe. A child engaged in imaginative play does not necessarily use raw material and semantic units in the ways they are commonly used in her culture or society. She can introduce in her play a lion toy, but from the contexts in which she uses this toy one can learn that she created in her private world something different from a conventional lion. The lion in her play is much more a frightened little baby than King of the Beasts. A boy is spreading his fingers to signify "sun". But the meaning of "sun" for him is "grandfather". Such private raw material signs and meanings can be understood only if the contexts in which they occur are taken into account, hence the need for CDCA. With the aid of CDCA, the contextualized uses of both raw material units and semantic units are systematically categorized into sets defined by dimensions and subdimensions. The final result of each such analysis is a map exhibiting the hierarchical patterns of relations among the various signifying (raw material) dimensions and signified (semantic) dimensions and subdimensions. These hierarchical patterns are cross-classified with the degrees of emotional intensities associated with the various dimensions and subdimensions. Such a map constitutes a partial description of the deep, covert structures underlying the observed behavior or text. It is a kind of x-ray picture of the emotives and emotional balancing mechanisms that underlie the observed behavior and a kind of dictionary of the observed person's private language. CDCA helps us to learn the client's private language so that we can communicate with them in their own language. Furthermore, it facilitates the further discovery and formulation of more rules representing the hidden patterns lying behind the surface of the observed verbal and non-verbal behaviors.

A full demonstration of the CDCA technique is beyond the scope of this book. Such a full demonstration is found in Ariel (1992, 1999, 2002). To

134 Multi-systemic diagnosis

give an idea of what some of the CDCA discovery procedures and the final map look like, let me show how CDCA could be applied to Aaron's play in Observation 6.1. The following illustration applies just to the semantic level, although CDCA can be performed on the raw material level too.

Step 1. Listing all the activity units (AUs) of Aaron's play, with their contexts.

AU1: shark.
Contexts: attacking fish with sharp thrusts; squeaking violently; biting Alan's and then Sofia's arm; eating up fish; wanting to eat up more fish; swimming away from fish with wavy movements; not hungry anymore.

AU2: fish.
Contexts: doesn't eat up; swims; only he swims; doesn't want to be petted; not outside but at home, waiting for another fish; lets the other fish come too.

AU3: outside (in the sea).
Contexts: not at home; shark is outside; fish is outside.

AU4: home (inside).
Contexts: fish is at home; fish is waiting for another fish to come home.

AU5: attacking.
Contexts: shark attacks fish with sharp thrusts, squeaking violently.

AU6: biting.
Context: shark bites fish.

AU7: eating up.
Contexts: shark is eating up a fish; shark wants to eat up more fish; shark is not hungry; shark doesn't want to eat up more fish.

AU8: swimming.
Context: fish is swimming away.

AU9: waiting.
Context: fish is waiting for another fish to visit him.

AU10: inviting.
Context: fish invites other fish to follow him from a distance.

Step 2. Finding semantic dimensions that are common to all the contexts of each AU.

Collecting and analyzing diagnostic data 135

It will be noted that this and the following steps in the procedure are not mechanical, but subject to the intuition and creative thinking of the analyzer. This step is illustrated below just with reference to a sample of AUs.

AU1: shark.
The common dimensions of the contexts of shark seem to be: *degrees of aggression* [attacking, biting, eating up]; *hunger* [hungry, not hungry]; *intensity of action* [very intense, intense, mild]; and *direction of movement* [toward prey, away from prey].

AU2: fish.
The common dimensions of the contexts of fish seem to be: d*egree of aggression* [no aggression]; *movement* [moving (swimming) vs. *being static* (at home)]; *location* [outside, inside (at home)]; and *degrees of looking for company* [does not want company, wants company but doesn't want it too close nor to be touched by it].

AU3: hungry.
The common dimensions of *hunger* are: *degree of hunger* [high (wants to eat up many fish), intermediate (wants to eat up just one fish), low (not hungry)].

Step 3. Comparing all the pairs of the semantically interpreted AUs with their dimensions found in Step 2 and finding common dimensions and differentiating values.

This step will not be fully performed here. The main dimensions have already been specified above. A full analysis would probably yield more dimensions: *aggression* [high, low, no aggression]; *hunger* [very hungry, hungry, not hungry]; *intensity of action* [very intense, intense, mild]; *motion* [dynamic, static]; *direction of movement* [toward, away from]; *location* [outside, inside (at home)]; *degrees of looking for company* [does not want company, wants company but does not want it too close or to be touched].

Step 4. Looking for super-dimensions (i.e. dimensions that are common to the dimensions specified in Step 3).

The super-dimensions found seem to be: *intensity* (of aggression, hunger, action and movement); *location* (outside, inside); and *attachment* (strong, weak, detachment).

Step 5. Looking for a super-super-dimension (common to all the dimensions of Step 4) and charting the dimensions, subdimensions and semantically interpreted AUs in a single map, arranged according to the degree of intensity of specific emotions.

136 Multi-systemic diagnosis

Table 6.2 The results of the semantic CDCA of Aaron's play

Super-super-dimension: interpersonal distance	**Close:** *strong attachment; high intensity; outside*	**Medium:** *weak attachment; reduced intensity; outside*	**Far:** *detachment; low intensity; inside*
Level of arousal of anger vs. loneliness			
High anger, low loneliness	Shark very hungry, attacking, biting, moving forward in a straight line, squeaking violently, powerful		
Medium anger, medium loneliness		Fish not hungry, not aggressive, moving away, swimming with wavy movements, outside	
Low anger, high loneliness			Fish inside home, static, looking for friends

The super-super-dimension seems to be *interpersonal distance*. Its subdimensions are *attachment* (strong, weak, low); *intensity* (high, medium, low); and *location* (outside, inside). The associated emotions are anger vs. feeling lonely. The final map is displayed in Table 6.2.

Table 6.2 holds a great deal of information. It presents what seems to be one of Aaron's central emotives and the mechanism of emotion-balancing applying to this emotive, fluctuating between aggressive attachment and detachment. It exposes Aaron's central dilemma: fight or flight in his relationship with his adoptive parents. The turning points in his play behavior can be explained by the structure of this table. Furthermore, the table can serve as a kind of dictionary, defining the main private signified contents in Aaron's make-believe play and their emotional valence. In his play, for instance, *shark* is defined as an angry, hungry, powerful animal striving for strong and aggressive attachment and not so lonely, whereas *fish* is defined as a less angry, less powerful, less hungry and less aggressive but also more lonely animal looking for a relatively weak attachment or detachment as a defense against being rejected because of his aggression.

Fuller presentations and illustrations of the techniques of collecting and analyzing diagnostic information proposed in this chapter are found in Ariel (1992, 1999, 2002).

Collecting and analyzing diagnostic data 137

Trainees often ask me: is it really necessary to perform such time-consuming, meticulous analyses of observations and interviews that go into such minute detail? Is conducting such analyses even possible in the timeframe of psychotherapy? Why not rely on the observer's or interviewer's intuitive understanding of the data? The answers I usually give are: first, such an analysis provides information about deep structures that cannot be obtained by sheer intuition. It reveals covert patterns that are not easily accessible. Second, these methods of analysis can serve the function of validating and objectifying one's intuition. Third, these techniques are used primarily as training methods. Once internalized, they shape therapists' modes of thought and action even when they are not formally and fully implemented. These techniques do not replace but supplement natural discourse. Fourth, these methods of analysis can be used, at least in part, in the presentation of cases, case studies and research.

Summary of Chapter 6

This chapter presents various methods and techniques for collecting and analyzing multi-systemic diagnostic data that can assist the therapist to explain and understand the case and choose an effective therapeutic strategy. The techniques presented are: (a) presenting problems interview, whose purpose is to get a more objective picture of the difficulties to be treated than the characteristically vague, subjective picture given by the clients. The interviewer attempts to learn about the contexts in which the problematic behavior occurs (time, place, antecedent stimuli and responses by people in the environment) and its raw material manifestations (spatial, vocal–linguistic, movement and touching). Then the interviewer can attempt to interpret the data on the semantic and pragmatic levels. (b) Case history interview, whose purpose is to get diachronic information about the development of the case and the etiology of the symptoms. Information is elicited about the development of the various relevant internal and external subsystems, with special attention to the situation of change and crisis. The interview is not a rigid questionnaire. The interviewer forms hypotheses in his or her mind during the interview and asks further questions to confirm or refute his or her hypotheses. (c) Daily life interview – the client or clients (in a family or group setting) recount all their day's activities in minute detail. (d) Family interviews. Three requests – each family or group member asks each other three requests referring to their relationship. (e) The puppet show techniques in family or group therapy. Each participant chooses a puppet, gives it a name and makes up a show in which his or her puppet and the puppets of the other participants participate. (f) Observations of the free play and non-play behaviors of individuals, groups and families. A microscopic and macroscopic semiotic analysis is conducted. The syntactic rules underlying the observed behavior on the raw material, semantic and pragmatic levels are formulated. The information processing programs generating these rules are formulated. And (g) CDCA, in which the basic raw material or semantic dimensions of the observed behavior, their interrelations and their various emotional intensities are described.

Assignments

(a) Conduct a presenting problems interview, a case history interview, a daily life interview, three requests and the puppet show technique with clients. Interpret the data obtained in the ways presented in this chapter. If you don't have access to clients, you may interview people you know. You may also interview yourself.

(b) Observe the free play behaviors of children, families and groups, preferably clients. Videotape or hand-record the observations and transcribe them. Analyze them using the techniques of analysis proposed in this chapter. Attempt also to apply CDCA to these observations. In doing these tasks, you may be also assisted by Ariel (2002, pp.153–184), where these techniques are explained and illustrated in full detail.

A classified list of publications

Clinical interviews

McConaughy, S.H. (2013). *Clinical interviews for children and adolescents: Assessment to intervention*. 2nd ed. New York, NY: Guilford.

Transcription and notation techniques

Ekman, P. (2015). *Emotions in the human face*. 2nd ed. Los Altos, CA: Malor Books.
Eshkol. N. and Wachman, A. (1958). *Movement notation*. London, UK: Weidenfeld and Nicolson.
Kipling Brown, A. (2008). *Labanotation for beginners*. Hightstown, NJ: Princeton Book Co. Publications.

Semiotic analysis of observations

Ariel, S. (1992). *Strategic family play therapy*. Chichester, UK: Wiley.
Ariel, S. (1999). *Culturally competent family therapy*. Westport, CT: Praeger.
Ariel, S. (2002). *Children's imaginative play: A visit to Wonderland*. Westport, CT: Praeger.

Componential analysis

Hammel, E.A., ed. (1965). *Formal semantic analysis*. Special publication, American Anthropologist, 67(5), pt. 2.

Chapter 7

Organizing the multi-systemic diagnostic data

The purpose of this stage of the diagnostic evaluation is to expose the multi-systemic dynamics that enables us to understand the development of the case with all its complexity and base our therapeutic strategy and treatment on such deep understanding. An organized analysis of the data is an explanatory idiographic theory about the case. The data can be analyzed and organized in many different ways. No way is the correct one. The only test of validity that can be applied is to propose a number of alternative idiographic theories and choose the simplest one, the one that is the most comprehensive, parsimonious, consistent and plausible. Each such theory will be formulated in the languages of information processing, semiotics and cybernetics.

The distinction between a diachronic perspective and a synchronic perspective has already been mentioned. The two perspectives are important for understanding the case and for choosing the right treatment, but one should not confuse them with one another. It is not that everything that was true in the past is true at a later time. For example, in Case 6.1 (Moran), one learns from the data of Tikva's childhood that she was orphaned when she was eleven and witnessed a mother figure that had to work very hard and devote herself totally to her children. Daliah, the interviewer, hypothesized that Tikva had internalized this model and attempted to apply it in her current life – marginalizing her husband and shouldering all the parental and familial duties. This is thinking from a diachronic perspective that makes sense. But looking at the data solely from a synchronic perspective is likely to lead to different hypotheses (e.g. that at the present Tikva, omitting the declarative level, does not believe anymore that her sole role is to serve her family, hence her refusal to file a complaint with the police and her preference to work until late at night out of the home). The past can help us understand the present, but we should not confuse the past with the present.

Programs that are related to each other diachronically (i.e. a program follows another program through the axis of time) can be in *linear causality*. Programs that are related to each other *synchronically* cannot be in linear causality, but can be in *mutual, circular causality.* Returning to Example 6.1, Mosheh, following the death of his brother, developed programs that, without trying to formulate them in detail, led him to devote himself totally to his family of origin and to army service. Diachronically, these programs caused him (linear causality) to develop another program – of being marginal in his new family. Synchronically, however, the latter program causes his wife, Tikva, to function according to a program of shouldering the whole burden of the family. This program of hers, however, causes Mosheh to function according to his program of being uninvolved with his current family. This is mutual, circular causality. Synchronically, these two programs reinforce each other.

A multi-systemic idiographic theory may be constructed in stages. First, the programs of each specific subsystem can be formulated and then the programs of all the subsystems can be combined into a single multi-program idiographic theory.

Putting it all together

Despite the multiplicity of events and programs influencing the development of the case, a good idiographic theory exhibits a clear line of thinking, emphasizing the most important interrelated aspects of the development of the case in a way that throws light on what has happened. It is like a well-designed story or screenplay that gives the reader or the spectator a feeling of order and meaningfulness.

Although building a synchronic or diachronic idiographic theory about a particular case is done with the aid of intuition and creativity, this does not mean that the construction process is arbitrary, haphazard and capricious. An idiographic theory is cast into a given format, which delimits in advance, in principle, the kinds of possible interrelations between all the relevant entities. These interrelations will only belong to the following kinds:

(a) Relations of uni-directional, bi-directional or multi-directional influence between two or more programs. The possible kinds of such relations of influence are given in advance.
(b) Adverse effects of such relations of influence. The possible kinds of such adverse effects are given in advance.
(c) Possible ways in which such adverse effects are reflected in the presenting problems. These possible ways are also given in advance.

Types of uni-directional, bi-directional or multi-directional relations between programs or events and programs

First type: restriction of choice

One or more events, or one or more programs of the same or different subsystem(s), restrict the possibility of choosing a program or programs from the same or different subsystem(s).

Example: In Case 1.1 (Nonny), Shalom's total dependence on his achievements as a soccer player limited his ability to rehabilitate after the end of his career as a soccer player.

Second type: shaping form or content

An event or a program shapes the form or content of a program.

Example: In Case 6.1, the fact that Mosheh's brother was killed in the war shaped his over-devotion to his family of origin.

Third type: strengthening or weakening

An event or a program strengthens or weakens an already-shaped program.

In Example 5.3, Gabriel's having continued to stalk Ella strengthened her rejection of his attempts to enter into a relationship with him until she filed a complaint with the police.

Fourth type: mobilizing defensive responses

An event or a program mobilizes a program that serves as a defense.

The concept of *defensive responses* has wider applicability than the psycho-dynamic concept of *defenses* or *defense mechanism*. For example, a boy whose parents fight all the time may stay away from home as much as he can as a defensive response against his being exposed to their aggression.

Fifth type: influencing the tempo or nature of change

Diachronically, an event or a program quickens or slows down or influences the nature of change in some programs.

A child in a parental role can exhibit premature development in various respects.

An over-protective mother can slow down her child's development of autonomy.

Types of adverse effects of such relations of influence

First type: lacuna

A lacuna is lack of programs required for proper functioning. A lacuna prevents certain subsystems from having the optimal simplicity required for adequate functioning. It is very difficult but not necessarily impossible to acquire the lacking program by learning. For example, research has shown

142 Multi-systemic diagnosis

that children who grew up in conditions of extreme deprivation of parental touch, warmth and care (e.g. in orphanages of a bad kind) suffer later in life from lacuna in attachment abilities. In my view, such correlations are not deterministic. They are only probabilistic. The likelihood of a lacuna being repaired depends on the interaction between programs from all the subsystems in the course of development.

Lacunae can be manifested in programs belonging to any of the internal or external subsystems. There are lacunae in cognitive programs such as perception and conceptualization, in emotion regulation programs, in object relations programs or in interpersonal programs such as parental relationships. Some lacunae are genetically inherited. Other lacunae appear at a very early stage of the development of certain internal or external subsystems.

One should distinguish between a lacuna and dysfunctional programs. In Example 6.1, Tikva's inability to deal with her child's problems was not due to a lack of attachment and empathy, but to her being overburdened.

Second type: distortion

What I call a distorted program is a program that is extremely bugged. An example is the anorexic girl who is absolutely certain that she is fat (an extreme example of the non-sense bug).

Third type: shattering

What I call shattering is extreme weakening or disintegration of an already-acquired program. One of the manifestations of shattering is an extreme flip-flop bug as a part of a post-traumatic syndrome in a person who was stable before the trauma (e.g. extreme mood swings and extreme fluctuations between being nice and considerate and being violent toward loved ones without any apparent reason).

Fourth type: fixation and regression

Case 7.1 Natalie

Twelve-year-old Natalie was the daughter of Violet, a forty-year-old single parent. Violet was depressed. She neglected Natalie. In a dyadic therapy session, Natalie exhibited extremely regressed behavior. She tried to force Violet to literally breast-feed her.

Mosheh in Case 6.1 was fixated to the stage of his life following his brother's death.

Fifth type: insoluble conflict

Insoluble conflict is a conflict within the same program (flip-flop) or between two or more programs that cannot be solved, because the two sides of the conflict are equally powerful.

> Example: After the parents of a boy divorced, each of them tried to convince the boy that the other parent was a bad person. This created an insoluble identification conflict inside the boy's mind.
>
> A typical approach–avoidance conflict: a young man is extremely attracted to a particular young woman. He has a strong drive to court her, but a powerful fear of being rejected and humiliated. He is paralyzed by this insoluble conflict.

Sixth type: dysfunctional defensive response

Bugs are often dysfunctional defensive responses in the sense that, instead of solving the difficulty, they defend against it and aggravate it (feed-forward, deviation-amplifying). In the above example, if the young man yields to the dysfunctional defensive response of avoiding any attempt to court the girl, this can only exacerbate his fear of being rejected.

Possible ways in which such adverse effects are reflected in the presenting problems

The adverse effects can be reflected in the presenting problems directly, as for instance in Case 7.1 (Natalie) or indirectly, metaphorically, e.g. compulsive hand-washing as a metaphor for cleansing one's bad conscience. These kinds of possible interrelations among all the relevant entities constitute together the format into which the multi-systemic diagnostic data can be cast. This format makes it easier to organize and order the abundance of raw and analyzed data. The organization is hierarchical: first layer – relations of influence; second layer – adverse effects; third layer – reflection in the presenting problems.

It will be stressed that all these terms are not just words chosen arbitrarily. They in fact summarize and classify numerous concepts found in the literature. These terms constitute theoretical statements about various psychopathological phenomena, their etiologies and their external manifestations. They do not just describe the phenomena, but also form a part of their explanations. Saying that Tikva's failure to protect her daughter against the abuser reflects a lacuna of attachment on Tikva's side (Case 6.1) is very different from saying it is an inadequate defense against her being over-burdened with family duties out of choice. Each of these alternative formulations makes for a different idiographic theory about the case and predicts different therapeutic prognoses. If it is a lacuna, it will be difficult to repair it. If it is a defense, it will be easier to help Tikva to change it.

It should be emphasized, however, that all the above terms are just titles, abbreviations, names for very complex semiotic information processing and cybernetic processes. A fuller multi-systemic diagnosis will not only give the titles, but will also specify in some detail the processes named by these titles. The detailed specification will demonstrate how an event, or the output of each program in a particular subsystem, becomes input to another program in the same or a different subsystem.

Case 7.2 Amir

Amir was adopted by Basil and his wife, Sabina, both immigrants from a Middle Eastern country, when he was two years old. Before his adoption, Amir had stayed in a foster care institution, where he was said to have been physically abused by some of the caretakers.

Basil was a hard-working factory laborer, a shy, silent, dutiful man. Sabina was a warm, industrious housewife.

Basil and Sabina saw eye-to-eye in everything concerning Amir's upbringing. They both were loving and accepting, maintaining adequate parental authority without being overly strict. When Amir was five, Sabina died of a fatal disease. Basil and Amir did not show any dramatic external manifestations of grief and bereavement, but Basil became sullen and dejected, unable to speak. For a few months, Amir slept in Basil's bed.

A year later, Basil married another woman, Badra, of the same country of origin as himself. Badra was very different from Sabina. She was an extrovert, emotionally expressive, dramatic and domineering. She considered herself intelligent and talented. She recalled with bitterness that her father, having held a traditional tenet that study and work out of home were not meant for women, would not allow her to complete her high school education and confiscated her books. Nevertheless, she continued studying secretly, with the aid of her older sister, and completed her matriculation on her own. After she got married to Basil, she devoted a great deal of time to taking various kinds of courses out of the home. Basil complained that she was spending too much time and money on these courses, straining the tight family budget and neglecting her home duties. She justified herself by saying that some of these courses would help her be a better wife and mother, because they dealt with topics related to psychology and education. She accused Basil of being ignorant and lacking ambition. He retorted that none of these courses had made her any cleverer.

Amir was a smart little boy, but he did poorly in school. He was restless and lazy. He associated with some unruly fourth-grade children, doing with them all kinds of mischief.

Organizing the multi-systemic data 145

Soon after Basil married Badra, a severe conflict developed between her and Amir, with Basil taking Amir's side. Badra attempted to impose strict limits on Amir, to structure his afternoons and holidays with many hours devoted to study and family duties. When he did not comply, she would use threats and punishments. Amir reacted by being disobedient and insolent. Often he would run away from home and hide somewhere for hours. Basil passively supported Amir by not going along with Badra's demands that he should cooperate with her policy of limit-setting. She, however, never consulted Basil about this policy. She thought Basil too unintelligent and indifferent for her to bother asking for his advice. Badra often made dramatic scenes, crying and yelling, accusing both Basil and Amir of hating her and wanting her out of the home.

Amir's school performance and behavior were gradually deteriorating, until he was transferred to a therapeutic day school. For a short period, his behavior and performance improved. The school was located near a neighborhood considered "bad" and dangerous, with occasional street gang shootouts. Amir was attracted to that neighborhood like a moth to a burning lamp. One day, he witnessed a shootout followed by a police raid. Two youngsters were killed and a policeman was seriously injured. After that event, his behavior became much more problematic. He spent more time out of class than in. His behavior toward the teachers was extremely insolent and disrespectful. He often got entangled in brawls with other pupils. He would climb over the school's fence and go to the "bad" neighborhood, spending the whole day who knows where. At home, he stole money from Badra's purse. He began associating with delinquent boys in the neighborhood. Badra and Basil almost totally lost control over him. Badra blamed Basil. She said he was too weak and permissive and complained that he left her to struggle with the problem alone.

Therapy started when Amir was nine years old.

Let me analyze parts of this case, using the above concepts, without attempting a full technical formulation. The analysis will not adhere only to the sheer facts, but will raise hypotheses to be confirmed or refuted.

First life event: Amir stayed in a foster care institution. There was no single caretaker there who could serve as a main good-enough parental figure for him. Some caretakers were abusive. The caretakers' conduct was unpredictable (the ecological and social subsystems). Amir suffered from a *restriction of choice* of parental environment needed for healthy development.

The *adverse effects* of this situation were *lacunae* in attachment, in internalization of parental objects and in basic trust. An *insoluble conflict* was *shaped* between Amir's dependency on the caretakers on the one hand and his fear of them, as well as his inability to trust them, on the other hand. An *emotive*

146   Multi-systemic diagnosis

was *shaped* in Amir's mind: fear of aggression and of being neglected by caretakers and anger at them.

These lacunae, insoluble conflict and emotive *shaped* in Amir proximity and control goals with respect to caretakers in general: not letting any caretaker neglect or abuse him. His plan for achieving these goals was avoiding caretakers whenever possible. This plan was materialized later in his life. This interpersonal program was bugged with horse blinders: He preferred consistency at the cost of comprehensiveness (being in touch only with caretakers' neglect, aggression and abuse).

Second life event: adoption (the family subsystem). Amir got consistent and appropriate parental love and caring (family system input). These circumstances gradually *weakened* the *adverse effects* of the pre-adoption period and *affected the tempo and nature of change.* Amir began to *shape* an emotive of love and gratefulness with respect to his adoptive parents. He *shaped* a new family program whose goal was to preserve the proximity between them and himself and let them control him in a benign way. His new program was not bugged. He began to *evaluate the behavior of his adoptive parents as positive with respect to his own self.* The consistent warm and caring parenting from the side of Basil and Sabina sprouted in him buds of an ability to trust parental figures. He began to internalize Basil and Sabina as good-enough parents and to form more or less secure attachments with them, despite his *lacunae* in these respects.

Third life event: the death of Sabina when Amir was five. Amir and Basil suffered another blow, another *restriction of choice* of a spouse and of a parental figure.

This tragedy *shaped* in Basil an emotive of sadness and loneliness related to the loss. As an *inadequate defense* he chose not to externalize his grief. He *shaped* a family program with respect to Amir that had a proximity goal but not a control goal. He gave up the possibility of applying parental authority. His plan for achieving proximity with Amir didn't include communication about the loss, only physical closeness, sleeping in the same bed. This program was a response to his own emotional needs, but he failed to consider Amir's needs. His program was consistent, parsimonious (no redundant information) and plausible (no misinterpretation of input), but not comprehensive (horse blinders). It did not consider the traumatic effect of the loss on Amir, nor his need for parental control. It prevented Amir from working through his loss (*restriction of choice*). The mutual physical closeness between Basil and Amir was the result of an *inadequate defense* on the side of both of them – physical closeness as a substitute for real attachment.

The loss of Sabina *restricted Amir's choice* of enjoying stable parenting. The previous parental programs were *weakened* considerably. Their simplicity was lost. The memory of the loss of his biological mother, even if Amir had only been told about it and had never experienced it directly, *shaped* in him an emotive of acute sadness about loss of a mother figure. Sabina's death *strengthened* this emotive and got the emotions even more off-balance. However, as an *inadequate defense*, these emotions were repressed and not consciously available to Amir. He preferred consistency and parsimony at the cost of comprehensiveness. He wasn't aware of his own emotions, of his real needs (horse blinders).

Fourth life event: Badra came into the picture; *restriction of choice* again. Amir was no longer allowed to sleep in Basil's bed. This *shaped* in him an emotive of anger at being rejected. He lost his last remnants of corrective emotional experience, of consistent, rehabilitated parenting. The additional *weakening* of the corrective programs caused deeper regression to his previous stage of lack of secure attachment and basic trust. The sadness and anger related to his early memories were aroused again.

Basil *shaped* a new program of proximity: getting closer to Badra and distancing himself from Amir, not letting him sleep in his bed any longer. This program failed to take into account the effect on Amir of his remarriage. He did not prepare Amir for the change (horse blinders; no corrective feedback).

Badra's father had a family cultural program (structural and functional rule). His program had a control goal of preventing Badra from studying when she was an adolescent. She *mobilized a defensive response* and *shaped* a cultural family program whose control goal was not to let him dominate her. Her plan included studying secretly with the aid of her sister. Her control goal was related to loss of simplicity in a period of cultural change, emigration to a country in which the dominant culture encourages rather than discourages women's studying and having a career out of the home. This *shaped* in her an emotive of anger at being prevented from studying. Her achievement also *shaped* in her self-concept program, "I am clever, intelligent, independent uncontrollable". She was *fixated* to this program and on her emotive, even after she got married to Basil. But then this program and the related emotive were not as relevant to her new life as before (fifth wheel).

The family program Badra *shaped* with respect to Basil and Amir had a proximity goal (not to be too close to Basil and Amir) and control goals (not to be controlled by Basil and to control Amir). Her plan of studying out of the home to become a better mother was infected with non-sense (the prediction that it would make her a better mother substitute was wrong). This plan was also infected with horse blinders and with fifth wheel. She did not take into account the fact that her studies were not relevant to what Amir needed. She did not try to understand what Amir's real needs were. She also *shaped* a program whose proximity goal was to be accepted and appreciated by Basil as a wife and a substitute mother. This program also had a control goal – to dictate to Basil how to raise Amir. She treated Basil with disrespect, seeing him as weak and uneducated. This program was infected with flip-flop. The goal of being accepted and appreciated clashed with her control goal and with treating Basil with disrespect. Her view of Basil was infected with non-sense. He was more clever and intelligent that she thought. Her program of domineering and diminishing her husband clashed with her program of needing his approval and appreciation (flip-flop). She used to complain that he did not understand, was not intelligent enough, was too indifferent and weak to know how to raise Amir, but she did not let him show his abilities, so her plan was infected with horse blinders and flip-flop.

Basil *shaped* a program with respect to Badra whose control goal was not to let Badra dominate Amir. His plan was to passively support Amir by not cooperating with Badra's demands that he should abide by her policy of limit-setting. She, however, never consulted Basil about this policy. She thought Basil too unintelligent and indifferent for her to bother asking for his advice. She saw Basil as passive, but at the same time projected onto him the controlling image of her father, because he objected to her studies. This projection was bugged with fifth wheel. Her father's attitude to her studies was not relevant to her relationship with Basil. Unlike her father, Basil had no parental authority over her. His objection had no cultural basis. Her program was therefore infected with non-sense and horse blinders.

Basil's program with respect to Badra had the proximity goal of not forming any real intimate relationship with her. He seemed to want her just for taking care of Amir and the home. Therefore, he criticized her studies and her spending time and money on them. His plan was infected with horse blinders. He did not see her emotional needs as a woman and her wish to prove herself as a mother substitute, competing with the late Sabina's success. He had never really worked thorough the loss of Sabina and was therefore still very much attached to her. He did not negotiate with Badra about her status and role in the family, so his plan was infected with horse blinders.

Badra, as a *defensive response* against her being rejected as a wife and a mother substitute, *shaped* a program with respect to Amir that had mainly a control goal. Maybe she had a proximity goal too, but this didn't show in her behavior. She believed that structuring Amir's daily life and setting strict limits were what Amir needed. Her plan, however, included a limited understanding of his behavior. She was not aware of the real sources of his difficulties and of his emotional needs (horse blinders). Her plan to reach her control goal included aggressive disciplinary measures: threats and punishments. Her prediction about the effects of these disciplinary measures was erroneous (non-sense). If these disciplinary measures didn't work, then, as an *inadequate defense*, she would make dramatic scenes, crying and yelling, accusing both Basil and Amir of hating her and wanting her out of the home. This plan included horse blinders. She was blind to the adverse effects on Amir and Basil of both her courses of action. Her plan was also infected with non-sense: wrong predictions. The bugs in her plan initiated feed-forward processes instead of mobilizing corrective feedback, escalating the conflict between her and them.

Badra's aggressive plan reminded Amir of his having been a victim of aggression in his early childhood. He *shaped* a program that retrieved from memory the inconsistent and aggressive parenting he had experienced before the adoption. His proximity and control goals with respect to Badra were not to let her be close to him or control him. His plan included being insolent, running away and hiding. This plan was infected with fifth wheel, because Badra's behavior toward him was very different from the inconsistent parenting, neglect and abuse he suffered in his early childhood.

Amir was not mentally ready to invest energies in studies. His ability to maintain basic trust in figures of authority was fatally *weakened*. He *shaped* a program whose control goal was rebelling against any kind of authority.

Amir, as mentioned above, experienced Badra's strict parenting measures as sheer aggression and abuse, which reminded him, unconsciously, of the aggression he had suffered from some of his caretakers in the foster institution. As *an inadequate defense* he *shaped* an ecological program with a proximity goal, attraction to "bad" neighborhoods and gangs. This was a repetition compulsion, replaying his early childhood experiences. He was attracted to and identified with both aggressors and victims of aggression. It also seems that he nourished suicidal wishes.

The loss of simplicity caused by the arrival of Badra and the dysfunctional relationship in the family triad led Amir to choose consistency (rejecting both his adoptive parents and the school and associating only with children he saw as being like him) over comprehensiveness (understanding and dealing with the complexities of his family life; horse blinders).

Fifth life event: the traumatic shootout scene Amir witnessed. This event totally *shattered* all the remnants of Amir's family programs. His only way to keep proximity to his home was stealing money from Badra's purse. His early childhood *lacunae* (lack of basic trust, avoidant attachment and inability to internalize any positive, consistent parental figures) came to the fore. His emotions became extremely unbalanced. His behavior was *a direct expression* of his emotions.

Basil and Badra lost control over him completely. Badra *shaped* a program toward Basil, of which the proximity and control goals were to urge him to exercise his authority over Amir and cooperate with her. Her plan to achieve these goals – accusations – was bugged with non-sense and horse blinders. This only made Basil leave her alone in the battlefield and become even more passive.

Summary of Chapter 7

This chapter deals with the question of how to organize all the collected data into a multi-systemic, diachronic and synchronic diagnostic evaluation. The joints that link the building blocks of this edifice are: (a) the types of uni-directional, bi-directional or multi-directional relations among programs, or events and program, belonging to the various subsystems (restriction of choice, shaping form or content, strengthening or weakening, mobilizing defensive responses, influencing the tempo or nature of change); (b) the types of adverse effects of such relations of influence (lacuna, distortion, shattering, fixation and regression, insoluble conflict, dysfunctional defensive response); and (c) the possible ways in which such adverse effects are reflected in the presenting problems (direct or metaphorical). These types of joints have not been chosen arbitrarily. They summarize and classify numerous concepts found in the literature. These terms constitute theoretical statements about various psychopathological phenomena, their etiologies and their external manifestations. They do not just describe the phenomena, but also constitute a part of their explanations. Nevertheless, these terms are no more than titles for very complex semiotic, information processing and cybernetic processes. A fuller multi-systemic diagnosis will not only give the titles, but will also specify in some detail the processes named by these titles.

Assignment

Attempt to reformulate Case 6.1 (Moran) using the format and the terminology illustrated in the analysis of Amir's case above.

A classified list of publications

Integrative assessment

Ariel, S. (1992). *Strategic family play therapy*. Chichester, UK: Wiley.

Ariel, S. (1999). *Culturally competent family therapy*. Westport, CT: Praeger.

Gersten, A. (2012). *Integrative assessment: A guide for counselors*. Cambridge, UK: Pearson.

Part 4

Therapy

Chapter 8

Planning and carrying out the therapy

Strategy

The diagnostic evaluation serves as a basis for designing an overall strategy, or a number of alternative strategies, for the therapy. A strategy determines the therapeutic goals and the main ways of reaching them. They attempt to predict obstacles in the way of reaching the goals and offer ways of removing or overcoming them.

In designing strategies, it is important to base every decision on explicit considerations that take into account the information collected in the evaluation phase. A strategy is just a general treatment plan. It should not be adhered to rigidly during the therapy. It will be modified flexibly, adapted to new data encountered in the various stages of therapy.

The questions that should be asked when a strategy is designed are:

(a) What are the specific targets of change?

In The Diamond Model, the main targets of change are the bugs in the various information processing programs. The therapy should concentrate primarily on removing or weakening such bugs. Bugs prevent the homeostasis-maintaining mechanisms from functioning properly. Removing or weakening the bugs can restore the systems' ability to mobilize corrective, balance-maintaining feedback. It will be recalled also that bugs are kinds of defenses, energized by over-heated emotions. A preliminary for removing or weakening the bugs is therefore restoring the balance of unbalanced emotions that are associated with the emotives to which the bugs are related.

In designing the strategy, one has to decide first which of the bugs to concentrate on.

(b) What kinds of difficulties can one expect to encounter on the way to trying to restore emotion balance and to removing the bugs?

The difficulties can come from various origins: lack of motivation or resistance to change, lack of strengths or skills required, failure of the therapeutic

154 Therapy

alliance, etc. Therefore, in the stage of planning strategies, it is necessary to assess in advance factors that can contribute to the therapy's success vs. factors that can adversely affect the therapy. Among such factors are, for instance, the nature and strength of motivation for therapy of each of the participants, sources and motives of resistance, strengths and weaknesses of the clients and cultural and personality traits that can assist or hamper the prospects of success.

(c)   What is the order of priorities in choosing intervention foci?

The main consideration is efficiency. One should concentrate first on trying to intervene in foci that are expected to get the best results with the least resistance and investment of time and effort. A relevant metaphor is the domino effect. One should prefer to achieve changes that will lead spontaneously to other changes in the desired directions. One should also try to predict possible adverse effects that can be caused by the intervention.

When designing a strategy, it is advisable first to make a list of the programs of the participants in the case and the bugs found in these programs. One should distinguish between programs that are still relevant on the one hand and programs that belong to the history of the case but are not relevant to its current state on the other.

Example 8.1   A strategy for the case of Amir

In Case 7.1 (Amir), there are many bugged, emotionally unbalanced programs of various subsystems that are relevant to the case, because each of them partly explains the presenting difficulties.

Targets of change. Here is a list of the main emotionally unbalanced programs and bugs:

Amir was referred to therapy after all his post-adoption family programs had been shattered. He was traumatized by the shootout he had witnessed. His basic lacunae came back to the fore. He was regressed to the stage of lack of basic trust in caretakers, no internalization of stable parental figures and avoidant attachment. He didn't trust Basil to protect him against Badra. His main emotive was heightened anger at parental figures in general and Badra in particular.

Among his programs were rebelling against any authority figures, including benevolent ones such as teachers. He distanced himself from them, preferring the company of "bad" peers. These programs were energized by the above-mentioned emotive and by his lacunae. These programs were bugged with fifth wheel, non-sense and horse blinders, but not with flip-flop. His early childhood experiences were irrelevant to his current relationships with Badra or with the other adults in his life. He misinterpreted the strict limits imposed by Badra as sheer aggression and abuse, but failed to understand her positive proximity and control goals. His proximity program – seeking the company of "bad" peers – was designed, unconsciously, to reduce the level of his anger and emotional distress. This program was infected with horse blinders and non-sense, because his repetition compulsion and identification with aggressors only intensified his anger and distress (feed-forward). The traumatic shootout scene he was a witness to totally shattered all the remnants of his family programs and got his emotions more off-balance. Contrary to common sense, stealing money from Badra's purse was a positive sign of not severing any contact with her.

At the onset of therapy, Basil and Badra found themselves helpless, unable to resume parental control over Amir and stop his deterioration. All their previous dysfunctional programs were considerably strengthened. Badra's program to urge Basil to exercise his authority over Amir and cooperate with her through accusations was bugged with non-sense and horse blinders. This program only made Basil leave her alone in the battlefield and become even more passive (feed-forward).

Badra and Basil's proximity and control goals with respect to Amir were infected with horse blinders. They had no idea why Amir was behaving the way he did, nor what were the sources of his difficulties.

Priorities. In designing the strategy for this case, the first consideration will be priorities. Which bugs should be concentrated on, taking into account obstacles and adverse effects of the chosen interventions?

Obviously, the first priority would be restoring Amir's trust in his adoptive parents and in his teachers. To achieve this, helping him rebalance his emotions related to his emotive of anger at and fear of the parental figures that he considered abusive and neglecting will be required. Helping him rebalance his emotions related to the traumatic shootout event will also be needed. He should be helped to get rid of the horse blinders and non-sense bugs in his program of identification with the "bad" peers. This could be a preliminary to removing the horse blinders and non-sense bugs in his family programs.

Resistance. Any attempt to achieve these goals would, however, be met with unbending resistance on the side of Amir. In all probability, any therapist would be rejected by him because of his total lack of trust in any authority figure. It would be almost impossible to persuade him to enter into any therapeutic relationship.

An alternative course. Another course could be couple therapy along with parental guidance with Basil and Badra. They can be helped to balance their emotions with respect to each other and to Amir and then to weaken the bugs in their mutual relationship and in their relationship with Amir. They will be likely to cooperate because of their being helpless and needing help. However, even if they change in the relevant respects and reconsider their attitudes and behavior toward Amir, it would perhaps be too late, because Amir would not believe or trust them.

In order to get results in this therapy, a way to attain cooperation on the part of Amir must be found. This could perhaps be achieved in either of two ways: to buy his cooperation by offering him something that he would have an interest in receiving (e.g. some electronic device his parents had refused to buy him because of his misbehavior); or to find and establish a connection with an influential youth in the peer group Amir has been associated with. Although it is definitely not advisable to pay a minor to get him into therapy, this would be legitimate in this case if it were the only way to get his initial cooperation. If he complies, it will be advantageous to have him meet two co-therapists, a man and a woman, who would take a one-down, non-authoritative, non-directive, accepting position. He would be encouraged to engage in play or another form of expressive therapy in which he would be permitted to express his anger freely. He would be allowed to attack the therapists verbally and non-verbally, without touching them physically, transferring to them his anger at his parental figures. After he lets himself trust the therapists up to a certain extent, more subtle emotion-balancing techniques could be applied (see Chapters 9 and 10).

The couple therapy with Basil and Badra would be carried out simultaneously. Emotion-balancing techniques would be followed by bug-busters, weakening the bugs in Basil and Badra's mutual programs and in their parenting programs. When Amir was ready, family therapy with the three of them would be conducted, using emotion-balancing techniques, followed by applying debugging techniques to remove the bugs in the parenting programs. A deeper individual psychotherapy with Amir would be postponed to a later stage in his life.

The therapeutic alliance

A good therapeutic rapport between therapist and client is crucial for the success of the therapy.

Therapeutic contract

At the onset of the therapy, a therapeutic contract, usually oral, is discussed between therapist and client. The contract will cover the goals of the therapy, its structure and the methods by which it will be conducted. It will address subjects such as who is to be asked to participate in the session, the expected number of sessions, fees, rules concerning missing sessions and being late and the nature of the relationship between therapist and client.

One should distinguish between a direct, explicit contract and a tacit contract. The latter is an unspoken, tacit agreement on things both sides prefer not to talk about openly. For example, in the case of Amir, the explicit contract between the therapist and the adoptive parents would state that the purpose of the meetings is parental guidance, but the tacit agreement would include also treating Basil and Badra's marital problems.

Culturally sensitive therapeutic alliance

Every good therapeutic alliance is based on mutual respect and trust and unconditional, non-judgmental, empathetic acceptance of the client, their personalities and their difficulties. The therapist will attempt to understand the client's world – all the more so if the therapist and client do not share the same culture. To achieve a good culturally sensitive alliance, the therapist is advised to adopt the following principles:

(a) Try to learn and accept the client's own culturally determined conceptions of the nature and causes of their difficulties and of their preferred ways to be helped (see Chapter 5).
(b) Know your own culture. Be aware of your cultural biases and ethnocentric conceptions.
(c) Openly acknowledge the differences between your own culture and theirs and adopt the position of a learner. If necessary and possible, use mediators.
(d) Try to achieve an insider status and find or create a common cultural ground between you and the clients.
(e) Beware of bugs in the therapeutic communication between you and your clients. Attempt to remove the bugs.
(f) Be aware of the fact that some clients will not fully trust you, will be reluctant to share with you important information or will give you incorrect information, especially if they see themselves as members of a disadvantaged section of the population and you as a member of a privileged section.

Carrying out the therapy

The main purposes of therapy are to remove or weaken bugs. For these purposes, it is necessary to find ways of balancing the emotions maintaining the bugs. If a bug is horse blinders, the therapy should somehow help the client process the missing information required for good functioning. If the bug is fifth wheel, the therapy will concentrate on removing superfluous information that burdens proper functioning. If the bug is flip-flop, the therapy

158 Therapy

should help the client to be aware of contradictions in their information processing programs and settle these contradictions. If the bug is non-sense, the client will be helped to become aware of the irrationality of their interpretations or predictions and adopt more rational ones.

These purposes are achieved by the *main therapeutic moves* made by the therapist. In such moves, bug-busters are activated. However, in order to prepare the ground for the main moves, the therapist often needs to make various *preparatory moves*. The purposes of the latter are to secure the client's cooperation, to survey their readiness for the main moves and their responses to previous main moves and to help them get ready for the main moves. One has also to make *auxiliary moves* for monitoring unwanted side effects of main moves.

The approach to the use of therapeutic methods and techniques in The Diamond Model is systematic technical eclecticism; that is, one can use or make up any techniques whatsoever from any source, providing that the techniques chosen are informed by the diagnostic evaluation, the therapeutic strategy and the particular purpose of each session. For this purpose, the therapist must understand the mechanism of change of the chosen technique – what makes it work (see below and Chapter 10). It follows that in therapy informed by The Diamond Model there is no room for standard interventions that follow a preset protocol. Each intervention will be tailor-made according to the specific characteristics of the client and the case. Admittedly, it is easier to learn and apply standardized protocols. Individualized methods and techniques require the therapist to be always insightful, creative and imaginative, an artisan and an artist. This is sometimes easier said than done, but I believe it is unavoidable, because no method or technique can suit every client, every situation and every difficulty. Moreover, individualized interventions make the therapy more exciting and challenging and therefore more rewarding.

In choosing or creating techniques, one has to take into account factors such as the motivation, strengths and cultural and personal styles of the client, the stage of therapy and other considerations. Every aspect of the diagnostic evaluation and strategy can influence the choice of intervention methods and techniques. For instance, we will not use techniques based on insight with people whose capacity for abstract thinking and emotional intelligence are low. We will not use techniques based on dancing in mixed groups (males and females) if the client comes from a culture in which such an activity is considered immodest. We will choose or create techniques that are likely to be effective and really produce the require results because they suit the client's personality, cognitive style, emotional responsiveness, biological makeup and, of course, culture.

The frameworks in which the therapeutic intervention are carried out are also not fixed, but chosen according to the stage of the therapeutic process and the multi-systemic dynamics in each stage of therapy. One can combine,

Planning and carrying out the therapy 159

in working with the same case, individual, family, group and community therapy, consultation to the school, etc., simultaneously or in sequence.

When a therapeutic setting and techniques are chosen, one should ask oneself the following questions:

(a) What are *the targets of change*? What is the purpose of the intervention? What emotive-related emotions need to be balanced? Which bugs need to be weakened or removed?
(b) What is the mechanism of change? How is the chosen technique supposed to achieve the purpose of emotion-balancing and bug-removing or softening?
(c) What are the means of change? What kinds of preparatory, auxiliary and main moves (the therapist's verbal or non-verbal acts) should the therapist make to activate the technique?
(d) What are the expected results of our intervention?

Example 8.2 *Individual therapy with Avner*

Let's go back to Case 5.4 (Avner).

The above-listed goals of the therapy were:

(a) Helping Avner create new, optimally simple (comprehensive, parsimonious, consistent and plausible) cultural programs.
(b) Assisting him to realize that, at least for the time being, his religious faith with all its implications and ramifications could not be revived or replaced by a substitute and helping him to mourn its loss. However, even if he no longer believed in an all-knowing, omnipotent deity external to his own self, he could still find within himself the correlate of such a spiritual entity.
(c) Encouraging him to recognize that secular life without absolute faith can be meaningful and satisfying if a person sets himself a worthy goal in this world.

In terms of debugging, the goals are weakening his fifth wheel (the irrelevance of his previous faith to his current life), his non-sense (erroneously predicting that he can find a substitute to his lost religious faith) and his horse blinders (failing to see spiritual meaning and purpose in his current life).

Description of some sessions

(a) First purpose: help Avner rebalance his unbalanced emotions of deep sadness and fear related to his emotive of the loss of his religious faith.

Preparatory moves: I got Avner's consent to participate in psycho-physical and other activities that are not just conventional talk therapy. Then I helped him enter into a state of relaxation.

Main moves: I asked Avner to locate the part of his body in which he was feeling emptiness. He located it inside his chest. Then I asked him to identify those parts of his body in which he had been feeling pains and other unpleasant sensations. He described pains, trembling and other odd sensations in his feet and hands. I instructed him to transfer these unpleasant feeling to his chest, concentrate all of them inside his chest and fill it with them. He managed to do so. Then I asked him whether he still felt the emptiness in his chest. He said no, he experienced his chest as full, but full of pain. And he started to cry. He cried bitterly for a long time. When he calmed down, I asked him to continue concentrating on his chest and to tell me whatever would come into his mind. His immediate association was of himself as a baby, sitting astride his father's shoulders. His father played as if he were a galloping horse. In my mind, this childhood memory was immediately associated with his admiration of the authoritative headmaster who he claimed was very different from his own father, who he saw as weak and indifferent. This memory was also associated in my mind with his previous belief in God. However, I didn't attempt to share these thoughts with him.

Avner had big and wide feet and hands. I asked him to get up and stand firmly while looking at the palms of his hands, with his fingers spread in front of his face. I turned his attention to the size of his feet and hands and asked him to imagine that he was a bronze statue attached firmly to its base.

The mechanism of change: Suggestion and guided imagination, using concrete images; catharsis.

As stated above, the choice of technique has to take into consideration the client's special characteristics, such as their cognitive style and threshold of sensory sensitivity. Avner was prone to somatization. I often found clients with somatization highly suggestible. There is some research evidence, though not very strong, for this correlation (see Brown, Schraq, Krinamoorthy and Trimble, 2008). I suggested that his feeling of emptiness covered acute mental pain related to his losses. The mental pain was partly somatized as unpleasant sensations in his feet and hands. The pains and trembling in his feet were raw material manifestations of the idea and feeling (on the semantic level) that he was no longer standing on sure ground. The unpleasant sensations in his hands were raw material manifestations of the idea (on the semantic level) that everything he used to have had slipped out of his hands.

Avner was very analytic and verbal. I predicted that verbal interpretations and analysis would not do the trick with him. Imaginary concentration of all his unpleasant somatic experiences in his "empty" chest would fill it with the emotions he experienced as emptiness. His chest

Planning and carrying out the therapy 161

would become so full that his emotions would need to be poured out in a purifying catharsis. Turning his attention to his big, strong feet and hands and guiding him to imagine that he was a bronze statue would counter his feelings of weakness.

After these emotion-balancing main moves, Amir was ready for further main moves whose purpose was to debug some of his programs.

(b) Second purpose: assist Avner to realize that, at least for the time being, his religious faith with all its implications and ramifications could not be revived or replaced by a substitute and help him to mourn its loss (removing non-sense). However, even if he no longer believed in an all-knowing, omnipotent deity external to his own self, he could still find within himself the correlate of such a spiritual entity.

Preparatory move: I asked Avner to devote the time until the next session to considering very seriously the question of whether he would be able to revive his religious faith or find a satisfactory substitute. I also asked him to bring the object that most symbolized his religious faith next time.

In the next session, he said that he could not find an unequivocal answer, but his answer was ninety percent "no, impossible". The object he brought was his *Siddur*, the Jewish prayer book.

Main moves: Avner's home village was situated in the Negev, Israel's southern desert. I suggested to Avner to camp alone in the desert near his village for three days with the *Siddur*. His time there would be devoted to parting with his religious faith (not the *Siddur*) and mourning the separation. He did so. He told me that during these three days he was flooded with past memories. He had cried and asked for God's forgiveness, although in the back of his mind he knew all the time that God was just an idea. After these three days, he felt relief and a sense of freedom.

The chief purpose of these moves was rebalancing Avner's emotive-related emotions, but they also had a secondary purpose: debugging Avner's non-sense, his erroneous prediction that he could find a substitute for his lost religious belief in sources external to himself.

(c) Third purpose: help Avner get in touch with his real needs.

Preparatory move: I gave Avner a paper of mine in Hebrew in which the classification of cultural programs introduced in Chapter 5 was presented. I asked him to read and keep it.

Main move: I reminded Avner of the memory of his father carrying him as a baby on his shoulders that had been evoked in a previous session. I told him that although as an adult he sees his father as somewhat weak and indifferent, the memory of a powerful father that loved and protected him was still vivid in his mind. Memories have a life of their own. Even deceased loved ones continue living inside us.

Then I asked Avner to enter again into a state of relaxation, concentrate on his chest, shut his eyes and be attentive to any memories, images and thoughts associated with his former religious identity and style of life. He said he preferred to concentrate on the inside of his head. I asked him to share with me in real time whatever came into his mind. I got his permission to record everything he said on a recording machine. After the session, I gave him what I had recorded and instructed him to write down all the positive things included in his soliloquy, classified according to the following headings: experiences that had given him a sense of well-being, security and confidence; people he loved and who loved him; and his cultural makeup, organized according the classification of cultural programs presented in the Hebrew article I gave him.

He did this assignment dutifully. Among the experiences that gave him a sense of security and peace of mind he recalled bedtime intimate conversations with his boarding school roommates, especially with a specific boy who loved and understood him. When he had difficult moments of loneliness and sadness, he silently prayed to God and asked Him to help him. He recalled the thundering voice of the teacher he admired, which gave him the feeling that this teacher had the answer to every question. He enjoyed studying with his peers and teachers complex Talmudic problems.

He said that the attempt to define his internalized culture was important and fascinating. Cultural programs that were high on his mind were, among others, the axiom of an all-knowing, omnipotent God and the rule "love your neighbor as yourself".

I turned his attention to the features shared by the memories to which he attributed special importance: intimacy and lack of ambiguity and uncertainly. I said that this realization can orient us in our future meetings: how to find and create intimacy and certitude in his current secular life. I told him that everything he recounted and wrote down had always been and still remained inside him, independent of any external circumstances. Praying to God and asking for His help were internal mental activities independent of the question of the objective existence of God. Avner could find the answers himself with my assistance and with the aid of other people.

Then I asked him to read aloud each part of what he had written and let it enter his brain and settle there. He could feel the words getting into his brain through his ears, swirling inside and then filling the space and taking roots. I asked him, "Can you feel that all these are still integral parts of you?" He said, "Yes."

Mechanisms of change employed in these sessions: evoking memories by free association; organizing, classifying and writing the retrieved information; teaching and instructing; encouraging transference (me as his teacher and father figure); reframing; suggestion.

Planning and carrying out the therapy 163

These main moves may be viewed as bug-busters whose purpose was to weaken Avner's fifth wheel (get rid of parts of his programs that are no longer relevant to the current situation) and horse blinders (ignoring benefits that can be accrued in the current situation).

In choosing and making up these interventions, I took into consideration Avner's need for an authority figure to guide him and tell him what to do. That is why I adopted the directive, authoritative attitude of a teacher and instructor whose purpose was not to dominate him, but to teach him not to need such a mentor in the future. (This is likely to read like a paradox, but it is not so. The role of a teacher is to serve temporarily as an authority until the student is ready to go his or her own way without a guide.) I also took into account his inclination to studying and thinking deeply. I reframed some relevant aspects of his lost religious belief as being motivated by a need for intimacy, guidance and reassurance. I helped him, by suggestion, to feel that he had not really lost anything that could not be found inside him and outside of himself in his current life.

As a result of these and other moves, Avner's distress was greatly diminished. He was able to devote himself to his studies, began to adapt himself to his new environment, found new friends and was interested in the company of girls. His spiritual void didn't disappear and never would, but it stopped having such a detrimental effect on his emotions and his functioning.

Example 8.3 Family therapy with Amir

Let us go back to Case 7.2 (Amir).

Goals of the sessions with Basil and Badra:

(a) Restoring partially the simplicity of the programs of the mutual relationship between Basil and Badra and of their processing of Amir's difficulties. To attain this, the therapist should attempt to remove the bugs in their mutual plans to achieve their proximity and control goals with respect to one another.

As stated in Chapter 7, Badra's plan was infected with flip-flop and horse blinders. She was urging Basil to exercise his authority over Amir and cooperate with her, but at the same time would not let him adopt such an active position. Her plan included mainly accusations, conveying to him the message that he is no good, weak, indifferent and unwise (flip-flop). Her plan was also infected with horse blinders because she failed to process Basil's strong sides and was blind to her own share in his passivity.

(b) Weakening the horse blinders and non-sense in Basil's plan. He erroneously believed that he had no chance to win against her and that the best tactic with her was not to confront her. Therefore, he adopted a passive stance.

164 Therapy

(c) Removing the horse blinders in their proximity and control programs with respect to Amir. They were ignorant of the reasons and motives for his difficulties and of their own share in them.

Descriptions of some sessions:

(a) First purpose: rebalancing the unbalanced emotions in Basil and Badra's emotive of helplessness, frustration and worry with respect to Amir's problematic behavior.

Preparatory and auxiliary moves: I asked Basil and Badra to refrain from arguing during the following activity and to follow my instructions without being distracted. They gave me their consent.

I asked each of them to close their eyes and to see Amir in their minds' eyes for ten minutes. I watched them. When I saw expressions of sadness on their faces or tears in their eyes I didn't say anything. When I observed signs of stress such as muscle tension or heavy breathing I told them in a calm voice to quieten the tense part of the body (e.g. "Breathe more slowly and deeply"; "Relax your neck muscles by imagining that the muscle melts down like a melting ice cream"). After ten minutes I asked them to open their eyes. Each of them was asked to share with us his or her mental experiences during the ten minutes of silence. Badra reported that she remembered situations in which Amir annoyed her and worried her, but also situations in which he was sweet and loveable. She said she felt sorry for him because of his past. When she spoke, Basil nodded as if identifying with her. He also said that he recalled situations in which Amir was cute and clever. He remembered the first days after the adoption. He spoke of this memory with great warmth. He said he believed that Amir would overcome his current difficulties and he on his side was willing to do his utmost to make this happen.

Mechanisms of change: Blocking (not letting Badra and Basil divert their attention from concentrating on their task to their usual mutual bickering); physical relaxation by mental images; reflecting; retrieving materials from memory.

These moves at least partially achieved their purpose of restoring the emotional balance, among other things, because they raised in each partner more varied and softer feelings than just frustration and concern.

A side effect of these moves was a partial attainment of one of the additional goals of the therapeutic intervention: partially removing the horse blinders in their proximity and control programs with respect to Amir. The therapeutic moves helped them partly get in touch with the reasons and motives for his difficulties.

(b) Second purpose: removing the bugs in Basil and Badra's proximity and control programs with respect to one another and to Amir.

Preparatory moves: In my therapy room, there is a whiteboard with markers. I had a small drum that I had ready.

Main moves:

I asked Badra what she wanted and hoped to achieve from Basil. She said, "Not to sit like a dummy and do nothing. To take a more active role in treating Amir's problems. To be with me and support me."

I told Badra, "But Basil doesn't know how to be active and how to be with you and support you. You have to teach him."

"She doesn't have to teach me," said Basil. "I know perfectly well how to be active."

"Let's pretend you don't," I said. "Just sit here like a dummy and Badra will teach you how to be active and how to be with her and support her."

I gave Badra a marker and I asked her to go to the whiteboard and give Basil a lesson, teaching him how to be active, how to solve Amir's problems and how to support her. "You should make the lesson very simple," I said, "otherwise Basil will not understand it. Write the main things on the whiteboard in simple sentences."

She said, "That's ridiculous. Why should I do it?"

I said, "Otherwise Basil will not know how to do what you want him to do."

She said, "I know what you are trying to do, Shlomo. I got the message."

"OK," I said. "Let's do something that is still ridiculous, but not so ridiculous."

I asked Badra and Basil to face each other, resting their forearms on their own knees. Badra was to lay the palm of her right hand on the palm of Basil's left hand and the palm of her left hand under Basil's right hand. They were not supposed to grip or apply pressure on each other's hands. They were asked to leave their palms placed on each other's palms during the conversation. I held the small drum and told them that if I called the name of one of them and beat the drum more loudly, the one I had addressed should speak louder, and the other way around; if I beat the drum more lightly, the one I had addressed should speak in a lower voice. The same applied to the speed of drumming: if I called the name of one of them and drummed faster, he or she should speak faster, and if I drummed slower, he or she should speak more slowly. If I beat the drum one time they should stop talking.

Then I asked them to discuss Amir's difficulties, listening to each other and joining forces to help them. I told them to concentrate first on understanding the causes of Amir's problems before offering any solutions. They began by accusing each other. Badra attributed Amir's difficulties to a lack of a strong, caring, involved masculine role model. Basil ascribed Amir's problems to Badra's having imposed on him rigid limits in an aggressive way. During the conversation, I monitored their non-verbal responses by the drum, attempting to create a more harmonious coordination between the volumes and speeds of their speech. When one of them withdrew his or her hand or applied pressure on the other one's hand, I beat the drum once to stop their talk and asked the other one why his or her partner withdrew his or her hand or held his or her hand less gently.

Then I asked them to keep quiet for five minutes and close their eyes. I instructed each of them to ask himself or herself if there was something in what his or her partner had said or whether it was just false accusations. After five minutes, they were asked to join the palms of their hands as before and hold eye contact with each other. Each of them admitted that there was some truth in what the other had said, but each of them insisted that the other one's arguments were not the whole truth nor nothing but the truth. Then I asked each of them to close their eyes for another five minutes. Badra was to reflect on why she had imposed on Amir such strict limits. Basil's task was to reflect on why he was so passive, permissive and uninvolved. After five minutes, they joined the palms of their hands again. Badra talked about her fear of failing to live up to the standards of the late Sabina as a parental figure. She didn't want to disappoint Basil. She also referred to her worry that Amir would not realize his potential and deteriorate. She talked about her own struggle to study and realize herself despite all odds and about her wish to serve as a model for Amir in this respect. Basil said that Amir had suffered enough in the past and what he needed was love, warmth and acceptance, not discipline and pushing. He said that he did want Badra closer to himself and to reach a common educational policy with her, but she scorned him and did not cooperate.

Then I asked the two of them to close their eyes for another five minutes and reflect about other causes of Amir's difficulties, unrelated to their different educational approaches. Afterwards, both of them talked about his having been abused before he was adopted and about the losses he suffered. This opened the way to a deeper discussion about the past and present difficulties and possible ways to solve them, with my more active participation.

Mechanisms of change: paradoxical injunction (telling Badra to be the teacher) that made Badra aware of her flip-flop in her attitude toward Basil; making unspoken thoughts explicit; reflecting without being disturbed; cognitive restructuring; facilitating physical intimacy between Basil and Badra; monitoring their physical responses with respect to one another to achieve better coordination and harmony between their expressions through pacing; and helping them listen to one another. Toning down the levels of emotional arousal enabled both of them to process information that had been prevented from being processed, hence the weakening of the horse blinders.

Summary of Chapter 8

The treatment plan includes designing a strategy for the entire therapy, agreeing on a therapeutic contract and forming a therapeutic alliance. A good strategy is based on the multi-systemic diagnostic analysis. It specifies the overall goals of the therapy – the bugs to be removed in the various relevant programs in order to restore the simplicity of the multi-system and renew its ability to mobilize corrective feedback. Priority should be given to removing bugs whose elimination will initiate the domino effect, causing other bugs to disappear spontaneously. However, the choice of bugs to concentrate on should take into consideration likely obstacles to achieving the desired results and predict possible adverse effects of the interventions. A therapeutic contract, usually oral, will detail the agreed-upon terms and conditions of the therapy. Side by side with the explicit contract, there is often a tacit contract, an unspoken agreement between therapist and client on goals and ways to achieve them that both sides prefer not to talk about explicitly. A culturally sensitive therapeutic alliance requires, beyond the generally agreed-upon characteristics, special attention to the differences between the therapist's culture and that of the client. A list of guiding principles for a culturally sensitive alliance is proposed. Therapy sessions informed by The Diamond Model can be conducted in any framework, as dictated by the strategy: individual, family, group and community, simultaneously or in succession. In each session, the therapist makes therapeutic moves. There are three types of moves: main moves, whose purpose is to rebalance the emotions that maintain the bugs and remove the bugs by bug-busters; preparatory moves, whose purpose is to prepare the ground for the main moves; and auxiliary moves, whose purpose is to monitor, especially in family or group therapy, clients' actions that can interfere with the successful achievement of the main moves. These three types of moves can be made, according to the principle of systematic technical eclecticism, by any suitable existing therapeutic technique or by techniques made up by the therapist, as long as the techniques chosen or created are tailored to the clients' personalities, styles and cultures and can effectively rebalance the emotive-related emotions and remove the bugs. In using a technique, the therapist is advised to have in mind the target of change, the mechanism of changes, the means of change and the desired results of the intervention.

Assignments

(a) Design two alternative strategies for Case 1.1 (Nonny). Decide which of the two is the better one and why.

(b) If you are an experienced therapist, describe the details of the explicit and tacit therapeutic contracts agreed upon with your clients in some of your cases. Describe the characteristics of the therapeutic alliance in these cases. Describe difficulties you have encountered in working with clients of various cultures and how you tried to overcome them.

(c) Find or create some techniques of intervention in individual, family and group therapy that are likely to be effective for Case 6.1 (Moran). Describe and analyze each technique as follows: what is the purpose of the intervention? What emotive-related emotions need to be balanced? Which bugs you want to weaken or remove? What kinds of preparatory, auxiliary and main moves should you make to activate the desired change? What are the mechanisms of change? How is the technique you would choose or create supposed to achieve the purpose of emotional balancing and bug-removing?

A classified list of publications

Psychotherapy integration

Norcross, J.C. and Goldfried, M.R. (2005). *Handbook of psychotherapy integration.* Oxford, UK: Oxford University Press.

Planning and carrying out the therapy

Ariel, S. (1992). *Strategic family play therapy.* Chichester, UK: Wiley.
Ariel, S. (1999). *Culturally competent family therapy.* Westport, CT: Praeger.

Suggestibility and somatization

Brown, R.J., Schraq, A., Krinamoorthy, E. and Trimble, M.R. (2008). Are patients with somatization disorder highly suggestible? *Acta Psychiatrica Scandinavica,* 117(3), pp.232–235.

Chapter 9

The healing power of various therapeutic techniques

The choice of therapeutic techniques in The Diamond Model is subject to the principle of systematic technical eclecticism. Any method and technique borrowed from any source or made up by the therapist may be applied in the therapeutic process as long as it can hit the chosen target of change: rebalancing unbalanced emotions and debugging bugged programs. The helping professions and other relevant fields such as management sciences include numerous relevant methods and techniques. A great number of traditional healing methods exist in all human societies.

Most methods and techniques are based on specific theoretical assumptions, ideologies or beliefs. Many of these are speculative or dogmatic and are not supported by any solid research evidence. My view is that borrowing a method or technique for achieving emotion balancing or debugging does not necessarily require adopting the theories, tenets or beliefs on which it rests. I share this view with some proponents of the psychotherapy integration movement (see, for instance, Stricker and Gold, 2013). Close scrutiny reveals that most methods and techniques share the same limited number of change mechanisms and means for achieving the change. Understanding these mechanisms and tools can enable the therapist to apply many of these methods and techniques successfully or to create his or her own. This by no means implies that I do not recommend studying any therapeutic approach in depth. It only means that understanding the main existing change mechanisms is essential for carrying out an effective therapy informed by The Diamond Model. It is impossible for any single person to specialize in all the numerous existing therapeutic approaches, but understanding the limited number of mechanisms that make the most of these approaches work is manageable.

Types of mechanisms of change

The following typology is not clear-cut, because many techniques use more than one kind of change mechanism and means of change and some techniques

170 Therapy

share mechanisms and means with other techniques. The techniques that make use of these change mechanisms are surveyed briefly below.

First type. Working through the body; changing body functions.

These are cybernetic techniques, which are assumed to change various physiological functions that influence emotions, moods and cognitions. They work in two opposite directions, as required by the nature of the emotional dysregulation and of the bugs: relaxation or activation.

Techniques that use relaxation are, for instance, biofeedback, gradual relaxation, systematic desensitization, yoga and meditation, mindfulness and massage.

Activation techniques are, among others, movement and dance therapies, Some Neuro-Linguistic Programming (NLP) techniques, trance and Eye Movement Desensitization Reprocessing (EMDR).

Second type. Enhancing alertness, attention and concentration.

These techniques too can be guided to two opposite directions: amplifying one's awareness of the external environment (input) or filtering out external stimuli and concentrating on one's inner experiences. The emotion regulation functions of these mechanisms are derived from their alleged ability to increase awareness of positive external or internal information. Their debugging power is derived from the fact that they make unavailable information accessible (busting horse blinders, flip-flop and non-sense) and filter out redundant information (getting rid of fifth wheel).

Some of the techniques listed above employ this mechanism too (e.g. systematic desensitization, EMDR, yoga, meditation and mindfulness). Other techniques that use this mechanism are Gestalt therapy, free association, locating emotions and cognitions inside the body, exposure techniques, some art therapies and bibliotherapy.

Third type. Mechanisms based on influence.

The mechanisms discussed above are based on a person's ability to monitor and control his or her own body states, emotions and cognitions. The present type is based on the ability of one person to monitor and control another person's body states, emotions and cognitions.

Emotion regulation and debugging techniques belonging to this type are, among others, hypnosis and suggestion, inducing trance, magic and sorcery, healing ceremonies, induction and modification of dreams, locating the emotions and changing them, some techniques of the creative arts, guided imagination, music and drama therapy and some paradoxical techniques.

Fourth type. Mechanisms of expression and catharsis.

These mechanisms are built on inborn emotion-balancing expressive and cathartic responses such as crying, shouting and laughing. These responses develop along the parameters discussed in Chapter 4: growth; internalization; complexity; coordination and integration; differentiation; depth of processing; concreteness vs, abstraction; constancy and stability; objectivity; and monitoring and control. The expressive repertoire grows with age. More and more verbal means of expression are acquired. The expressive means become partly internalized. People can cry, shout and pour out their hearts inside without easily discernible external manifestations. More and more nuances of verbal and non-verbal expressions become available. People can monitor and control their expressive and cathartic behavior and let it out or hold back.

Techniques based on encouraging expression and catharsis are, for instance, movement and dance therapy, psychodrama and drama therapy, music therapy, healing ceremonies, mourning and bereavement ceremonies and rituals and sharing.

Fifth type. Positive reinforcement and support.

The main mechanism of change employed in such techniques is operant conditioning. Providing rewarding input can ameliorate unbalanced emotions and open blocked information channels, lifting horse blinders and removing non-sense. Such mechanisms are activated in the accepting and encouraging atmosphere of psychotherapy, which provides corrective emotional experiences, in healing ceremonies and rites of passage, in humor therapy, in bereavement and mourning ceremonies and in atonement rituals.

Sixth type. Habituation.

This mechanism is based on the realization that repeated and prolonged exposure to stressing stimuli, coupled with positive reinforcement, has the effect of blunting their impact. This applies both to sensory stimuli such as noise as well as to emotional stimuli such as traumatic experiences.

Techniques using this mechanism are, for instance, flooding, *in vivo* exposure, prolonged exposure and repeated exposure. Exposure to music, art, theater and films in creative arts therapies and bibliotherapy also has an ameliorating, habituation effect.

Seventh type. Concretization.

These mechanisms are based on the assumption that concrete, raw material stimuli are easier to process than abstract semantic concepts or pragmatic messages. These mechanisms are also founded on the idea that concrete representations are easier to accept because they bypass the defenses.

Concretization techniques are, for instance, using symbolic objects such as talismans and amulets, sculpting techniques, speaking in metaphors, fables and allegories. Gestalt therapy has a collection of concretization techniques.

Eighth type. Influencing information processing.

This type of mechanism involves debugging by adding or filtering out input, retrieving data from memory, introducing changes in internal processing and changing output. Techniques employing change mechanisms of this type are, among other, free association, encouraging internal or external debate and dialogue, interpretation and reflection, reframing, rational-emotive behavior therapy and some other CBT techniques, narrative techniques, strategic and paradoxical techniques and interpretation and manipulation of dreams.

172 Therapy

A survey of therapeutic techniques, classified according to their main change mechanisms

Here is a succinct summary of some of the key features of most of the above-mentioned techniques, classified according to the types of change mechanisms employed, with some examples. The analysis of the change mechanisms will be elaborated a bit. It must be stressed that the only purpose of these summaries is general orientation. By no means do they purport to present a comprehensive and in-depth picture of any of these techniques. Fuller introductions to these techniques are included in the classified list of references. It will be stressed again, however, that some techniques belong to more than one class and use more than one mechanism. Therefore, the following classification is somewhat arbitrary.

Working through the body; changing body functions

Techniques using these mechanisms are based on the following assumptions:

> The memory stored in the brain is transmitted to the various body organs and to the physiological processes taking place in them. Therefore, the body, its organs and its processes remember past events and experiences (kinesthetic memory). The various parts of the body have learned to behave in certain ways.
>
> Information processing in the brain can be infected with bugs such as horse blinders, fifth wheel, flip-flop and non-sense. These bugs influence the various body organs and the ways they function.
>
> Physiological processes such as muscle tension, sweating, breathing, heart rate, electrical conductivity of the skin, body temperature and brain wave conductivity can be voluntarily controlled.

Certain types of postures and movements of different body parts can affect these physiological processes in various ways.

Changes in these physiological processes can alter emotional responses such as fear, anxiety, depression, anger, etc., and thus lead to emotion balance.

Changes in these physiological processes can affect information processing operations in the brain and their manifestations in the body organs; for example, giving access to unavailable memories and other types of information (removing horse blinders), cleansing redundant, damaging information (removing fifth wheel), settling inconsistencies in information processing (removing flip-flop) and correcting misinterpreted information (correcting non-sense).

In many techniques, these physiological changes are also mediated by verbal and non-verbal input by the therapist.

The above assumptions have been formulated in my own language. In many cases they are not formulated as such, if at all, by the creators of the techniques.

The following techniques have been founded, wholly or partly, explicitly or implicitly, on the above assumptions.

Biofeedback

This method is based on the use of a computerized electronic system that presents the client with feedback and ongoing information about the physiological processes and changes taking place in his or her body in real time. The client can voluntarily change the relevant parameters and, in this way, achieve emotion regulation that opens the way to debugging.

Gradual relaxation

Some parts of the body "remember" stressful events and experiences. These memories are manifested in muscle tension in particular parts of the body. The purpose of this technique is to counter the muscle tension. The client is sitting comfortably or is lying in a quiet and pleasant environment and is breathing slowly. The therapist, in a low, calming voice, instructs the client to concentrate each time on a different body organ, starting with the toes and feet and ending with the head, or vice versa. Each time that the client is focusing on a particular organ, the therapist asks him or her to feel whether the muscles in that organ are constricted or not. If not, the client is asked to contract the muscles and then release them. Often the therapist uses images such as, "Imagine that the organ is melting like ice cream." The relaxation leads to emotion regulation and helps filter out negative data (removing fifth wheel).

Systematic desensitization

The process is carried out in a gradual manner. First, the therapist and the client prepare together a list of emotion-arousing situations, scaled according to the degree of intensity (e.g. agoraphobia, social anxiety, etc.). Then, when the client is at maximum relaxation, he or she is asked to imagine various situations, from the lowest to the highest on the intensity scale.

The mechanism of change seems to be operant conditioning – positive reinforcement – but it can also be defined in information processing terms. The brain processes new information about the anxiety-provoking situations (removing horse blinders and non-sense). Another explanation, proposed by Wolpe (1958), is reciprocal inhibition (i.e. the assumption that different physiological responses are incompatible with each other). Wolpe hypothesized that a state incompatible with anxiety, such as relaxation, inhibits the anxiety and eventually leads to its extinction. In our terms, this may be viewed as a cybernetic process that removes the bug flip-flop.

174 Therapy

Yoga and meditation

What interests us here is less the different underlying philosophies and more the emotion-balancing techniques developed in these frameworks.

There are many yoga exercises that combine special body positions with breathing. These exercises are alleged to induce serenity and expand one's consciousness. In our language, they contribute to emotion balancing and to removing horse blinders and non-sense.

Meditation is a collection of techniques, some of which are within the framework of yoga. Meditation is supposed to train the body and brain to control attention and concentration and to expand one's consciousness. The client remains in a static, passive body posture, with relaxed muscles, for a long time, with eyes closed, while filtering out all external stimuli (input), memories and thoughts, often with eyes closed, and focusing on one thing, usually an emotionally neutral word or a meaningless series of letters or numbers. This technique leads to emotion balancing and at least temporarily prevents the brain from processing disturbing information (removing fifth wheel).

Mindfulness (mindfulness-based stress reduction)

This is a currently popular technique, inspired by yoga and meditation.

The client is sitting with eyes closed in a comfortable position. Attention is concentrated on the movement of the abdomen when breathing in and out. The main ingredient of this method is non-judgmental attention to every moment. Clients increase self-awareness to the different aspects of the experience: the body, the senses, the feelings and the thoughts. Non-judgmental attention helps the clients be aware of automatic responses and replace them with conscious, elected responses. This is an emotion regulation technique and also a debugger. It makes available useful information that is not usually processed in real time (removing horse blinders).

Massage

There is a wide variety of medical massage methods, such as *shiatsu* massage, reflexology, deep tissue massage, hot stones and facial massage (tactile input).

Mechanism of change: muscle relaxation and facilitating blood flow.

Targets of change: emotion regulation.

Movement and dance therapies

These techniques belong both to psychophysical and to expressive and creative therapies. Dance and movement, accompanied by percussion and chanting, are integral parts of traditional healing rituals and ceremonies all over the world. This attests to a universal recognition of their therapeutic powers.

As stated above, movement can express emotions and other internal experiences that are not available to consciousness and are difficult to verbalize. There is a kinesthetic memory. The conscious and unconscious memories of a person are impressed upon and represented in the body. These memories can be retrieved by spontaneous movements. Therefore, movement and dance therapies can serve as debuggers, lifting horse blinders. Movement usually has symbolic meaning. In our semiotic language, we can say that body language belongs to the level of raw material, but it expresses semantic, thematic and emotional entities and has communicative functions on the pragmatic level. A change in habitual gestures, motions and postures can modify the functioning of the mind. Movement and dance therapy can therefore contribute to emotion regulation and to reprocessing.

There are many movement and dance therapy techniques, some directive, some non-directive. Particularly effective are techniques employing spontaneous movement, unaccompanied by music and percussion, and followed by verbalizing what the movements have expressed.

NLP

This is a collection of techniques designed to change automatic emotional, cognitive and behavioral responses.

One of the techniques is related to eye movements. The hypothesis is that the way the eyes are turned (e.g. during a conversation) indicates the type of data the brain is processing and the ways in which the brain processes them. It follows that changing the direction of the client's gaze will change his or her pattern of information processing.

I have often observed that some of my clients used to turn their eyes to one direction when they expressed unbalanced emotions such as fear, anxiety or anger. I asked them to go on talking about what they were feeling while turning their eyes in the opposite direction. In many cases they reported altered, more balanced emotions when their eyes changed direction. They could process horse-blindered information and put misinterpretations right (correcting non-sense).

In another technique practiced in NLP, the client is asked, following conventional wisdom, to change his posture or action: "If you sit bent and withdrawn, do the opposite. Get up, straighten up and move energetically. Breathe fast and powerfully. If, contrariwise, you move restlessly, sit down or slow down and breathe slowly."

One of the things I have tried, not in the framework of NLP, is asking the client to change the speed of their speech. Some clients of mine with anxiety disorders used to speak very fast. They swallowed words, sometimes to the point of unintelligibility. I asked them to speak very slowly, excessively, and to separate words. In most cases this caused a significant reduction in anxiety. The same can be done with the volume of speech. If someone talks very loudly, ask him or her to whisper, and if he or she whispers, ask him or her to speak loudly.

Trance

Powerful rhythmical movements to the beating of percussion instruments and chanting induce an altered state of consciousness characterized by profound mental absorption, suspension of full consciousness and suggestibility.

In traditional healing ceremonies all over the world, trance states are used for the exorcism of evil spirits and getting in touch with the supernatural (see below).

The cathartic effect of trance contributes to emotion balancing. This technique enables the brain to process unconscious information and be susceptible to input data that have not been processed by the client's programs (removing horse blinders).

EMDR

The main feature of this technique is bilateral stimulation of the two hemispheres of the brain, usually with alternating lateral eye movements, but often with alternating auditory or sensory stimulation of both sides of the body. Simultaneously or immediately afterwards, the client tells of an experience that causes him or her emotional imbalance, anxiety, fear, anger or other kinds of mental stress. The bilateral stimulation is alleged to cause the integration of unprocessed information related to the stress or trauma with the other ongoing data processing. Allegedly, this results in emotion balancing and rapid working through of the stressful event (removing horse blinders and getting rid of the fifth wheel).

Enhancing alertness, attention and concentration

Some of the techniques listed above employ this mechanism too (e.g. systematic desensitization, EMDR, yoga, meditation and mindfulness). Here are some other techniques that use this mechanism: Gestalt therapy, locating the emotions and cognitions inside the body and changing them, exposure techniques, creative arts therapies and bibliotherapy. All these techniques are introduced briefly further below.

Techniques using influence by suggestion and magic

Suggestion is the activity by which one person influences and guides the thoughts, feelings or behaviors of another person, directly or indirectly. Magic is a form of suggestion. It is a very common therapeutic method in cultures all over the world. Its effectiveness is based on the realization that a person can voluntarily control his or her own physiological, cognitive and emotional responses; in other words, his or her information processing activities. If so, a therapist who has succeeded in winning the total confidence of the client can control the client's information processing activities.

Hypnosis and suggestion

Milton Erickson, a famous hypnotist and one of the initiators of strategic, solution- focused psychotherapy, saw suggestion as a form of indirect communication that resonates in the unconscious mind (see below, strategic and paradoxical techniques). When that happens, the client's unconscious mind becomes responsive to the therapeutic process and ready to actively participate in it. In our language, it gets in touch with the bugs and becomes ready to get rid of them.

Erickson developed many suggestion techniques. One of them is *artful vagueness*, deliberately getting the client into a state of confusion. Allegedly, this causes the client to embark on an *transderivational search*, an intensive and extensive scanning of his or her own mind to make his or her own sense of the therapist's messages.

A central principle in Erickson's method is *go with the client*. Do not try to impose your own wishes or ideas on the client, but help him or her change from his or her own frame of reference.

Healing ceremonies

Many traditional healing ceremonies such as exorcisms of evil spirits make use of suggestion, magic and sorcery, coupled with concretization. Often, during the healing procedure, the client is entered into a state of trance (see above) to make him or her more prone to the influence of the shaman, the healer. Shamans receive messages from the supernatural entities, who cannot be contacted directly, explaining the sources of the difficulties and saying what should be done to solve the problems. Often the explanations provided by the supernatural beings refer to violations of the balance between different, usually opposing forces whose names and meanings are understood by members of the cultures (e.g. *yin* and *yang* in some Chinese philosophical traditions) or to violation of basic laws of nature. Healing will be achieved if the balance is restored. The suffering person must recognize the parts in him or herself or in his or her behavior that are contributing to the violation of balance or stand in opposition to the laws of nature. He or she is required to create order in his or her life in accordance with the laws of nature.

178 Therapy

Induction and modification of dreams

One of the traditional Jewish therapeutic dream techniques is called *dream improvement*. A rabbi specializing in this technique performs a ceremony in which the client who had a bad dream is commanded to improve the dream, to dream another dream of a more positive nature. This suggestion works in many cases. This is an emotion-balancing as well as a debugging technique. The improved dream can include information missing from the original dream or reframes the messages conveyed by the original dream (removing horse blinders and non-sense). For instance, if in the original dream the client dreamt that he or she was punished because of some religious transgression, in the improved dream, he or she dreams about extenuating circumstances.

Locating the emotions and cognitions and changing them

This is a form of suggestion that is also a psychophysical technique.

I often employ techniques of emotion balancing that work through the body. For example, if the client feels emotional stress – anxiety, fear, depression, anger, etc. – I ask him or her to locate the emotion and the cognition associated with it in a particular area of the body. Almost always clients are able to identify a specific area where the emotion is located – the head, the throat, the stomach, etc. Then I ask the client to move the emotion to another area of the body or to melt it and let it flush out of the body. It is astonishing how this technique succeeds in balancing the emotions.

Guided imagination

This is a collection of techniques that uses concrete images and imagination to achieve emotional balance, usually in a state of relaxation. Examples include: "Imagine a pleasant light illuminating the insides of your body," and, "Imagine being in a pleasant, enchanting, paradise-like place, on another planet or in a magical, mythical world." If the client finds it difficult to conjure up such images, the therapist can start by inventing such fantasies and then encouraging the client to continue the process, the imaginary journey or the like, using his or her own imagination. This technique removes horse blinders by making the client aware of unrealized possibilities.

Other relevant techniques are included in creative arts, drama and music therapies. Paradoxical techniques are also a form of influence (see below).

Techniques using expression and catharsis

Expressing one's feelings verbally and non-verbally has a cleansing, cathartic effect due to releasing the physiological tension associated with strong emotions. Externalizing one's emotions can also serve debugging purposes because it helps the client get in touch with arrested, subconscious, emotive-related emotions (removing horse blinders).

Creative arts therapies

Expressing oneself through such media has an emotion-balancing effect. The emotion-regulating effect of such expression is also due to its sublimation function. Direct, raw expression of emotions such as anger and sadness often escalates the emotions through feed-forward instead of ameliorating them.

Music therapy

The human voice is one of the major means of emotional expression from infancy. The use of the voice in all its variations, with or without speech, activates the lungs, and therefore the breathing, the diaphragm, the abdominal muscles, the neck, the vocal cords, the tongue and various areas of the brain. Therefore, vocal expression affects the blood flow and the amount of oxygen absorbed or emitted. Improvised singing with or without words can open arrested emotions. Changes in the use of voice can modulate the emotional valence. In voice improvisations, clients can change the pitch, the intensity, the speed of production, the intonation and other vocal parameters. The changes will affect their emotions. The use of voice can also open real or imagined blocks, such as in the chest or throat, alleviating a feeling of suffocation resulting from muscle contraction due to mental stress. Wind instruments such as flutes and whistles can have similar functions.

Percussion can also have two opposite functions: expressing emotions for the purpose of catharsis or modulation of emotions to balance them. It is possible to drum, for example, at different intensities. Drumming with high intensity can express anger or frustration. Soft drumming can express depression. A change in the intensity of drumming can lead to a change in the emotional state. A key role percussion has is rhythm and tempo. Too fast or too slow drumming express different emotions such as anger, joy or sadness. Regular and uniform rhythm relaxes, creates order in confused and disorganized emotions and also regulates physiological mechanisms such as the heartbeat and breathing. A too regular and non-variable rhythm can indicate emotional fixation. If the client is encouraged to change the rhythm, this can help him or her to get out of the fixation.

Psychodrama and drama therapy

Drama therapy is a method of group therapy, the main means of which is improvisation drama. Psychodrama is a sub-genre of drama therapy. What is common to all forms of drama therapy is activating in tangible ways, using symbols and metaphors, unresolved, emotionally charged situations from the present or the past. The participants use soliloquy and role play to express feelings and thoughts that they find difficult to express because of shame, guilt, mental restraint, politeness and over-consideration, fear or anger. Like play therapy, drama therapy bypasses the defenses. The participants can observe their own selves from outside by mirroring, doubling and role reversal, and in this way get in touch with information that had not been fully available to them (removing horse blinders). One of the functions of drama therapy is catharsis. Drama therapy and psychodrama are closest to play therapy. The mechanisms and means of change of play therapy are applicable to drama therapy too (see Chapter 10).

Visual arts

Visual arts can exteriorize feelings that the client is not aware of, when he or she has no suitable words or when words serve as a barrier rather than a means of expression.

The client does not necessarily need prior knowledge to undergo art therapy. One can use a very wide range of means – several types of pencils and colors, clay or Plasticine, collages and all sorts of accessories and materials.

Case 9.1 Abigail

Abigail was an artist. She would mostly draw miniature, framed, decorative paintings. After her husband had an affair and began divorce proceedings, she moved to a city near their hometown. On the way from her hometown to the city, there were wheat fields. She began painting these fields in larger, less stylized and less decorative paintings. Two years after her therapy had been terminated, she invited me to an exhibition of her works. One of the exhibits was an expressionistic painting the size of an entire wall, full of rich and passionate colors.

Ameliorating grief

One of the functions of mourning ceremonies is working through the grief of loss.

Grief is a powerful, moving emotion that throws the emotion system out of balance. Grief is not only a reaction to the death of a loved one. It can be a reaction to any kind of loss (e.g. separation, loss of a job or loss of health or youth). Cultures all over the world have developed various strategies and ceremonies to cope with loss. These include stylized outward verbal and non-verbal cathartic expressions of grief, often by professional mourners.

Unconventional bereavement practices can be invented by the therapist and client as part of the therapeutic process.

Case 9.2 Scarlett

Scarlett was obsessively preoccupied with the possibility of losing loved ones, especially her father, who had grown old and was less healthy than he used to be. The fear of losing him and other people in her life, and the associated sadness, were with her incessantly, especially at night. She generalized this emotive to refusal to accept the fact that people die, grow old or separate. I suggested to Scarlett that she should go through a private bereavement ceremony. We decided together on the details. The purpose was to mourn the very fact that people die, grow old and separate, with special reference to her father. Scarlett stayed alone in a camping site in a forest for five days. She was dressed in black. She erected a pile of stones that symbolized the tomb of immortality and of an unchanging world. Each day was devoted to one stage of working through the grief of loss. This was carried out by reflection, crying, cursing, kicking the pile of stones and other actions initiated by Scarlett. After these five days, Scarlett reported a considerable reduction in her symptoms.

The above-mentioned healing ceremonies have a cathartic function too.

Techniques employing positive reinforcement and support

Reparenting

A common view is that the very therapeutic alliance enables the client to go through a corrective emotional experience. *Reparenting* is an elaboration of this idea. It is a collection of techniques designed to facilitate a multi-faceted corrective parenting experience, provided by the therapist, in clients who had internalized inadequate parental objects in their childhood. These techniques were developed by Young in the framework of his eclectic *schema therapy* model (see Young, Klosko and Weisner, 2003).

Techniques facilitating transition and change

As stated in Chapters 3 and 7, in times of transition and change, programs lose their previous simplicity. These techniques are designed to alleviate the distress caused by such change by providing support and reassurance. They prepare the concerned parties for change and supply them with information on the new situation, which they had not previously had. Emotion regulation

182 Therapy

is facilitated by the ability to influence another person's feelings, thoughts and behavior.

Very common transition-facilitating techniques are *rites of passage*. Take, for instance, a marriage ceremony in a modern, liberal, urban society. Even though the relationships between men and women in this society are relatively open and free, society has imposed restrictive rules on this freedom. The programs prescribing these rules delimit the choice of sexual partners and the range of acceptable behaviors (comprehensiveness, parsimony), require consistency and dictate how to interpret certain behaviors (plausibility). The marriage ceremonies affirm these programs and make them publicly recognized. The expressions of ritualized joy at wedding ceremonies are designed, along with other things, to calm the couple's anxiety about the new situation, in which they give up some of the freedoms and rights they enjoyed before marriage.

Other celebration ceremonies mark the transition from one stage of life to another (from early childhood to school age, from childhood to puberty, from puberty to adulthood and leaving home, etc.). Such rites exist in all known societies.

Example 9.1 Supporting a bride

Some traditional healing ceremonies for treating culture-bound syndromes have the function of facilitating transition. Freed and Freed (1964) describe a case of spirit possession in a north Indian village:

The victim was a newly married young woman who, as prescribed by custom, had just left her father's home village and was moved to her husband's parents' home, in a village far away from her home village. Her symptoms included loss of consciousness, shivering and convulsions, dizziness and a sensation as if her stomach was swelling. The treatment was performed by a local shaman. She gathered the young girl's husband's mother and sisters around her and instructed them to sing verses expressing their love and support. The shaman also took measures to make the ghost uncomfortable by beating parts of the young woman's body with straw, cursing and smoking burning dung.

In this example, like in most traditional healing ceremonies, the treatment had the cybernetic function of enlisting corrective feedback – the massive expressions of love and emotional support by the women in the girl's new family – in order to counteract her loss of simplicity and restore homeostasis.

Families and individuals create their own rituals and ceremonies (not necessarily conventional ones) that serve the same functions (e.g. bedtime stories to facilitate the transition into the loneliness of sleep and family dinners).

In individual and family therapy, old rituals and ceremonies can be revived or new ones created to prevent the onset of bugs or to remove bugs that have already invaded the relevant programs.

Mourning ceremonies can also be viewed as rites of passage. In most societies, such ceremonies include external signs such as wearing black or partly torn garments. The emotional balancing mechanisms of change in such ceremonies and customs include catharsis, sharing the grief with loved ones and other members of the community, raising memories and expressing them orally or in writing and other expressive means. In the Jewish bereavement custom of *Sitting Shiva*, the mourners stay in one apartment for seven days. The mourners and their visitors often talk about the deceased, sharing stories of his or her life. Some mourners use the *Shiva* as a distraction from their loss; other mourners prefer to openly experience their grief together with friends and family.

A ceremony documented by Lee (1988) in Korea was a kind of family therapy that included some features of drama therapy. It involved the spirit of a deceased head of the family and the living members of the family he left behind. Unresolved conflicts and unfinished business between the deceased, represented by a shaman, and the living were discussed and debated. The dialogue was very emotional, with expressions of anger and weeping, until finally reconciliation was reached and the deceased was asked to leave his family alone, to rest in peace and not bother them again. The emotion-balancing and debugging techniques are evident in this example.

Case 9.3 Kidist

Thirty-two-year-old Kidist was in therapy with me because of free-floating anxiety and depression. She was having short-lived relationships with men who treated her badly and exploited her. She was experiencing a general feeling that her life was going nowhere.

Kidist had emigrated to Israel with her family from a small village in Ethiopia when she was five. Her father died when he was seventy-five, leaving behind a wife and six children. He passed away during a journey on foot to the Sudanese border on the way to Israel. He was buried in the desert. There was no possibility of holding a mourning ceremony as was customary. Kidist was twenty-eight when he died. After his death, all her brothers and sisters developed psychopathological symptoms or substance addictions. Kidist was the only one who remained "normal". Although she was the youngest of the siblings, she was taking care of them all, even of her mother, who was helpless. But when she reached the age of thirty, she decided to build an independent life for herself. She left home and reduced her contact with her family of origin to a minimum. Her symptoms appeared soon after she left home.

184 Therapy

In therapy, Kidist became aware of the source of her difficulties (horse blinders removed). The death of the father, who was the mainstay of the family, caused the disintegration of the seams that tied the family together. She was the youngest of the siblings and therefore the most integrated in the dominant Western culture of Israel. For the same reasons, she had the best mastery of the Hebrew language. These assets gave her an advantage over her siblings and her mother. Her culturally prescribed allegiance to her family, typical of collectivistic cultures, compelled her to take care of her family at the cost of her own self-interests. However, when she felt at the age of thirty that she was wasting her own life and letting her youth slip away, she decided, apparently under the influence of the individualist Israeli culture, to leave. In our terms, she chose partial simplicity to preserve consistency (being independent) at the cost of comprehensiveness (ignoring the internal conflict between her loyalty to her family and to herself). But the flip-flop was there under the surface. Unconsciously, she chose non-committal relationships with men in order to stay virtually in her previous role with respect to her family. Perhaps she also punished herself for betraying the family by choosing men who treated her badly. Her symptoms were the external manifestations of her internal conflict.

When we talked about her late father, she told me about a regular family ritual her family used to hold back in Ethiopia. Once a week, the family would sit in a circle on the carpet in the living room. Only the parents would sit on padded stools, above the children. Like in group therapy, the children would share with the rest their experiences and concerns and listen to their siblings' responses and advice. The father would just listen patiently and speak only after the other had finished talking. He never gave direct instructions or solutions. He used to say, "Who am I to cut the meat for the lion?" He would only deliver educational messages by telling folk stories or fables about animals. After his death, the family didn't continue to observe this custom.

I suggested to Kidist that she should persuade her family to sit a belated *Shiva*, mourning the loss of their father, and afterwards resume this ritual. They did, with Kidist's mother and her oldest brother sitting on stools and her oldest brother serving as the facilitator. Kidist didn't take any leading role. She just behaved like the youngest sibling that she was. Since this ritual had been held again, Kidist's symptoms disappeared and the conditions of the other siblings improved.

Atonement rituals and ceremonies

Guilt is a major emotion that often gets off-balance. Many cultures all over the world have developed atonement, penance and repentance practices and ceremonies that relieve guilt associated with sins against deities or humans. These include prayers, sacrifices to deities and self-punishment by abstaining from pleasures. Examples of such practices are apology and asking for forgiveness, fasting, financial and other kinds of compensation and doing good deeds anonymously.

Such ritualized customs are the Catholic confession and the Jewish Day of Atonement, devoted to fasting and prayers. In culturally competent psychotherapy, traditional customs of atonement can be coupled with private acts to achieve balanced emotive-related guilt. This can open the way to removing or weakening bugs.

Example 9.2 Atonement

Bilu and Witztum combined modern methods with traditional practices in working with the ultra-Orthodox Jewish community in Jerusalem. They describe the case of a young man who suffered from depression and anxiety attacks because he blamed himself for the death of his alcoholic father by neglecting him. He was a repentant Jew; that is to say, a secular Jew who had converted to Orthodox Judaism. He heard the voice of an angel demanding him to fast and avoid sexual relations with his wife and he went to prostrate himself on the graves of the righteous. The treatment went the other way. He was persuaded to confess to his dead father and ask his forgiveness, but also to avoid excessive mourning and self-neglect by relying on such prohibitions in Jewish religious law (Bilu and Witztum, 1993).

Seeking such reassuring responses from the deceased or from supernatural beings and deities by prayers, spiritualistic ceremonies with or without a medium, etc., is very common in many cultures.

Techniques based on habituation

Repeating emotive-related negative emotions in a benign, supporting environment has a habituating effect. The client feels safe and in control of his or her emotions.

Prolonged exposure, flooding, implosive therapy, repeated exposure and in vivo exposure

Most of the techniques for treating PTSD, phobias and other anxiety disorders are based on the same principle. Instead of avoiding the stressing input and memory, as common sense would have it, the client is engaged in a prolonged or repeated gradual exposure to direct or simulated distressing stimuli that are related to his or her emotives (input) or to retrieved distressing memories. For

186 Therapy

example, soldiers who suffer from combat stress reaction are asked to describe their experiences vividly. Later they are exposed to video simulations or actual battle scenes and finally they are sometimes asked to return to the real battle-field. These techniques are supposed to reduce the level of emotion arousal and immunize the client to subsequent traumatic reactions. To make it easier for the client, the *ups and downs* technique can be used: exposing the client to the most stressing stimuli, retreating to less stressing stimuli and going back to the most stressing, over and over again. Systematic desensitization (see above) is also an exposure technique (see Chapters 4 and 10).

Exposure to music, art, theater and films in creative arts therapies and bibliotherapy

In these genres of therapy, the client can be an active creator or a passive consumer. As a passive consumer, the client can meet contents related directly or indirectly to his or her emotives. Such exposure can have the same ameliorating effect as in the above techniques. Furthermore, such works of art and literature can serve as bug-busters, since they often provide information that has not been available to the client (removing horse blinders; see Hynes and Hynes-Berry, 1986).

Techniques based on concretization, symbolization and metaphors

These mechanisms are often coupled with outward expression and catharsis, as in creative arts therapy. Thoughts, emotions and ideas are often easier to identify, express and understand when materialized by concrete images, symbols and metaphors, analogies, figures of speech and allegories that externalize information that would otherwise be difficult to identify and relate to. It is sometimes possible to overcome resistance to listening to verbal messages or difficulties in understanding them if the debugging information is conveyed through concrete, non-verbal means.

Gestalt therapy

The emphasis in Gestalt therapy, like in mindfulness, is on the development of awareness of the surrounding (input) sensations, memories, one's own body and thoughts (internal processing). It is therefore not only an emotion-balancing method, but also a bug-buster.

Various techniques of Gestalt therapy fall within the present category, for example:

> Description in the present tense. The client is asked to describe an event or a dream as if it is happening in the immediate present.

Be the emotion. Sometimes, in order to experience the emotion fully, to identify with it or to get to know it more closely, the therapist asks the client to play out the emotion, to speak in its name, to dramatize it.

Resuscitation of a metaphor. When the client uses a metaphor or a figurative expression to describe his or her condition, the therapist asks the client to make it tangible by performing it in practice (e.g. the client has said, "When my husband talks this way, it makes me sick." The therapist imitates her husband's talk and the client is asked to behave as if he or she is really sick).

Symbolic objects and acts in rituals and ceremonies

In many cultures, symbolic pictures and objects such as icons, talismans, amulets, etc., serve as therapeutic tools. Such traditional or makeshift means can be used as bug-busters in psychotherapy. For instance, the Jewish Day of Atonement is devoted to fasting and prayers. This day is preceded by *Tashlich*, symbolically casting sins into a lake or a river.

Example 9.3. Boris

Boris, who had sexual functioning difficulties with his second wife, believed that this was caused by his first wife, who had put a spell on him. The therapist gave him an amulet that was supposed to undo the spell. As a result, Boris' sexual functioning improved. The amulet served as a partial debugger, annulling the non-sense bug.

Concrete messages in therapy

In family or group therapy, the therapist may sit next to a person who has been ignored to turn attention to this fact and encourage the other participants to relate to this person (debugging horse blinders).

If two participants are overinvolved with one another and ignore the rest, the therapist can sit between them or put a physical barrier like a chair between them.

The meanings and communicative functions of body gestures vary from culture to culture. The therapist may use conventional gestures to convey messages like "This is an old, irrelevant stuff" (debugging fifth wheel) or "I am confused" (debugging flip-flop).

Sculpting

Techniques of family or group sculpting also belong to this category. The therapist asks the group or family members to turn the bodies of the participants into a sculpture, representing the ways they see each other and

188 Therapy

their relationships. Then they are asked to make changes to the sculpture to suggest what improvements they would like to make in the mutual images and relationships.

Example 9.4 Family sculpting

In family therapy with a father, a mother and a teenage son, the family members presented their mutual relationships as perfect. They were asked, each in his or her turn, to create a family sculpture. The father sculpted himself and his son as embracing each other and the mother as standing at a distance from them, holding out her arms and palms with a gesture of pushing, aimed at both of them. The mother sculpted the father as strangling her and the son as hiding behind her back. The son sculpted the father and mother as directing threatening gestures at each other and himself as standing aside with his back turned on both. The sculpting served as a powerful bug-buster, exposing their horse blinders. This family sculpting opened heated discussions about their covert interrelationships. Following the discussions, all three family members sculpted the interrelationships they aspired to as all three of the embracing each other.

Case 9.4 Lily

When Lily started therapy, the relationship between her and her husband was flawless. However, she found it difficult to suppress her bitterness toward him in connection with their past. She could not forgive him for having neglected her many years before when she had been ill and needed him. She could not forget and forgive his short-lived extra-marital affair and their violent, merciless fights. The therapist used a metaphor as a debugger of the fifth wheel bug: throwing all that refuse into the garbage can. He actually asked Lily to write all of her past grievances on a sheet of paper, accompanied with simple illustrations, and then tear the paper into small pieces and throw them into the waste basket in his office. The idea of useless refuse that is not needed anymore was a symbol of the past difficulties with her husband.

Fables and allegories

In many cultures, fables and allegories are used as therapeutic devices. Such texts can be used in therapy as bug-busters.

In the biblical Second Book of Samuel, a story is told about King David, who committed adultery with Bathsheba and sent her husband, Uriah, to be killed in war. Then the Lord sent the prophet Nathan to confront King David with his guilt. Nathan chose not to accuse King David directly of his transgression, apparently because direct blaming would have been met with denial and refusal to take responsibility for the sin. He told King David a story about a rich man who had great many flocks. He slaughtered a poor man's only lamb. When King David heard the story, he said to Nathan, "As surely as the Lord lives, the man who did this deserves to die, because he committed this cold-hearted crime." Nathan said to King David, "You are that man!"

In our terms, the prophet Nathan used a story as a bug-buster, removing King David's horse blinders concerning his own immorality.

Mechanisms based on changing information processing patterns

These mechanisms debug information processing programs by changing them. There are methods that work on the input – diminishing the exposure to input that causes emotional distress and filtering out redundant information (removing fifth wheel). There are methods that work on memory – free associations, gradual and non-flooding exposure to memory materials, disconnecting memory materials from input materials and softening the connection between memory materials and emotional arousal. There are methods that work on internal processing – reshuffling the wrong organization of input and memory material and correcting erroneous interpretations of these materials. And there are methods that work on output – changing external behavioral responses to the inner processing that has caused too much emotional arousal. What is common to most of these methods is that the therapist exposes the cognitive dissonance inherent in the bugs until the clients can no longer hold the bugs and need to weaken or remove them.

Free associations

This technique was developed by Sigmund Freud. In free associations, the client relates whatever comes into his or her mind without censoring the emerging materials. This technique helps the client get in touch with current and memory materials that have not been available to consciousness or were not high on his or her mind. It is therefore a debugging technique, removing horse blinders.

Encouraging external or internal debate and dialogue

In family or group therapy, the therapist may encourage the members to expose each other's bugs by debating the validity of things the others say about themselves, about other people or about the world.

190 Therapy

Example 9.5 Challenging

In a group therapy, one of the participants said, "Nobody wants me because I'm ugly." The other participants gave this person counter-evidence and in this way exposed his horse blinders and non-sense bugs.

Another participant said, "You were saying positive things about me just to cheer me up, not because you really think so." The other participants reassured this person that the compliments were sincere, debugging his non-sense.

Another participant told about his achievements and then qualified himself as a complete failure. The other participants exposed his flip-flop.

In a group therapy I facilitated, one of the men complained that women were not interested in him because he was considered a nerd. The women in the group explained to him that he was wrong. They recoiled from him because he was passive-aggressive, insulting women passively. He behaved this way because he thought himself a nerd and wanted to show that he wasn't.

Another man in that group therapy was also concerned that women didn't want him. He thought that this was because they saw him as ugly and stupid. This man was physically attractive and intelligent. Again, the women in the group helped him understand the real reason why they hesitated to let him get close. They told him things like, "We cannot make out who you are. You are confusing, you project contradictory things. You seem to be aloof and unapproachable." These women helped him debug his non-sense. Their responses led to discussions that exposed the non-sense bugs in this man's internal and external programs.

Debate and dialogue between internal characters can also be encouraged. The idea is that a person is not one thing. Inside a person there are all kinds of internal characters, some innate and some acquired during the course of life. Some characters conflict with one another or dominate other characters. This is so not only in states of dissociation, but also in normal mental states. In drama therapy and psychodrama, one externalizes these characters, gives them concrete form and manages their relationships in the external world, not only in the internal world, and thus perhaps resolves conflicts between them, turning a negative dominant figure into a marginal one or into a more positive dominant figure.

The idea that we have conflicting internal characters also appears in Eric Berne's transaction analysis method, according to which we have three ego states – the child, the adult and the parent – and there are relationships and struggles between these three ego states within us. A debate or a dialogue between internal characters can help with debugging bugged programs.

Case 9.5 Joshua

Thirty-year-old Joshua suffered from panic attacks and phobias. He was afraid to fly in airplanes, travel long distances or stay alone in places he didn't know. He was more relaxed in these situations if his mother was with him. Although he was intelligent, he did not complete high school studies and did not acquire a profession. He spent his youth gambling, partying and chasing women. He hooked up with youngsters who engaged in petty thefts and other minor acts of delinquency. When he was twenty-seven, he married, and at the age of thirty he had a son and a daughter. His anxiety disorders and phobias began after he got married. Because of his lack of formal education or training, he could only get simple jobs. On the way to a job interview, he would have a panic attack and call his mother to calm him down. He often changed jobs. When he worked as a salesman or a cashier, he was afraid of being accused of stealing money, although he never did so. As a child, he suffered from asthma attacks. His mother and father were over-worried about him and over-protective. When he reached thirteen he was perfectly healthy. His older brother, Jacob, was a very successful businessman. Jacob treated Joshua with a mixture of contempt and concern.

The crucial turning point in Joshua's life was his marriage and having become a father. This led to a loss of simplicity. His previous programs couldn't serve him well anymore. He had to become a serious, responsible person, a decent breadwinner. He gave up comprehensiveness, information that his previous programs used to process, for the sake of consistency. Therefore, his programs were bugged with horse blinders. But all the suppressed data crept in through the back door and caused the panic attacks and phobias.

One of the techniques Joshua's therapist used as a way of debugging his programs was encouraging a dialogue and debate between the internal parts of his personality. Joshua was asked to identify a number of characters within himself and to give them names. He identified the following figures: (a) the serious, honest, self-reliant, independent and responsible adult who is devoted to his wife and children. For this figure he preferred to preserve his real name, Joshua. (b) The frightened, frail child, over-protected by his parents, especially his mother, who is worried about his health. He called this figure Crybaby. And (c) the wild, dishonest, lazy, irresponsible womanizer, gambler and spendthrift. He called this figure Al Capone.

Joshua spoke alternately from the mouth of each of these three figures. He accused Al Capone of trying to entice him to betray his wife, gamble, steal and drink and to destroy his family and his life. Al Capone mocked Joshua, called him a nerd, a loser, chickenshit. Al Capone told

Joshua that he was jealous of the success of his older brother. That's why he was gambling and spending all his money – to play the big shot – but he would never be like his older brother, because he was lazy and had no talent for business. Al Capone told Joshua that he was still a crybaby and would remain a crybaby all his life. Joshua told Al Capone that he was just struggling not to be like Crybaby. He told Al Capone that he resisted working in simple jobs that were beneath his abilities and dignity. He told Crybaby that he was perfectly healthy and only wanted to be pampered by Mommy.

This dialogue lifted the horse blinders because it opened channels of information that had previously been locked.

In the next stage of therapy, Joshua attempted to amalgamate the three characters in ways that wouldn't interfere with proper functioning. He could give vent to his babyish dependency needs in make-believe play with his wife. He could make money by starting his own small business. He could realize his adventurousness by betting for small sums, playing soccer and going on jeep tours with his pals.

His phobias and panic attacks and his dependence on his mother dwindled gradually until they were completely gone.

Reframing

Debugging involves challenging the bugged parts of the client's programs, questioning and undermining their validity. This is one of the goals of strategic, cognitive and narrative therapies. Since direct confrontation invites resistance, these schools of psychotherapy have developed various indirect challenging methods.

Reframing, in our terminology, means suggesting the re-evaluation of certain regularly processed data as positive rather than negative with respect to the self. For example, in Case 9.5, Joshua had panic attacks on his way to job interviews. He saw this as a sign that he was not a man, that he was a frightened little baby. He despised himself for that. The therapist reframed this by saying that the panic attacks protected him against settling on a job below his capacity. They showed that underneath the surface he saw himself as a capable man.

Rational-emotive behavior therapy

This is a collection of cognitive-behavioral techniques whose purpose is to help the client challenge and dispute their own irrational, destructive and self-defeating cognitions, emotions and behaviors and replace them with more functional ones.

Narrative techniques

These techniques are based on the hypothesis that the problems individuals and families have to contend with are cultivated by narratives that these people have created and see as a genuine characterization of their past and present realities and as valid explanations of their current difficulties. Some narratives are shared by all the family members and some are stories that individuals tell themselves. The narratives are often groundless, inaccurate or misconceived and therefore harmful. In our terminology, the routine internal processing of input or memory information is bugged, failing to take into account all and only the relevant data in a consistent and plausible manner.

Narrative psychotherapists have developed numerous re-storying techniques. A small sample includes:

(a) Exposing the relativity of the family narrative by having each member tell his or her own story that doesn't necessarily match the family story. This is followed by building a new shared story that emphasizes the positive aspects of the past.
(b) Asking leading questions whose purposes are to fill out missing details, to contextualize recalled events, to question the sequence and causal relations among events, to examine each person's contribution to what had happened, etc.
(c) Re-examining the past by checking documents such as letters, pictures, diaries, etc., like in a crime investigation or history research.
(d) Concentrating on the description of facts rather than on inferences, interpretations and generalizations.
(e) Writing or recording memoirs and then editing them, changing the times and grammatical forms, adding data, including other points of view, etc.

Case 9.6 Benjamin

Benjamin, thirty-five, was a shrewd, successful businessman. He looked athletic, muscular, with carved, prominent facial features. He had a booming bass voice. He was charismatic, popular and had an excellent sense of humor, but he lacked self-confidence and felt inferior. He believed that his business successes resulted from sheer luck. When people would consult him about business matters, he was convinced that they were better than him and were just misled by his accidental successes. He avoided trying to meet attractive women because he was sure they would reject him and say to themselves or straight to his face, "How does such a stupid and ugly guy dare making a pass at me?" When attractive women showed interest in him, he was convinced that they were mocking him or wanting his money. In therapy, he attributed all these weaknesses to his own past. His narrative included the following stories: he was the worst student in school. The teachers and students would mock him and call him "Caveman". The girls used to call him "Stinky". His father would beat him up, saying he was lazy, no good.

After a period of individual psychotherapy, Benjamin took part in family therapy, in which the therapist applied some of the above-listed techniques. Benjamin learned various facts that he hadn't remembered about himself. He had ADHD and dyslexia and was treated using Ritalin and corrective teaching. He had regular meetings with the school counselor, who was warm and supportive. He was a member of the school soccer team. Friends would come to visit him at home. Even in primary school he would make business deals with friends. His father beat him up once and cursed him after Benjamin had thrown a chair at him and injured him. But then his father apologized and asked him to forgive him. Benjamin had to apologize too and they reconciled. His mother used to call him Schwarzenegger. After a few family meetings, there was a marked improvement in Benjamin's symptoms.

Reflection and interpretation

Reflection refers to the therapist's mirroring of the client's verbal or non-verbal acts, often in the therapist's own words. The therapist can also reflect the feelings expressed by the client (e.g. "When you said that you missed your sister you had a sad expression of your face"). This is a supporting technique, letting the client know that the therapist paid attention and listened empathetically. This is also a debugging technique that sharpens the client's awareness of his or her own words and acts.

Interpretation means sharing with the client the therapist's insights about what lies behind the former's verbal and non-verbal behavior in the clinic and in the real world. It is a debugging technique because it is designed to help the client become aware of bugs in his or her conscious or unconscious thoughts and feelings.

Mentalization and meta-cognition

Mentalization-Based Treatment is based on enhancing the client's ability to self-reflect and read other people's minds by meta-cognition (i.e. cognition about cognition). In the terms of The Diamond Model, this collection of methods is designed to help clients become aware of their own information processing programs and the bugs they are infected with.

Strategic and paradoxical techniques

Milton Erickson's suggestion techniques have been discussed above. His work, alongside the work of other pioneers, started the strategic tradition in psychotherapy. There are many streams within this tradition. What is common to all of them is the principle of "go with the client", do not resist resistance, help the client change from his or her own frame of reference. Proponents of this approach have often compared this to the guiding principle of martial arts of the Far East, like judo and jiujitsu, in which the warrior is assisted not by his or her own power, but by the power of the opponent in order to defeat the latter.

One of the main strategic techniques is paradoxical injunctions. A stock example is prescribing the symptom.

Case 9.7 Samuel

Samuel used to work long hours. When he came home from work tired and hungry, he was immediately asked by his wife to help her with something that was difficult for her to do, such as carrying heavy things from the car. Then he burst out screaming that she was mistreating and exploiting him. He shrieked so loudly that the children were terribly scared and the neighbors came to ask what had happened. In therapy, Samuel refused to listen to reason. He insisted that he was right and that his responses were appropriate for the situation (non-sense and horse blinders). The therapist prescribed the symptom by telling him, "If you don't burst out and exhale all your anger out, then you will be in danger of bursting like a balloon. So, don't try to control yourself, continue exploding. Your wife will have to accept it for the sake of your own health." As a result, Samuel told the therapist that he understood that his behavior was inappropriate and that his wife's request was justified. He said he had been tired and hungry and if his wife had waited for him to eat and rest for a while all of that would not have happened.

Obviously, the paradoxical injunction helped Samuel to soften the bugs in his program. One can only speculate about the mechanism of change that worked in this case. Maybe what he perceived as empathic acceptance of his difficulty on the part of the therapist brought about the restoration of emotional balance and therefore opened the way to self-awareness. But perhaps the paradoxical injunction opened his eyes to the absurdity of the way he conceived of his reactions.

Other standard paradoxical interventions are:

(a) Acceptance and exaggeration of a negative position. For example, if a member of the family expresses pessimism and the others try to encourage

196 Therapy

him, the therapist claims that the situation is even worse than the pessimist described.

(b) Consent with self-humiliation. For example, if the client says, "I'm stupid," the therapist agrees.

(c) Declaration of helplessness. The therapist takes no credit for change and declares that he or she has been making great effort to help the client but has failed.

(d) Dictating a symbolic, make-believe representation of the symptom. For example, in working with a client suffering from bulimia, instead of gorging and then throwing up, he or she is instructed to pretend to eat some porridge and then throw it into the toilet.

(e) Instructing the client to exaggerate and amplify certain problematic behaviors. For example, a woman blames her husband aggressively for not giving her enough attention and not allowing closeness. The accusation and the aggressive tone distance him even further from her. The therapist tells her that apparently her accusations are not sufficiently powerful or aggressive, because they have failed to achieve the desire result. She should be louder and more aggressive to achieve her goal.

(f) Prescribing a time and a place in which the symptom should occur. For example, telling the client to have his panic attack only at home in the evenings.

(g) Grotesquely exaggerating a real problem. For example, if parents complain that their child is not disciplined and they cannot control him, they are told, "Tie him to the bed and scream your demands into his ear through a loudspeaker."

(h) Imagining the worst options.

Example 9.6 Joshua again

Joshua in Case 9.5, who had gambled in his early youth, developed extreme reaction formation. When he played poker with his friends for very small sums, he would go into a panic attack and retire from the game. The therapist asked him to imagine the worst possible consequences of continuing playing. He started by imagining that he would be tempted to play for larger and larger sums and ended by imagining that he would lose his house and his family, become homeless and die on the street. At this point, he said that what he had imagined was idiotic and began to laugh.

Interpretation and manipulation of dreams.

According to Sigmund Freud, dreams are "the royal road to the unconscious."

Freud's dream interpretation method may be viewed, in our terms, as a debugging technique, accessing information that had not been available to the conscious mind.

Here, we will focus not on Freud's dream interpretation technique, but on more traditional techniques.

In some traditional cultures, dreams are not understood as expressions of the dreamer's conscious or unconscious concerns. Bilu and Witztum, who had done therapeutic worked with ultra-Orthodox Jews in Jerusalem, relate the fact that in one of the mystical Jewish traditions, during sleep, the soul exits from the body and ascends to heaven in order to unite with the Divine Presence. According to this tradition, dreams reflect the experiences of the wandering soul. The nature of dreams and their consequences are derived from what the soul encounters in its way. Great importance is attributed to the moral position of the soul and the characters it encounters in its path. In some cases, the soul brings the dreamer to visit relatives who have passed away.

Example 9.7 The bazaar

Bilu and Witztum based their modern professional therapeutic approach on these traditional beliefs. In one of the cases they reported, a woman who had lost her husband and could not cope with the loss dreamt that she was stranded in a closed bazaar with the gatekeeper until nightfall. She herself interpreted the day in the bazaar as a symbol of life and the night with the gatekeeper as a symbol of death. But she saw this dream not as a psychological entity, but as a sinister communication from the world of the dead. The therapist instructed her to prostrate herself on her late husband's grave and ask him to let her continue with her life. She did so. Following that, she dreamt that her late husband asked her to bring him wine for *Havdala* (a religious ritual conducted on Saturday evening to separate between the holiness of the departing Sabbath and the mundane quality of the coming week). The widow interpreted this as permission from her late husband to go on with her normal life.

This case reminds one of the above-mentioned ceremony of communication between the deceased head of the family, impersonated by a shaman, and his living family members, documented in Korea by Lee (1988). In our terms, the death of an important family member causes loss of the previous simplicity of some programs. Inability to work through the mourning and go on with normal life may be viewed as an attempt to sacrifice comprehensiveness (horse blinders) for the sake of consistency (avoiding flip-flop). Although the mourning is hard to bear, the mourner prefers to immerse him or herself in it rather than deal with the unfinished business in his or her relationship with

198 Therapy

the deceased, betraying him, as it were, by going on with his or her life in all
its complexity. In the above case, the therapist helped the widow remove the
horse blinders and cope with the inconsistencies and complexities involved in
really coping with her loss.

Summary of Chapter 9

The choice of therapeutic technique in The Diamond Model is subject to the
principle of systematic technical eclecticism. Any technique borrowed from
any source or made up by the therapist may be applied in the therapeutic process as long as it can hit the chosen target of change: rebalancing unbalanced
emotions and debugging bugged programs. Borrowing a method or technique
does not necessarily require adopting the theories, tenets or beliefs on which it
rests. Most techniques share the same limited number of change mechanisms
and means for achieving the change. Understanding these mechanisms and
tools can enable the therapist to apply almost any method and technique successfully or to create his or her own. The techniques presented succinctly in this
chapter are classified according to their leading change mechanisms: working
through the body (relaxation and activation); enhancing alertness, attention
and concentration; exercising influence; expression and catharsis; reinforcement and support; habituation; concretization; and changing information
processing patterns.

Assignments

(a) If you are an active therapist, specify the therapeutic techniques
you have used, whether they are included in the above list or not.
Define each technique by its targets of change, mechanisms of
changes and means of change.
(b) Suggest the use of techniques described in this chapter in the
treatment of Cases 1.1 (Nonny) and 7.2 (Amir). Define each technique by its targets of change, mechanisms of changes and means
of change.

A classified list of publications

Technical eclecticism

Lazarus, A.A. and Madanes, C. (1985). *Need for technical eclecticism.* An audio
cassette. The Evolution of Psychotherapy, L330–331. Infodemix. Phoenix, AZ: The
Milton Erickson Foundation.
Stricker, G. (2010). *Psychotherapy integration.* Washington, DC: American
Psychological Association.

Psychological healing mechanisms

Young, G. (2016). *Unifying causality and psychology: Being, brain, and behavior.* New York, NY: Springer.

Operant conditioning

Jones, B. (2012). *The conditioning handbook* [ebook]. Nevada City, CA: IronMind Enterprises, Inc. Sold by Amazon Digital Series LLC.

Biofeedback

Schwartz, M.S. and Andrasik, F. (2016). *Biofeedback: A practitioner guide.* 4th ed. New York, NY: Guilford.

EMDR

Shapiro, F. (2013). *Getting past your past: Take control of your life with self-help techniques from EMDR therapy.* Emmaus, PA: Rodale.

NLP

Dotz, T. (2013). *NLP: The essential guide to Neuro-Linguistic Programming.* New York: William Morrow Paperbacks.

Yoga and meditation

Brooks, J. (2014). *The meditation transformation: How to relax and revitalize body, your work, and your perspective today.* (N.P.): Empowerment Nation.
Brown, C. (2017). *The yoga bible.* London, UK: Godsfield Press.

Mindfulness

Kabat-Zinn, J. (2012). *Mindfulness for beginners: Reclaiming the present moment and your life.* Louisville, KY: Sounds True.

Mentalization

Fonagy, P., Gergely, G., Jurist, E.L. and, Target, M. (2002). *Affect regulation, mentalization and the development of the self.* New York, NY: Other Press.

Gestalt therapy

Mann, D. (2010). *Gestalt therapy: 100 key points and techniques.* London, UK: Routledge.

Gradual relaxation

Nejad, L. and Volny, K. (2008). *Relaxation techniques: Reduce stress and anxiety and enhance well-being.* Audio CD. Carmarthen, UK: Crown House Publishing.

Systematic desensitization

Wenrich, W. and Dawley, H. (1976). *Self-directed systematic desensitization: A guide for the student, client and therapist.* (N.P.): Behaviordella.

Wolpe, J. (1958), *Psychotherapy by reciprocal inhibition.* Stanford, CA: Stanford University Press.

Trance

Smith, W. (2012). *The trance state as a religious experience: A monograph.* Kindle edition.

Massage

Liddell, L. and Thomas, S. (2012). *The book of massage: The complete step-by-step guide to Eastern and Western techniques.* 2nd ed. Greenwich, CT: Touchstone.

Movement and dance therapies

Payne, H. (2017). *Essentials of dance movement psychotherapy: International perspectives on theory, research and practice.* London, UK: Routledge.

Art therapy

Buchalter, S. and Navarro, T. (2009). *Art therapy techniques and applications.* London, UK: Jessica Kingsley Publishers.

Music therapy

Wheeler, B.L. (2016). *Music therapy handbook.* New York, NY: Guilford.

Drama therapy and psychodrama

Karp, M. and Holmes, P. (1998). *The handbook of psychodrama.* London, UK: Routledge.

Swart, J. (2015). *Get to know drama therapy: Using play and pretend techniques to heal* Kindle edition.

Bibliotherapy

Hynes, A. and Hynes-Berry, M. (1986). *Bibliotherapy – The interactive process.* Boulder, CO: Westview Press.

Humor therapy

Mann, D. (2015). *Humor therapy: The art of smiling for others.* Bloomington, IN: iUniverse.

Suggestion and magic

Silvester, T. (2010). *Wordweaving: The science of suggestion: A comprehensive guide to creating hypnotic language.* Hetherset, UK: Quest Institute.

Stein, R. and Stein, P.L. (2017). *The anthropology of religion, magic and witchcraft.* 4th ed. London, UK: Routledge.

Guided imagination

Hart, J. (2008). Guided imagery. *Alternative and Complementary Therapies,* 14(6), pp.295–299.

Reparenting

Young, J.E, Klosko, J.S. and Weishaar, M.E. (2003). *Schema therapy: A practitioner's guide.* New York, NY: Guilford.

Healing ceremonies

Freed, S.A. and Freed, R.S. (1964). Spirit possession as illness in a North Indian village. *Ethnology,* 3(2), pp.152–171.

Hammerschlag, C. and Silverman, D. (1997). *Healing ceremonies.* New York, NY: Perigee Books.

Strathern, A. and Stewart, P.J. (2010). *Curing and healing: Medical anthropology in global perspective.* 2nd ed. Durham, NC: Carolina Academic Press.

Rites of passage

Van Gennep, A., Vizedon, M. and Caffee, G.L. (1961). *The rites of passage.* Chicago, IL: The University of Chicago Press.

Mourning ceremonies

Bilu, Y. and Witztum, E. (1993). Working with Jewish ultra-Orthodox patients: Guidelines for a culturally sensitive therapy. *Culture, Medicine and Psychiatry,* 17(2), pp.197–233.

Lee, D.H. (1988). Korean shamans: Role playing through trance possession. In: Schechner, R. and Appel, W., eds. *By means of performance: Intercultural studies of theater and ritual.* Cambridge, UK: Cambridge University Press, pp.149–166.

Robben, A.C.G.M., ed. (2005). *Death, mourning, and burial: A cross-cultural reader.* Hoboken, NJ: Wiley-Blackwell.

202 Therapy

Atonement

Piers, G., Singer, M.B. and Grinker, R.R. (1972). *Shame, guilt and atonement: A psychoanalytic and cultural study.* New York, NY: Norton.

Zigo, S. (2008). *Morality: An anthropological perspective.* New York, NY: Berg.

Induction and modification of dreams

Bilu, Y. (1979). Sigmund Freud and Rabbi Yehuda: On the Jewish mystical tradition of "psychoanalytic" dream interpretation. *The Journal of Psychological Anthropology,* 2(4), pp.443–463.

Bilu, Y. (1986). Dreams and the wishes of the saint. In: Goldberg, H., ed. *Judaism viewed from within and from without: Anthropological exploration in the comparative study of Jewish culture.* New York, NY: SUNY Press, pp.285–314.

Exposure techniques

Bill, Y. (2016). *Cognitive behavioral therapy: CBT techniques to manage your anxiety, depression, compulsive behavior, PTSD, negative thoughts and phobias: A practical guide to self- empowerment and liberation.* San Diego, CA: JPL Publishing.

Boudewyns, P.A., ed. (1983). *Flooding and implosive therapy: Direct therapeutic exposure in clinical practice.* New York, NY: Springer

Foa, E., Hembree, E. and Rothbaum, B.O. (2007). *Prolonged exposure therapy for PTSD: Emotional processing of traumatic experiences.* Oxford, UK: Oxford University Press.

William, M.B. and Poijula, S. (2016). *The PTSD workbook: Simple, effective techniques for overcoming traumatic stress symptoms.* Oakland, CA: New Harbinger Publications.

Concretization, symbolization, fables and allegories

Baker, P.A. (1985). *Using metaphors in psychotherapy.* New York, NY: Brunner/Mazel.

Constantine, L.L. (1978). Family sculpting and relationship mapping techniques. *Journal of Family and Marriage Counseling,* 4(2), pp.13–24.

Lewis, L. and Langer, K.G. (1994). Symbolization in psychotherapy with patients who are disabled. *American Journal of Psychotherapy,* 48(3), pp.231–239.

Internal characters

Berne, E. (1961). *Transactional analysis in psychotherapy: A systemic individual and social psychiatry.* New York, NY: Glove Press.

Earley, J. (2012). *Resolving inner conflict.* Larkspur, CA: Pattern System Books.

Schwartz, R. C. (1995). *Internal family systems therapy,* New York, NY: Guilford.

CBT techniques

Ellis, A. (2004) *Rational-emotive behavior therapy: It works for me, it can work for you.* Amherst, NY: Prometheus Books.

Riggenback, J. (2012). *The CBT toolbox: A workbook for clients and clinicians.* (N.P.): Premier Publishing & Media.

Narrative techniques

Madigan, S. (2010). *Narrative therapy.* Washington, DC: American Psychological Association.

Strategic and paradoxical techniques

Quick, E.K. (2007). *Doing what works in brief therapy: A strategic solution focused approach.* 2nd ed. New York, NY: Academic Press.

Chapter 10

Make-believe play as a therapeutic instrument

The advantages of play therapy

Play therapy is a highly enjoyable activity. It is a rich and flexible activity. The therapist plays together with the client – a single child, a group of children or a family. Both the therapist and the client can set their imaginations free and create unlimited amusing situations. There is no end to the means of expression and communication at their disposal. They can talk, sing, play, paint, use all sorts of means and materials, move, dance, leap or roll on the carpet. Everything is possible. At the same time, the therapist should not, at the height of his or her enthusiasm, drift and forget his or her goals. He must carefully monitor what is going on in the room, decipher the events as they move and respond consciously to their goals. She must be constantly aware of all her actions and decide for herself why she chose to do what she did. The play therapeutic moves should be focused, like a laser beam in eye surgery.

The functions of play therapy

Play therapy has three different but interrelated functions:

(a) Play as an emotion-balancing device.
(b) Play as a debugging instrument. Play bug-busters are used as means of achieving therapeutic change by removing or weakening the bugs in the clients' information processing programs.
(c) Play as a means of therapeutic communication between the therapist and the clients and between the clients themselves.

The sub-model of integrative play therapy, a part of The Diamond Model, includes the following components:

(a) A formal, explicit definition of the concept of *make-believe play.*
(b) Make-believe play as a language, a semiotic system.
(c) Make-believe play as an information processing system.

(d) Make-believe play as a cognitive-affective regulative mechanism.
(e) Make-believe play as a social regulative mechanism.
(f) Make-believe play as a product of culture.
(g) Play development and the child's general development.
(h) Play therapy as a debugger: playful bug-busters.
(i) Play therapy as a manager of therapeutic sessions.
(j) Play therapy as a monitor of the therapeutic process, its termination and its outcomes.

A formal, explicit definition of the concept of make-believe play

In this definition, make-believe play is looked at as a product of the following simultaneous, not necessarily conscious, mental operations:

Realification of a purely mental entity (e.g. "The image of a lion in my mind is a real lion present in the immediate external environment here and now").

Identication: verbalizing the realification and/or choosing or creating a tangible external entity and *identicating* it with what has been realified (e.g. "These are not my twisted fingers and my voice; these are, together, the realified lion").

Denying the seriousness of the realification and the identication (e.g. "I don't really believe that there is a real lion hear and now, nor that my fingers and voice are its claws or its roar. I'm just making these mental claims for fun").

This definition covers all and only the phenomena constituting make-believe play properly so-called. It draws clear distinctions between make-believe play and akin phenomena such as imitation, errors of identification, delusions, attempts to mislead, fantasy or storytelling. It is fruitful in the sense that many corollaries about the linguistic, cognitive and therapeutic attributes of make-believe play can be logically and pragmatically derived from it. The peculiar linguistic characteristics of make-believe play, logically derived from the above definition, are discussed in Ariel (1984). For a more detailed discussion of this definition and its implications, see Ariel (2002, pp. 5–14).

Some change-effecting properties of make-believe play were logically and pragmatically derived from this definition (see below).

Make-believe play as a language, a semiotic system

Like every semiotic system, make-believe play has both expressive and communicative functions. The developmentally more advanced manifestations of make-believe play take the form of structured, rule-governed texts produced by a child individually or conjointly with other children or adults. Each make-believe text is structured on the raw material, semantic and pragmatic levels by hidden rules. This is true even of make-believe play texts that look to the observer like a haphazard, chaotic jumble of disconnected entities. There are universal rules, group-specific rules and rules applying to an individual player. The rules are generative (see Chomsky, 1957, 1965); that is, they may be viewed as information processing programs (i.e. formulas, algorithms or virtual "machines") that can generate all and only make-believe play texts that can, actually or potentially, be produced by a specific player or a group of players at a particular period of their lives. The term *generative information processing programs* or, more briefly, *programs* will be used below instead of the term *rules*.

Like every semiotic system, make-believe play can be analyzed on three levels:

(a) The raw material level (i.e. the level of tangible verbal and non-verbal signifying entities – verbal expressions or identicated non-verbal entities).
(b) The semantic level (i.e. the level of signified [realified] thematic and emotive contents).
(c) The pragmatic level (i.e. the level of the social-communicational uses of signifier–signified units and combinations of units).

Interpreting a make-believe text requires uncovering and formulating the raw material, semantic and pragmatic programs underlying it. An interpretation of this kind is not informed by some external theory such as psychoanalytic theory, but inductively extracted from the empirical data. The best interpretation will be the simplest one; that is to say, the best set of programs covers all and only the elements of a sample of make-believe play texts in a consistent and plausible manner. Such an interpretation is supposed to have the best predictive validity. The notion of simplicity is discussed in Chapters 1 and 3 and is taken up again below.

It should be noted that such an interpretation does not amount to a full diagnostic evaluation. It only serves as a basis for such a diagnostic evaluation. Make-believe play texts divulge multifarious kinds of information about the players' functional and dysfunctional developmental profiles, emotives and emotional conflicts, social behavior, culture, etc. A full diagnostic evaluation will expose complex links between the semiotic programs underlying play texts and the programs organizing all these other systems. It is, however, semiotically interpreted play texts, not raw play texts, that carry information about such complex links.

For a more detailed discussion of make-believe play as a semiotic system, including methods and techniques for analyzing it as such, see Ariel (2002).

Make-believe play as a cognitive-affective regulative mechanism

Make-believe play has been hypothesized to function as a cognitive-affective regulative (cybernetic) device. The Diamond Model comprises an explication, formalization and systematization of theoretical and empirical studies of the emotions by the language of information processing, semiotics and cybernetics (see Chapter 4). In The Diamond Model, human emotions are conceived of as a homeostatic feedback mechanism, a cybernetic system of control whose function is to balance the level of emotional arousal associated with a person's central concerns (emotives). The concept of an *emotive* is explicated in Chapter 4 as a potentially infinite semantic field, a kind of thesaurus entry whose core includes concern-related themes with the highest emotional valence (e.g. fear of mother's death) and its periphery includes milder concern-related themes (e.g. fear of losing a beloved toy animal). The central hypothesis is that all the higher mental faculties – attention, sense perception, memory, thinking, motivation for action, etc. – are more alert to themes and images belonging to the cores of the person's emotives (see Chapter 4). For example, a child whose central emotive is a fear of being rejected by his mother will retrieve from memory themes and images related to the core of this emotive more easily than themes and images belonging to the periphery of this emotive or unrelated to this emotive. The same child will also pay attention to and perceive external stimuli related to such core themes and images more readily than unrelated stimuli and so forth. But then the homeostatic feedback mechanism of emotion balancing is likely to be activated. The core themes and images retrieved or perceived will arouse intense feelings, which will heat up emotional tensions to boiling point. At this stage, all the cognitive faculties will abruptly or gradually switch off and cool down. Only themes and images belonging to the emotive's periphery or emotionally neutral themes and images will be retrieved from memory, thought about, attended to, perceived and so forth. But then, having cooled down, all the cognitive faculties will gradually become alert again to the emotive's core themes and images and a new emotion-balancing cycle will start.

The applicability of this mechanism to make-believe play is almost self-evident. Since the mental images and themes realified in make believe play are retrieved from memory, thought about and motivate action, themes and images belonging to the core of the child's main emotives are more likely to occur in his or her make-believe play than other themes and images. Likewise, the player will more readily pay attention to and perceive external stimuli reminding him or her of the core themes and images of his or her emotives and identicate the chosen stimuli with the realified contents. But then the realified contents and identicated stimuli are likely to arouse in the player intolerable feelings with respect to the core of his or her emotives. At this point, to reduce the heightened emotional tension, the player is likely to move

208 Therapy

to signified contents and identicated stimuli belonging to the periphery of his or her emotive or to neutral contents and stimuli. Having cooled down, the player will reintroduce core signifiers and signified contents into his or her play and a new cycle will start.

Children often introduce additional emotion-balancing devices into their make-believe play (e.g. bringing in protective signifiers and signified themes, strengthening vulnerable imagined characters or reversing unpleasant situations; see below).

Play therapists are advised to identify the client's emotives, apprehend the manifestations of the above-mentioned balancing mechanisms as part of the diagnostic evaluation and take this information into account when they decide on their play therapeutic moves. The therapist must be particularly alert to external manifestations of the client's inability or reduced ability to use the cognitive-affective balancing mechanisms of play during the session. In such a case, a directive intervention is required, in which the regulative function of play is reinforced by the therapist's playful moves.

The task of interpreting the cognitive-affective aspects of the child's play can be assisted by the heuristic technique of raw material and semantic analysis entitled Context-Dependent Componential Analysis (CDCA), introduced in Chapter 6. The meanings of signifiers and signified contents in a child's make-believe play are not always conventional, being often unconventional and private. What a particular signified content means for a specific playing child can often be understood only if one examines the contexts in which this child uses this signified content. For instance, a child plays with a devil toy and calls it "the devil", but an inspection of all the contexts in which he plays with this toy reveals that he always uses it as a kind, nurturing, good-mother-like figure. The original componential analysis technique (Hammel, 1965) had therefore to be varied and called CDCA. This technique can assist one to extract and formulate generative programs interpreting the hidden meanings of the player's raw material and semantic units, relating them to the child's emotives and unmasking the emotion-balancing mechanisms as manifested in the make-believe play of a specific child. Such programs constitute a kind of ultrasound, exposing the child's cognitive-emotive dynamics. This technique and its ramifications are described in detail and explained in Ariel (2002).

Make-believe play as a cybernetic social regulative device

Social systems such as families and peer groups are explicated in The Diamond Model as sets of generative programs regulating the mutual proximity and control goals that the members of a given social group have with respect to each other and the strategic plans these members have developed to overcome or bypass obstacles in the way of reaching these goals (see Chapters 5 and 6). Children's make-believe play is one way of managing interpersonal proximity and control conflicts in a manner that keeps the conflicts within tolerable limits, avoiding breakdown of relationships. The conflict is transferred from the level of reality to the level of make-believe. Instead of directly ordering a friend around, his playmate says, "Let's pretend the king, me, told his servant, you, to bring him his shield and sword." Make-believe play functions in this respect as a social control, interpersonal homeostatic feedback system.

The Diamond Model includes a heuristic semiotic procedure that facilitates the extraction and formulation of generative programs. These programs describe the goals, the plans and the make-believe play tactics that family or peer group members have adopted to regulate their level of social tension. This procedure is applied to the semiotic level of pragmatics. Using it can assist play therapists to obtain a diagnostic evaluation of family or peer group dynamics and choose effective family or group play therapeutic moves (see Chapters 5 and 6).

Another component of The Diamond Model, which is relevant to the role of make-believe play as a social regulative device, is the laws children's peer groups develop to manage play-related proximity and control conflicts with respect to the rights of use of toys and other play things, play territories, play group participation and play group leadership. I call such laws *mini legal systems*. Play therapists who work with peer groups and families, especially siblings, are advised to learn the unwritten book of laws the children have created and take it into account in their play therapeutic work. Such mini legal systems are discussed in Ariel (2002) (see Chapter 4).

Make-believe play as a product of culture

Theorists and researchers of play and play therapy have asserted that children of different socio-cultural groups play differently. Play therapists should be culturally competent and sensitive to these differences. Reviews of the literature have shown that most studies of the cultural characteristics of play are impressionistic or weak methodologically. Therefore, almost nothing can be stated about this subject with any degree of assurance. One can only summarize the main questions students of this fields have posed and suggest directions for further research. Here are some of the main questions:

(a) Is play in general or make-believe play in particular universal or a product of particular cultures? Are there cultures in which children do not play at all or are never engaged in make-believe play?
(b) Are the roles of make-believe play as emotionally and socially regulating mechanisms universal or culture-bound?
(c) Do children of all cultures create play-related mini legal systems?
(d) Are there cultures in which children play just traditional games?
(e) Are there cultures in which play is only produced collectively, as a structured social activity, and not as a product of individual minds?

(f) Is play a preparation for adult roles? Do children who work from an early age nevertheless play?

(g) Are there cultures in which play is purely mimetic and not creative?

These questions are discussed in Ariel (2002) (see Chapter 7) with reference to field research conducted by Ariel and Sever with Jewish, Arab and Bedouin children in Israel and the Sinai Desert (see Ariel, Sever and Kam, 1980; Sever, 1980). In Ariel (1999), specific concepts and techniques are proposed for learning the therapy-relevant aspects of a client's culture from the clients themselves during therapy and for conducting therapy in a culturally competent manners (see Chapter 5).

Play development and the child's general development

The Diamond Model also includes a synthesis of theoretical and research studies about the development of play and its interface with the child's physical, neuropsychological, psychomotor, cognitive and socio-emotional development (Ariel, 2002). It is hypothesized that the child's play in general and make-believe play in particular develop in growth, internalization, complexity, coordination and integration, differentiation, depth of processing, concreteness vs, abstraction, constancy and stability, objectivity and monitoring and control as a function of the child's development in all these areas (see Chapter 4). Play, however, is not only influenced by the child's general development, but also influences it. Play contributes to the child's acquisition and solidification of psychomotor, cognitive, linguistic and social skills and to the development of problem-solving abilities, self-concept, gender identity, self-control, empathy, body and self boundaries and other personality development achievements.

The Diamond Model includes heuristic procedures assisting the construction of a diagnostic evaluation of the child's profile in all these developmental lines on the basis of semiotically analyzed make-believe play texts (see Chapter 6).

Play therapists are offered techniques for helping the child mobilize the learning and development-enhancing powers of play during play therapy sessions.

The therapeutic power of play

The removal or weakening of the bugs from the information processing system leads to spontaneous healing. It enables the mobilization of resources to overcome the crisis and facilitates the creation of a new system of information processing, which makes enlisting corrective feedback possible.

Play therapy with an individual, a family or a group mobilizes *play bug-busters*, well-defined curative properties of play that have the power to weaken or remove bugs from infected programs. Once the programs have been cleansed of their bugs, they change spontaneously. They acquire a new simplicity, which renovates their capacity to process the new information in a comprehensive, parsimonious, consistent and plausible manner and to mobilize corrective feedback. The bug-busters are derived from three different sources:

(a) First source of bug-busters: the role of play as a homeostatic feedback mechanism for regulating the level of emotional arousal around the player's emotives.
(b) Second source of bug-busters: debugging properties of make-believe play that are logically derived from its very definition.
(c) Third source of bug-busters: the role of play as a homeostatic feedback mechanism for regulating social relations.

In my view, the therapist in play therapy should not be non-directive at all costs. If the spontaneous play of the clients brings about the desired therapeutic change, there is no need for the therapist to be directive. But if the clients do not have the necessary bug-busters in their repertoire of play techniques, the therapist has no choice but to be directive in order to help the clients activate the relevant bug-busters. However, even if the therapist has no choice but to be directive, it is always preferable that his or her interventions be integrated into the spontaneous play of the clients and respond to it.

Emotion balancing by means of play

If the child is not skilled in employing the emotion-balancing mechanisms of play, the therapist can join in as a playmate and help the child activate these mechanisms.

Here are some of the emotion-balancing techniques used by children in their play:

Repetition in a safe environment

When emotionally loaded themes are repeated over and over again in the safe environment of play, a habituating, positively reinforcing effect is created (see Chapter 9). The child, as the director of the play and as an actor, experiences a sense of mastery over the emotionally unbalanced events depicted in his or her play.

Distancing and ups and downs

This is actualized by moving from play behaviors reflecting unbalanced emotions to behaviors reflecting balanced emotions and then back to unbalanced emotions. The cycle repeats itself. Signified contents and signifiers

212 Therapy

belonging to the core of the player's emotives can be replaced by themes and signifiers belonging to the emotives' periphery (distancing), until the player is ready to realify and identicate core themes again.

Example 10.1 Nick

In make-believe play, six-year-old Nick, whose emotive was fear of dying or being seriously injured, brought to his play the most difficult contents (drowning, having fatal accidents) and then calmed himself down by switching to softer contents (sitting in a boat, resting on the beach, staying quietly at home watching TV). After he relaxed he returned to the more difficult contents. This cycle repeated itself over and over again.

In the following example, the boy was unable to use the emotion-balancing power of play. The therapist had to intervene to help him use the up-and-down mechanism.

Example 10.2 Ryan

Seven-year-old Ryan, whose father had cancer, was staging obsessively scenes of death and burial in his play. At first he used puppets and later he played as if he himself was the one who died and was buried under a stack of pillows. His play started a process of feed-forward. He became more and more distressed and restless. The therapist helped him use the up-and-down mechanism. She introduced into the play "a time machine" that takes people back in time. She played the role of the operator of the time machine. She let Ryan play as if he were dying and buried, but when she saw that his level of emotional distress was rising too high she operated the time machine and took him back to the time before he "was ill". Ryan liked the idea. When he went back in time, he played his favorite games like soccer and police. When he calmed down, he went back to his dying play, and so on.

A distancing move Ryan could but didn't use was replacing the theme of death by the theme of the loss of a valuable object.

The following is an example of distancing without up and down.

Example 10.3 Bella

Eight-year-old Bella was sexually abused by an uncle. Every time this event was mentioned, Bella would have an unbearable stomachache and start crying and shouting. She refused to talk about this traumatic experience.

The play therapist helped her process this experience. She encouraged her to choose raw material signifiers and semantic contents belonging to the emotive "fear of being attacked", but situated at the margins of the emotive's associative field (e.g. a cat lying in wait for a mouse, a pickpocket and a bothering friend). This play alluded to the traumatic event only indirectly.

Introducing protective devices

Example 10.4 Nick again

Nick (see Example 10.1) introduced the theme of "drowning submarines" into his play. Then he took a toy doctor's toolbox and called it "a redcross submarine."

Neutralizing

Example 10.5 Luna

Five-year-old Luna, who played with a threatening toy shark in children's group therapy, told her playmate Bob (as if from the mouth of the shark), "Don't worry, I'm hollow." Bob still feared the shark and was unable to relax. The therapist played as if she were a dentist who came to treat the shark because "he has weak teeth."

Empowering and immunization

Example 10.6 Bob

Bob (see Example 10.5), who was afraid of being a victim of violence, played as if his skin turned into a steel shield.

Compensation

The child compensates him or herself in play for deprivation or deficiency.

Example 10.7 Anita

Eight-year-old Anita, whose father went bankrupt and the family had to move to a lower-quality apartment, played as if her family had a one-hundred-room house.

214 Therapy

Example 10.8 Paul

Nine-year-old Paul, who suffers from muscle weakness (hypotonia), played games that expressed his weakness. The therapist gave him light black plastic sports weights and played with him as if he were a professional weight-lifter.

Example 10.9 Alex

Alex, a disabled five-year-old boy in a wheelchair, played games expressing his weakness. The therapist suggested that the wheelchair would "be" a racing car.

Reversing

Example 10.10 Max and Leo

Five-year-old Max and Leo, who were friends and neighbors, used to be harassed by a boy named Eric in their kindergarten. At home, they would take rather violent revenge on a doll they named Eric.

Example 10.11 Heidi

Heidi, who had lost her father, used to revive him in her play.

The play therapeutic uses of these emotion-balancing techniques are controlled applications of natural emotion-balancing uses of play observed in children's spontaneous play activities. The main play therapeutic effect of these techniques is preparing the ground for the operation of other play bug-busters. Since bugs are energized by unbalanced emotional responses to stress, clients are more likely to be receptive to corrective information after their relevant emotional balance has at least partly been restored.

Play as a debugging instrument

The second source of play bug-busters is, as stated above, the very definition of the concept *make-believe play*. Bug-busters of this kind are logically derived from this definition.

Owning and alienation

Since in the play the player performs the mental actions of realification and identication, he or she associates him or herself with his or her play's contents

Make-believe play 215

(i.e. sees them as real, as part of the immediate external reality). But since he or she also performs the mental act of denying seriousness, he or she is at the same time alienated from the same contents, not committed to their truth.

Example 10.12 Dean

Dean, who was jealous of his baby brother, played as if he had killed the baby's image, represented by a doll. He both associated himself with the jealousy and desire to get rid of the competing infant and alienated himself from these feelings and thoughts.

In therapy, activating this property of play can help the client retrieve and recognize unreachable information (because of the horse blinders bug) in the imaginary world of the play, and vice versa, to keep away information he or she is flooded with. This play bug-buster can be applied to help a client own rejected (horse-blindered) information in the fantasy world of play without disowning it explicitly, or vice versa.

Example 10.13 Daniel again

This property of play was used as a way to help Daniel (Case 3.1) to distance himself from his tendency to see his mother as a "witch" (alienate himself from this tendency). Consider, for example, the following play moves: the therapist suggested that Daniel and his mother would play "a masks procession". Each of the two tried several masks. Some of the masks represented good figures, such as a guardian angel or a loyal watchdog. Some other masks represented evil characters, such as a demon, a witch or a bird of prey. Each of the two pretended that his or her masked face was actually his or her real face. The property of owning and alienation was supposed to influence Daniel's perception of his mother and make him, at least subconsciously, question the truth of his vision of his mother as evil.

The same play property, owning and alienation, was used to help Daniel's mother own the fact that she had been transferring her anger at her husband onto Daniel. For example, the therapist gave himself a name that was a distorted version of the name of Daniel's father. He played a "boxing match" with Daniel's mother (of course, without really touching one another). Daniel played the role of the referee. The therapist avoided the fists of Daniel's mother and committed various offences. Daniel's mother demanded that Daniel tell the therapist off. If Daniel found it difficult to respond, his mother accused him of being on the therapist's side and began to fight with him instead of with the therapist.

Basic duality

Thanks to the mental claim *denial of seriousness*, a part of the definition of make-believe play, the player is both the actor that plays a role and the persona he or she is in the role of. For example, playing as if I am lying is forcing me to observe myself and examine my own habit of lying.

The "boxing match" play in Example 10.13 illustrates this application as well. Both Daniel and his mother were well aware that their play content referred not only to imaginary boxers, but also to the real people who embodied them: Daniel and his mother. Looking at themselves from the sidelines, as it were, while playing their roles in the play forced them to think, at least subconsciously, about the relationships between them in real life. It compelled them to feel what really happened in these relationships. And so the play weakened the horse blinders bug that caused them to ignore the true nature of their relationship. Another example: Daniel's mother played as if she punished her son for his unruly behavior although he didn't deserve to be punished.

Another role of the property of basic duality as a bug-buster is weakening the flip-flop bug by exposing the contradiction between different levels of communication.

Example 10.14 Kevin

Ten-year-old Kevin was suspended from school for two days because he beat up one of his classmates. Kevin's father decided to teach Kevin a lesson by beating Kevin up.

In a family play therapy session, the therapist suggested that Kevin's father would play as if he were hitting Kevin in order to teach him not to use violence.

In this play, basic duality was used as a way to expose an internal contradiction between two layers of communication, one visible and one hidden. On the visible level, hitting Kevin was an educational act. On the hidden level, Kevin's father used sheer aggression. The play implied denial of seriousness. It follows that Kevin's father did not really punish Kevin for his bad behavior. His motives were different, less pure. The use of basic duality made Kevin and his father aware of the flip-flop in the father's attitude, thus weakening this bug.

Arbitrariness of the signifier

In play, anything can signify anything. Thanks to the mental claims of realification and identication, there might not necessarily be any resemblance between the signifiers and the signified contents.

Make-believe play 217

Example 10.15 Zara

Nine-year-old Zara would refuse food. Her mother used to force-feed her. If she was ready to eat, her mother would give her a treat. In the play therapy session, Zara pretended that she did eat what her mother told her to eat. When her mother looked for a toy candy to give Zara as a reward, the therapist gave her mother a toy bee and said, "This is a honey cookie. It is sweet. Give it to Zara because she was a good girl and did eat."

The therapist used the bee, a stinging insect that produces honey, as an arbitrary signifier for a sweet cookie. This had the effect of weakening the mother's horse blinders, ignoring the aggressive side of her force-feeding, as well as weakening the flip-flop bug, showing the mother the contradiction between her benevolence and using force.

Example 10.16 Tessa and Kate

Tessa, a divorcee, wanted to send her ten-year-old daughter, Kate, to a boarding school. Both claimed they were not getting along. Both said that they "get on each other's nerves." The therapist understood their quarrels as reflecting their bugged (horse-blindered) plan to overcome their over-dependence on each other. Their mutual proximity–control goals were to separate, to create arbitrary boundaries between them.

In one of the therapeutic sessions, Tessa and Kate played out the following scene: Tessa as "a queen" expelled Kate "the princess" to the forest. The therapist played the role of a "good fairy". He promised to lead the princess to a hut in the forest where she would be protected. He led her to Tessa. Kate sat in her lap. Tessa's body, particularly her lap, served as an arbitrary signifier for the signified content "a hut in the forest", hinting at the boarding school. The contradiction between the physical proximity of the mother and the daughter, the warmth and tenderness of Tessa's lap on the one hand and the cold and distant hut on the other, meant to make Tessa and Kate feel and be aware of the strong emotional connection between them and the difficulty of disengaging from one another. The horse blinders were removed. That opened the way for them to explore more adequate ways for developing mutual autonomy without turning each other's life into hell and without losing each other.

Possible worlds

Thanks to the mental claims of realification and identication, any imaginable situation can be created in make-believe play. For example, a family torn by aggressive conflicts can play a family of angels.

218 Therapy

The "cabin in the forest" scene in Example 10.16 illustrates this bug-buster too. In this scene, a possible world was created in which the covert relationship between the two was brought to the surface.

The third source of bug-busters is make-believe play as a regulative mechanism for interpersonal conflicts with respect to proximity and control goals and plans (see above). The main bug-buster of this category is *covert communication*. Difficult proximity–control issues and conflicts are disguised as make-believe play communications. For example, a child who wants an overprotective mother to get off her back plays as if she is a magic woman who can take care of her own affairs.

These bug-busters bypass the defenses. Their power is drawn from their subversive activities in the twilight zone between cognition and emotions. They help the client whose emotional state has already been balanced by previous emotion-balancing techniques go through a corrective cognitive-emotional experience, without being required to leave the fantasy world of make-believe. Missing information (due to horse blinders) is retrieved, irrelevant information (due to fifth wheel) is removed and distorted information (due to non-sense) and inconsistent information (due to flip-flop) are exposed as such and put right.

The role of the play therapist

In this genre of therapy, the therapist is an active participant in the spontaneous play of the individual child, the family or the group. The therapeutic goals are achieved by three kinds of play moves: main moves, in which the emotion-balancing techniques and the bug-busters are subtly activated; preparatory moves, preparing the ground for the main moves; and auxiliary moves, controlling any side effects of the preparatory or main moves (see Chapter 8). Preparatory and auxiliary moves have various functions such as joining, influencing the course of the play, supporting, focusing attention and emphasizing, commenting, reflecting and interpreting. These are achieved by playful techniques, belonging to a given repertoire or made up by the therapist. Here is a sample of such techniques:

Mimicking the client's play

Therapeutic functions:

Joining. When children want to join a play activity, they simply imitate the play of children they want to play with. The therapist can do the same.

Reflecting, commenting. By imitating aspects of the client's play behavior, such as an accusing finger pointed by a mother at her daughter, the therapist reflects those aspects and comments on them.

Make-believe play   219

Pacing

Therapeutic functions: channeling play behavior to specific routes that prepare the ground for the main moves.

After the therapist mimics the play of a client, he or she gradually modifies her own play until the client begins to imitate his or her play. A child plays as if he is a very noisy elephant. The therapist mimics his play, pretending to be another noisy elephant. But then the therapist gradually lowers her voice until the child has become a quiet elephant.

Focusing

Therapeutic functions: stressing aspects of the play behavior by sound and lighting effects or by verbal and non-verbal comments; interpreting.

In a family play therapy session, a girl wanted her mother to play with her at leisure. She was impatient, as if hurrying to finish the game and move on to something else. The therapist reacted by whistling the song "I'm late, I'm late for a very important date" from Disney's adaptation of *Alice in Wonderland*.

Explicating

Therapeutic functions: making hidden entities explicit by verbalizing them or acting them out non-verbally; emphasizing important features; interpreting.

A family staged "a bank robbery" make-believe game. To explicate the family members' covert messages, the therapist assumed the role of a TV reporter at the end of the scene. She interviewed "the bank manager", "the police officer", "the witness" and "the robber" about their motives for acting as they did and about their feelings.

The double

Therapeutic functions: the therapist, directly or through a doll, speaks for a client who refuses to participate in the play activity or is unable to express his or her hidden feelings and thoughts. In a family play therapy session, a mother, speaking through a doll, poured a torrent of accusations on her son, who remained silent. His mother accused him of treating her with disrespect because he didn't answer her. The therapist took hold of a doll that was identical to the son's and said, "I'm afraid of you."

Providing stimuli

Therapeutic functions: encouraging certain kinds of activities or changing the course of an activity.

220 Therapy

To encourage a girl to express her jealousy of her newly born brother, the therapist placed near her a baby doll, a baby cradle and other baby things.

Illusion of alternatives

Therapeutic functions: the therapist suggests two alternative play ideas. The more attractive alternative is the one he or she wants the client to choose. This enables the therapist to join the client's play or influence its course.

A therapist who wanted to encourage a timid little boy to express his strong side in play asked the boy, "Do you prefer being Mickey Mouse or Mighty Mouse?"

Obedient actor

Therapeutic functions: the therapist asks their client for permission to join their play and lets them choose his or her role in it. Once inside, he or she is free to make his or her own choices. This enables the therapist to become an equal play partner.

Willy-nilly

Therapeutic functions: the therapist performs a play act that engages the client in a complementary play act. In this way, the therapist manages to engage the client in play or influence his or her play in accordance with the therapist's aims.

A therapist who wanted to cast a boy in the role of a hunter said to him, "I am the rabbit. Hunter, please don't shoot me!"

Some of these techniques have been observed in children's spontaneous play. Others have been borrowed from Milton Erickson and other strategic therapists (e.g. Erickson and Rossi, 1980; Madanes, 1991).

This approach to play therapy is different from the traditional psychoanalytic (therapist as interpreter) approach, from the child-centered, nondirective approach or from the currently in vogue directive, manualized treatment techniques. In my view, a play therapist should be admitted into the child's or the family's private, intimate world of make-believe before making any kind of comments about it or interfering with it from the position of an outsider. A play therapist should communicate with a child using the child's own language rather than some grown-up's language. One should also be cautious not to over-rely on children's own ability to work through their difficulties by spontaneous make-believe play. Not all children possess such skills and those who do are usually those who do not need therapy. There are perhaps also cultural differences in this respect. The ability to use all the emotion-regulating and bug-busting powers of play is severely reduced in many traumatized, bugged clients.

Make-believe play   221

Example 10.17 Amir again

Let us go back to Case 7.2 (Amir).

At the beginning of the therapy, an attempt was made to have Amir participate in individual play therapy with a supervisor of mine, male therapist Malik.

Here are some excerpts of the play therapy sessions.

The following interchange took place in the first individual play therapy sessions with Amir after the shootout incident:

> The first thing Amir said when he entered the play therapy room was, "There's nothing to do here, it's boring. Let me go home."
>
> Malik said, "OK, go home."
>
> Amir said, "You're a liar. You won't let me go." Then he started throwing pillows at Malik. Malik caught the pillows and started a pillow-throwing battle with Amir. Amir cooperated, trying to hide the fact that he enjoyed this game. He kept evading the pillows Malik threw at him, saying things like, "You're stupid! You can't hit me!" while throwing a pillow at Malik as hard as he could.
>
> Then Malik said, "Let's pretend you are stronger than me and you're not afraid of me!"

Here, Malik activated three play properties: *play framing* (turning the activity into make-believe play); *owning and alienation* and *basic duality.*

By activating owning and alienation, Malik let Amir own his omnipotence and denial of fear and think of himself and feel himself to be powerful and courageous. At this same time, activating this play property enabled Amir to alienate himself from his omnipotence and denial of fear and understand and feel that he was just pretending to be so powerful and courageous.

By activating basic duality, Malik, so to speak, divided Amir into two people: the one inside the play, who is powerful and brave, and the one outside the play, who just pretends to be strong and courageous. This had the effect of bypassing Amir's defenses, introducing information that was missing from his emotion programs. The absence of this information had made these programs less than optimally simple and therefore incapable of mobilizing corrective feedback.

> After this play move, Amir threw a pillow at Malik very hard and shouted, "Shut up! I killed you!"
>
> Amir was angry at Malik because the latter had managed to break through his defenses.
>
> Malik lay still for a while, pretending to be dead. Amir walked up and down restlessly and then stood and looked at Malik. He said, "Hey you!" He looked a bit frightened.

222 Therapy

Then Malik got up slowly. He wrapped himself with a white sheet and whispered in a "ghostly" voice, "I am the ghost of the man you killed. Why did you kill me?"

Amir whispered, "Because you were stupid."

Malik whispered, "You shouldn't have killed me. When I was alive I could help you and protect you, although we were fighting, but as a ghost I can't help you, and now you'll have to manage on your own in the cruel and frightening world of the living."

In this intervention, Malik activated the following two play properties: *arbitrariness of the signifier* – Malik transformed himself from a signifier of the man killed by Amir to a signifier of the ghost of this man, who came back from the dead; and *covert communication* – Malik conveyed within the make-believe world messages about Amir's real world. If such messages bypass the child's defenses and are difficult to swallow, placing them within the make-believe world sweetens the bitter pill. In this case, the covert communication alluded to Amir's defenses of omnipotence and rebelliousness. He, in a way, "killed" his foster parents, his teachers and the other adults in charge of helping and protecting him.

Then Malik whispered, "I'll tell you a secret no living human being is allowed to be told. But don't tell anyone that I revealed this to you. Do you want me to tell you this secret?"

Amir said, "OK, if you want to." He said this as if he were doing Malik a favor.

Malik said, "If you make this gesture three times" – he demonstrated a gesture of acceptance, an invitation to embrace – "then this will revive me and make me a living person again. Try it."

Amir hesitated but then performed a poor, incomplete version of the embracing gesture.

Malik said, "It's not going to work if you do it that way. You should do it this way, three times."

Then Amir performed the full gesture, three times.

Amir threw the white sheet away, rubbed his eyes and said, "What happened? Did I fall asleep? I'm sorry." Amir looked at him, dumbfounded.

Malik picked up a pillow and said, "Do you want to go on with our pillow-throwing battle?"

In this intervention, Malik activated the play properties *covert communication* and *possible worlds*. He communicated to Amir, covertly, within the world of make-believe play, a message about Amir's real life: "You have the power to get love, support and protection from your adult caretakers, you can even draw psychological support from the late Sabina. If you use your power in a constructive, loving, embracing way rather than a

Make-believe play   223

destructive way, they will reciprocate. Come with me to a possible world in which this can come true."

In the theoretical terms of the model, this introduced missing corrective feedback into Amir's less than optimally simple programs.

After a number of these sessions, Amir's parents reported improvements in his behavior. After some couple therapy sessions with them (see Chapter 8), Malik felt that the time was ripe to start family play therapy.

Here is a vignette from a family play therapy session with Amir's family:

Basil and Badra sat on chairs in two different corners of the room. Amir picked up a plastic toy shaped like a combat knife covered with mock blood. He approached Basil and aimed the knife at his face, with a rather threatening look on his face, putting the tip of the knife very close to Basil's right eye. Basil flinched, but said nothing.

Amir said, in a voice quite vile and thuggish, "I'm going to spill your eye out."

Badra said, "Amir! Stop it! You hear me? Stop it immediately!"

Amir said, "You shut up!"

Badra looked at Malik with a helpless expression on her face.

Then Malik put on a sheriff's hat, held a toy gun and handcuffs and called out to Amir, "Jack! Hands up! Throw that knife!" (willy-nilly).

Amir turned toward Malik with the knife pointed at him and yelled, "I'm gonna kill you! I'm not afraid of anybody!"

Malik said, "Go ahead! Make my day!" Then he whispered to Amir, "Amir, do you remember how I taught you to release your hands out of these handcuffs? Let me handcuff you and then you show them how you release yourself."

Amir let him do it.

In this move, Malik used the play property *possible worlds*, showing Amir that he can be in a one-down position and still be powerful.

Then Malik handcuffed Amir and said, "This man is a desperado. He is an expert at running away from custody. He ran away from our state prison for dangerous criminals and terrorized the whole town. He shows his bravado to overcome his own fears. He attacks people out of fear and panic."

In this move, Malik activated the property *covert communication* to introduce missing information. Amir yelled at him, "Stop talking, I'll kill you!" He released himself from the handcuffs and pointed the knife at Malik.

Malik whispered to him, "Let's pretend I'm handcuffing you again and then you are put on trial and get a fair trial." Amir agreed.

224 Therapy

Malik arranged a trial. Badra was the prosecutor, Basil the counsel for the defense and Malik the judge. The trial was an opportunity to discuss the various issues standing between the family members by *covert communication*.

After progress had been achieved in the family therapy, Amir joined group play therapy with three of his peers. Here is a vignette:

Malik and his co-therapist, Sarah, offered the children a selection of masks representing types of people and animals with various facial expressions. They asked each boy to choose a mask for himself and do some show with it. Afterwards they asked the children to choose masks for the other children and direct a show. One of the children, called Abe, chose a clown's mask and did a show in which the clown was making biting remarks at the other children's expense. The children chose a different mask for him, that of a dog with sharp teeth. They directed him to bark and bite the other children.

Amir chose for himself a mask of a frightening monster. In his show, he frightened the children and threatened to devour them. Other children chose for him a mask of a puppy. In their show, they found the puppy in the street and took it to their home. Let me remark that the children knew that Amir was an adopted child, but they also were in emotional touch with his forlorn side, which he wanted to hide from himself. The children helped Abe and Amir get rid of their horse blinders.

In this game, Abe and Amir came into touch with information that was missing from their respective less than optimally simple programs.

Malik and Sarah helped the children develop these shows further. The children staged a scene in which the two dogs, the biting dog (Abe) and the lost puppy (Amir), were going to a friendly "dogs school", in which the dogs learned to do useful jobs such as guarding the home, finding lost children and helping the police find criminals. Thus, they created a possible world in which these boys could materialize their positive, pro-social sides.

Summary of Chapter 10

Integrative play therapy is a part of The Diamond Model. This chapter is devoted to the main type of play that has effective therapeutic applications: make-believe play. This type of play can have the following functions: it is a semiotic system, a language for expression and communication; it is a cybernetic, cognitive-affective mechanism for regulating the level of emotion arousal; it is a cybernetic social mechanism for regulating social relations; it is a product of culture; and it is an instrument for learning and

Make-believe play 225

development. This type of play can be used as an emotion-balancing device and as a source of bug-busters in individual, family and group therapy. Make-believe play is defined formally as a mental activity with external behavioral manifestations. For a mental activity to be make-believe play properly so-called, the following three mental claims have to be made by the player simultaneously: *realification* – claiming that a mental entity inside the player's mind is present in the immediate external environment at the time in which this claim is being made; verbalizing the realified entity or making the mental claim of *identication,* which asserts that a tangible entity in the external environment is not what it really is, but instead is the realified mental entity; and *denying the seriousness* of the claims of realification and identication. The main types of bug-busters can be logically derived from this definition: owning and alienation (the player both owns the content of his or her play and alienates him or herself from it); basic duality (the player is both the actor and the role he or she plays); arbitrariness of the signifier (any tangible raw material entity can be identicated and signify any realified semantic entity), possible worlds (any imaginable entity can be realified in make-believe play) and covert communication (communication messages on the pragmatic level can be disguised as make-believe play). These bug-busters can be applied in order to remove or weaken the bugs horse blinders, fifth wheel, flip-flop and non-sense and can enable the players to restore their ability to mobilize corrective feedback. A precondition for the effective activation of these play bug-busters is rebalancing the emotions that maintain the bugs. Make-believe play is an emotion-balancing cybernetic mechanism. Emotion-balancing techniques used by children in their make-believe play are, among other, repetition, ups and downs, distancing, introducing protective devices, neutralizing, empowering and immunization, compensating and reversing. Play therapy sessions are conducted by preparatory moves, main moves and auxiliary moves. The moves are carried out by techniques such as mimicking, focusing, explicating, providing stimuli, illusion of alternatives, the obedient actor and willy-nilly. Play therapy according to The Diamond Model is partly directive. Although the therapeutic interventions are responses to the client's natural play, the therapist has to direct the play if the natural therapeutic properties of play fail to do the job.

Assignments

(a) If you an active individual, family or group therapist who works with children, attempt to apply the concepts, methods and techniques proposed in this chapter in your practice.

(b) Suggest individual, family and group play therapeutic interventions for Case 6.1 (Moran). Attempt to apply all the concepts, methods and techniques proposed in this chapter.

226   Therapy

A classified list of publications

Play research and play therapy

Ariel, S. (1984). Locutions and illocutions in make-believe play. *Journal of Pragmatics*, 8(2), pp.221–240.

Ariel, S. (1992a). Semiotic analysis of children's play: A method for investigating social development. *Merrill-Palmer Quarterly*, 38(1), pp.119–138.

Ariel, S. (1992b). *Strategic family play therapy*. Chichester, UK: Wiley.

Ariel, S. (1999). *Culturally competent family therapy*. Westport, CT: Praeger.

Ariel, S. (2002). *Children's imaginative play: A visit to Wonderland*. Westport, CT: Praeger.

Ariel, S., Sever, I. and Kam, M. (1980). Play in the desert and play in the town: On play activities of Bedouin Arab children. In: Schawartzman, H.B., ed. *Play and culture*. Westpoint, NY: Leisure Press, pp.164–175.

Mielcke, J. and Lowenstein, L. (2010). *Handbook of play therapy: Advances in assessment, theory, research and practice*. New York, NY: Jason Aronson.

Sever, I. (1980). *Conflict resolution and social control among preschoolers, Jews, Arabs and Bedouins*. MA dissertation. Haifa, Israel: Department of Sociology and Anthropology, Haifa University.

Heuristic procedures and idiographic theories

Chomsky, N. (1957). *Syntactic structures*. The Hague, the Netherlands: Mouton.

Chomsky, N. (1965). *Aspects of the theory of syntax*. Cambridge, MA: MIT Press.

Cohen, L.E. and Waite-Stupiansky, S. (2011). *Polyphony of research, theories and issues*. Lanhan, MD: University Press of America.

Hammel, E.A., ed. (1965). *Formal semantic analysis*. Special publication, American Anthropologist, 67(5), pt. 2.

Strategic and paradoxical techniques

Erickson, M.H. and Rossi, E. (1980). *Hypnotic alteration of sensory perceptual and psychophysical processes (collected papers of Milton H. Erickson)*. Irvington, NY: Irvington Pub.

Madanes, C. (1991). *Strategic family therapy*. San Francisco, CA: Jossey-Bass.

Chapter 11

Monitoring the therapeutic process

Changes in sessions and between sessions

The therapist should continuously monitor the process of therapy and repeatedly re-evaluate the original diagnostic evaluation, the strategies and the changes occurring both in and out of the therapy room. The evaluation will focus on the following questions:

(a) What changes were planned and what changes occurred spontaneously?
(b) How can one explain these two types of changes?
(c) What modifications should be introduced into the therapeutic strategies and tactics in light of the changes that have occurred?
(d) Which new difficulties have appeared, what are their causes and what can one do to overcome them?
(e) When has the time for termination arrived and how should the termination be managed?

Case 11.1 Donna

Donna's husband and their teenage daughter formed a coalition that continuously humiliated Donna and undermined her position as a parent. Donna used to endure this and respond by becoming depressed and listless. As a result of the therapy, Donna strengthened herself and was ready to fight for her rights as a wife and mother and restore her respect and parental authority. But she did this by having bursts of fury, in which she would yell at her husband and daughter uncontrollably, hitting her daughter and breaking dishes. The change was in principle in the right direction of restoring the balance in the family, but the aggressive and violent ways in which Donna fought were an adverse effect of the therapeutic process. The therapy took a turn and concentrated on getting her interested in adequate, effective ways of achieving her goals.

228 Therapy

The data for monitoring and re-evaluating the therapeutic process can be obtained during the therapeutic sessions, but can also be detected in reports of clients and other people (e.g. teachers), from home visits, etc.

The processes of therapeutic change in a multi-systemic therapy are extremely complex. They are the sum of small changes that occur as a result of all the therapeutic interventions in all the sessions. The gains achieved in one session often cause changes not immediately, but after several sessions. Often the changes that occur are unpredictable. Unexpected difficulties as a result of therapeutic interventions often emerge and the therapist has to keep an eye on them.

Case 11.2 Zehava, Nitzan and Barak

Eight-year-old Barak was brought to therapy because he was caught taking things from children's satchels in his class. Barak lived with his mother, Zehava, and his nine-year-old sister, Nitzan, in a room apartment in a low-socioeconomic neighborhood in the south of Tel Aviv. His father left the home two years earlier with Barak's two older brothers. He lives with another woman.

A trainee of mine, Ruth, formulated some of the family's dysfunctional programs:

Zehava's proximity and control goal: to keep her children close to her and to create together with them a strong and stable family that cannot fall apart.

Zehava's plan to achieve the goal included the following clauses, among other:

Presupposition: my husband left and took the two older sons with him *because* I did not fight hard enough to keep the whole family united around me.
Prediction: there is still a danger that my husband will steal the other children from me.
OUTPUT
I have to keep an eye on the children all the time.
I will not let them quarrel and make sure they play well together.
I will not allow any connection between the children and their father, nor between the young children and their older brothers who live with him. He himself, his new home, the older brothers who live with him and his new spouse will not be mentioned or spoken to in my home.

Nitzan's proximity goal: to keep Mom as close to me as possible.

Nitzan's plan:

Prediction: *IF* I'm a bad girl *AND* do things that Mom does not like, such as fighting with my brother Barak *OR* mentioning my dad *OR* my older brothers *THEN necessarily* my mother will be so unhappy and so angry that she will *probably* decide to give up on me and send me to live with Dad.

OUTPUT
I will never mention my father or my older brothers when Mom can hear me. *IF* my brother Barak annoys me *THEN* I will give in and avoid an open fight with him. To prevent the possibility of having a conflict with him, I will keep myself to myself *AND* try to abstain from any contact with him.
I will listen to Mom and do nothing against her will.

Barak's proximity and control goals: to be independent. To be as little as possible under the control of my mother and sister and as close as possible to my father and my older brothers.

Barak's plan:

Presupposition: my mother and sister want to control me completely and prevent me from having any contact with my father and brothers.

Predictions: *IF* I do things that my mother is unhappy with, especially *IF* I mention my father, his new partner, my older brothers *OR* their new home, *THEN* necessarily my mother will get very upset *AND* my sister Nitzan will not dare to disagree with her.
IF I am not close to my mother and sister *THEN* I can feel closer to my father and my older brothers.

OUTPUT
I will avoid contact with my mother and sister as much as possible. In this way I can evade their control without direct confrontation with them.
I will not behave well at school where my mother does not see me or control me. *IF* my mother hears complaints about me from school *THEN* she will *probably* decide she cannot raise me *AND* ask for help from my father and this will suit my goal.
Barak's main symptom, taking things from children's satchels, was an expression of the final part of his plan. It also seems to have metaphorical, symbolic meaning. He could not get what he wanted directly – being close to his father and his older brothers – so he "stole" what he wanted, metaphorically.

The main bugs Ruth identified were:

> Zehava's presupposition that her husband left because she did not fight hard enough to keep the family around her was not necessarily correct. Its validity was not checked (horse blinders, non-sense).

Her prediction that he would want to "steal" the other children was not necessarily valid either. There was a lack of information that could corroborate these conjectures (horse blinders) and perhaps also a misinterpretation (non-sense).

Her policy of banning any talk about her divorcee and about the older children did not allow her to get any information that would corroborate or disprove these thoughts. She also did not consider less extreme ways of keeping Nitzan and Barak close to her. She did not see the drawbacks of this attitude (horse blinders). Because Nitzan and Barak did not share with her their goals and plans, she had no idea what they wanted, thought and felt (horse blinders).

Nitzan's prediction that her mother might give her to her father did not take into consideration that her mother's main goal was to keep her and Barak close to her (horse blinders, non-sense).

Her decision to minimize the relationship with Barak did not consider her mother's desire that she would be close to her brother. She did not consider other, less harmful options to keep her mother close to her (horse blinders).

Barak's prediction that his problematic behavior at school may lead his mother to decide to seek help from his father did not take into account his mother's goal and plan (horse blinders, non-sense). He did not think of less harmful possibilities for achieving his goal (horse blinders).

Ruth has adopted a strategy to weaken these bugs.

Her tactic for one of the first family play therapy sessions was the following:

The target of change: to help Zehava understand that her goal could be achieved in more positive ways, such as developing an open, supportive and enjoyable mutual relationship with Nitzan and Barak; letting them understand that she wants them to be close to each other; and encouraging them to stop avoiding each other's company and engage in joint activities.

The therapeutic play properties to be applied and the ways in which they would be implemented are as follows:

Possible worlds for creating collaboration and mutual support within the play world.

Arbitrariness of the signifier to overcome the children's resistance to mutual proximity. The signs of avoidance at the raw material level, such as maintaining physical distance and lack of contact, will be playfully reframed by Ruth as signs of closeness and intimacy.

Monitoring the therapeutic process 231

Owning and alienation in order to encourage Zehava to adopt the role of a good parent who encourages the children to show openness and mutual support.

Zehava's messages will be transmitted in covert communication through the play. Ruth will play a role that would place her in a position of authority. She will appoint Zehava to be her assistant. Later, Ruth will ask Zehava to replace her as the leader. Ruth herself will move aside and serve only as "a consultant".

Here is a protocol of a part of the session in which some of these ideas were implemented:

Observation 11.1 Zehava, Barak and Nitzan again

Barak sits on the floor, playing with a doll house, trying to put little animal dolls into it through the window. Zehava stands over him, looking at him. Nitzan stands by her, holding her arm.

ZEHAVA: [Turns to Ruth] He always plays like a little boy.
RUTH: Me too sometimes. It's fun.
ZEHAVA: [Turns to Nitzan] You also have to do something.
NITZAN: I'm going to paint.
Nitzan takes sheets of paper and crayons. She sits down at a table and begins to draw trees.
ZEHAVA: What are you painting?
NITZAN: A forest.
Both children are immersed in their activities. Zehava looks lost and depressed.
ZEHAVA: Barak, why don't you sit next to Nitzan at the table? You'll be more comfortable there.
Barak ignores her. She takes a chair and sits down next to Nitzan, looking at Nitzan anxiously.
RUTH: I'm the forest manager's supervisor. Zehava, you are my chief assistant.
Ruth sits next to Zehava.
RUTH: I see you were waiting for me here in the jeep. Well, let's start the forest tour to see if everything is all right. This time I'll drive.

Ruth takes a toy rubber wheel, sits down on the chair, turns the wheel and makes engine noises. She says to Zehava, "Everything is in OK here. Let's go into the zoo, there [pointing to the doll house where Barak plays], under a tree. This is a shelter for animals. Well, now you will drive. I'm tired." She gives the wheel to Zehava.

232 Therapy

In our supervision meeting, Ruth said that the family's play behavior mirrored their dysfunctional programs. She said that Barak's putting little animals into the doll house probably symbolized his desire to move to his father's home.

Ruth's intervention was in accordance with the tactics she had planned in advance. The main aim of her intervention was to get the family to play together and enjoy it, but also to show Zehava that this can be achieved without begging or trying to force things that do not suit the children. She applied arbitrariness of the signifier to define the entire room as a single forest, connecting Nitzan, Barak and Zehava in the same make-believe space. She created a joint family activity in which Zehava played a leading parental role without requiring the children to do anything different from what they were doing anyway.

In the next session, the family continued the same play.

Observation 11.2 Zehava, Barak and Nitzan (continued)

Nitzan leaves her painting and approaches Barak. She kneels beside him and watches him put animal dolls into the doll house and take them back. Zehava, who had been appointed by Ruth as Chief Inspector of the Forest Authority, sits on a chair and watches them. Ruth, who retired as "counselor", sits on a chair beside her.

RUTH: I see that your teammates cooperate more than I did when I was the supervisor. The team member has finished planting trees and now she has come to help the crew member bring the animals into the animals' shelter. Are you in favor of this cooperation?
ZEHAVA: Absolutely!
RUTH: I envy you, you run things so well!

Zehava takes a toy cow and hands it to Nitzan and tells her, "You forgot to give the cow to the crew member who brings animals into the shelter."

In our supervision, Ruth realized that changes in the latter session appeared to have been affected by the changes in the previous part of the session. Nitzan realized she could play with Barak without getting into a fight with him. Barak realized that he could play with Nitzan and Zehava without being controlled. Zehava learned that she could unite the family without being constantly on guard.

Later in the session, Ruth reinforced what had been already achieved.

Observation 11.3 Zehava, Barak and Nitzan (continued further)

Nitzan and Barak sit on two chairs at the table. Zehava sits opposite them. There are two doll houses on the table. Nitzan and Barak transfer animals from one doll house to another and back.

Monitoring the therapeutic process 233

RUTH (AS "CONSULTANT"): I see that you have built another shelter for animals. The animals love to visit the second house.

ZEHAVA: At home they demanded that I'd buy another doll house, as if one is not enough.

RUTH: They prefer two separate houses, but the animals will visit both houses.

In our supervision session, Ruth realized that the two houses symbolized both children's desire to be in touch with their father and visit his home. They became closer to each other without losing their boundaries and separateness. The changes happened spontaneously, but previous meetings prepared the ground for the changes to take place. Ruth did not plan to get into the matter of the relationship with the father at that stage because she thought that Zehava was not ready for it yet. But she did raise this issue anyway by covert communication.

In a following meeting with Zehava, Ruth learned that Zehava had become less rigid in her attempts to control the children. She began participating in their activities as a supportive figure. The children stopped avoiding each other's company and began to get closer. That is why Nitzan was less afraid of being a "bad girl". She became a little insolent and disobedient.

In the following meetings, Ruth wanted to preserve and reinforce what had been achieved. But this did not work as she had expected. The children came to the meeting in holiday clothes. They all seemed calm and happy. The children left the room a lot to drink water and go to the bathroom. Barak hid the doll house behind cushions. Nitzan put the toy animals on the window sill and said, "I'm driving a bus. We're going for a fun trip."

After that meeting, Zehava announced that they would quit therapy. She did not answer Ruth's phone call. They did not return to therapy.

Ruth and I tried to figure out what had happened. We understood that even though the subject of both houses was only hinted at, it threatened Zehava and the children. They really were not yet ready to enter into this subject and therefore left the therapy. Apparently, Zehava initiated the termination prematurely.

The behavior of the family in the room at the last meeting was interpreted as a symbolic way of conveying the message of termination and separation implicitly. The session looked like a farewell party. The festive atmosphere was also a way to balance the anxiety that has arisen because of the subject of the father having been raised. Perhaps it was also a way to hide the sadness of separation and the anger at parting.

Barak hid the house as if to say, "It is no longer appropriate to play with this." The direction of everything was outwards: the toys on the window sill and the bus ride away, leaving the room again and again to drink and going to the bathroom.

It seems that it is impossible to really predict whether our strategies will work or not. One can plan, but when things happen, things happen spontaneously. Therefore, it is important to get feedback from the family in and between the meetings in order to monitor the process and prevent undesirable developments. In the session, we get a lot of information, but not always all the information we need.

Ruth and I tried to deepen our understanding of the between-sessions developments. The bug-busters that were activated managed to balance the emotions that maintained the bugs. They succeeded in weakening the bugs. But maybe this change caused changes in other programs included in the diagnostic assessment. For example, Nitzan's avoidance of being connected with Barak stemmed from the same source as the failure to mention the subject of the father, the unwillingness to annoy the mother. But as soon as the bug preventing a close relationship with Barak had been attenuated, the fear of the mother also lost its vigor. This opened a door to hinting at the subject of the father, deterring the mother. Weakening the bugs sometimes deprives the defenses of their power too soon. Debugging one person's programs causes some bugs in another person's programs to be removed, even if the latter is not ready yet for the change.

Termination

In the latter case, the therapy was interrupted prematurely. We should also try to detect signs that the therapy is nearing its natural end.

If the client has not dropped out of therapy prematurely, the therapist has to decide when it is time to terminate. Finding a perfect solution to all the treated problems is a rare occurrence. Termination should take place when the therapist and the client feel that they have acquired the tools to work through their difficulties on their own and that remaining in therapy will create over-dependence on the therapist.

Termination should not be done abruptly. A number of sessions should be devoted to parting and preparing the ground for separation. The therapist is advised to be sensitive to various signs of approaching termination and not be misled by behaviors that disguise the client's wish to terminate. Such signs can be manifested on the raw material, semantic and pragmatic levels.

Spatial signs on the raw material level have been mentioned in the above case: keeping at a distance, leaving the room, facing outdoors and hiding.

Motional signs can be closing up physically.

Typical tactile signs are avoiding touch or touching aggressively.

On the semantic level, separation signs are:

Avoiding painful themes previously brought up
Introducing themes related to parting
Expressing anger at the therapist or avoiding any expression of anger
Being unusually sad or unusually cheerful

Typical signs on the pragmatic level are:

Expressing distancing
Anger at the therapist or over-appreciation of the therapist

Example 11.1 Amir's termination

After two years of therapy, Malik and I decided that it was time to terminate. When Malik raised the possibility of termination, Basil and Badra expressed concern and apprehension. They feared that without the support of the therapy the difficulties would re-emerge. Their behavior in the last sessions reflected their concerns, but also indicated a gradual process of readiness to continue without the therapy.

One of the contents that Amir introduced into the family play in the last session was a train ride. He ran a toy train very quickly with a lot of noise around his parents and then sounded a loud whistle and stopped the train. He told Basil, Badra and Malik to get little dolls into the train, each doll in a separate car. After they did so, he drove the train again with great speed and noise. At one point, he took Malik's doll out of the car and threw it aside.

Separation is usually not easy for the client nor for the therapist. In play or drama therapy, it is possible to soften the difficulty by passing the separation process to the world of make-believe. Some principles that should be adopted are:

Not letting the client feel rejected
Praising them for their achievements
Allowing them to express resistance to termination, anxiety or anger
Encouraging regression: going back to earlier stages of the therapy by
    acting them in role play
Summarizing the stages of the therapeutic process and pointing out what
    has been achieved in each stage
Continuing the therapy in make-believe
Staging a role play of a future meeting between the client and the therapist

All of these can be expressed metaphorically in make-believe, drawing, stories or other expressive means.

Summary of Chapter 11

The therapist should continuously monitor the process of therapy over and over again and re-evaluate the original diagnostic evaluation, the strategies

236 Therapy

and the changes occurring both in and out of the therapy room. The evaluation will focus on the following questions: (a) what changes were planned and what changes occurred spontaneously? (b) How can one explain these two types of changes? (c) Which modifications should be introduced into the therapeutic strategies and tactics in light of the changes that have occurred? (d) What new difficulties have appeared? What are their causes and what can one do to overcome them? (e) When has the time for termination arrived and how should the termination be managed? The processes in multi-systemic psychotherapy are very complex. Often changes within sessions and between sessions cannot be predicted. Well-designed interventions can go astray and lead to undesirable results. A therapist should do his or her best to understand such occurrences and make corrective therapeutic moves. One of the undesirable results is premature termination by the clients. A therapist should learn to read the early signs of premature termination, as well as of termination at the right time. Various techniques for preventing premature separation are proposed. If it is advisable, termination should be encouraged and facilitated. There are various signs of approaching spontaneous (not premature) termination. Some of these signs are subtle. The therapist should know how to read and interpret them. Various techniques for facilitating termination are proposed.

Assignments

(a) Try to analyze the processes and techniques specified in this chapter in cases you have treated or cases described by your colleagues or found in the literature. Case descriptions can be found in Wedding and Corsini (2004).

(b) Attempt to apply the various methods and techniques proposed in this chapter in your own practice.

A classified list of publications

The psychotherapeutic process and termination

Ariel, S. (1992). *Strategic family play therapy*. Chichester, UK: Wiley.

Ariel, S. (2009). *Culturally competent family therapy*. Westport, CT: Praeger.

Joyce, A.S., Piper, W.E. and Ogrodniczuk, J.S. (2006). *Termination in psychotherapy: A psychodynamic model of processes and outcomes*. Washington, DC: American Psychological Association.

Pinsof, W.M. and Greenberg, L.S. (1986). *The psychotherapeutic process: A research handbook*. New York, NY: Guilford.

Swift, J.K. and Greenberg, R.P. (2014). *Premature termination in psychotherapy: Strategies for engaging clients and improving outcomes*. Washington, DC: American Psychological Association.

Case studies

Wedding, D. and Corsini, R.J. (2004). *Case studies in psychotherapy*. 4th ed. Pacific Grove, CA: Brooks Cole.

Epilogue

Humanity has an insatiable thirst for knowledge. Enriching our knowledge is rewarding, but also frustrating, unsettling, disquieting and even dangerous. The more a person knows, the more aware he or she becomes of his or her ignorance. Biblical wisdom warned against an excessive thirst for knowledge. Adam and Eve were expelled from the Garden of Eden because they had eaten from the Tree of Knowledge. The Tower of Babel story in the Book of Genesis tells of people who had aspired to reach the knowledge reserved for the Lord. Then the Lord said, "If as one people speaking the same language they have begun to do this, then nothing they plan to do will be impossible for them. Come, let us go down and confuse their language so they will not understand each other." Ecclesiastes warned, "And furthermore, my son, be admonished: Of making many books there is no end; and much study is a weariness of the flesh."

It was that insatiable thirst for knowledge with the ensuing anxiety, frustration and weariness of the flesh that led me to invest years and years in developing The Diamond Model. I was overwhelmed by the endless abundance of therapeutic lore. My agenda was therefore to create a common language that would enable professionals who speak different languages to build a new Tower of Babel, a modest one, without the arrogance and megalomania that had brought the wrath of the Lord upon the builders of the original one.

List of cases, examples and observations

Cases

1.1	Nonny	7
1.2	Joyce	22
2.1	Linda	27
3.1	Daniel	45
4.1	Emma	63
4.2	Matthew and Olivia	67
5.1	Adelina	78
5.2	The Jaja family	79
5.3	Giorgi	81
5.4	Avner	92
5.5	Ethan	98
5.6	Kye	100
6.1	Moran	111
6.2	Ron	119
7.1	Natalie	142
7.2	Amir	144
9.1	Abigail	180
9.2	Scarlett	181
9.3	Kidist	183
9.4	Lily	188
9.5	Joshua	191
9.6	Benjamin	193
9.7	Samuel	195
11.1	Donna	227
11.2	Zehava, Nitzan and Barak	228

Examples

1.1	Nonny again	19
1.2	Autism	21
2.1	Jill	26

240　List of cases, examples and observations

3.1	The Death of Ivan Ilyich	48
4.1	Jack's body image	67
4.2	Julian	73
5.1	Grisli Siknis	80
5.2	Malgri	86
5.3	Gabriel and Ella	96
6.1	Nathan, a presenting problems interview	108
8.1	A strategy for the case of Amir	154
8.2	Individual therapy with Avner	159
8.3	Family therapy with Amir	163
9.1	Supporting a bride	182
9.2	Atonement	185
9.3	Boris	187
9.4	Family sculpting	188
9.5	Challenging	190
9.6	Joshua again	196
9.7	The bazaar	197
10.1	Nick	212
10.2	Ryan	212
10.3	Bella	212
10.4	Nick again	213
10.5	Luna	213
10.6	Bob	213
10.7	Anita	213
10.8	Paul	214
10.9	Alex	214
10.10	Max and Leo	214
10.11	Heidi	214
10.12	Dean	215
10.13	Daniel again	215
10.14	Kevin	216
10.15	Zara	217
10.16	Tessa and Kate	217
10.17	Amir again	221
11.1	Amir's termination	235

Observations

2.1	Liam and Andrew	38
2.2	Dan and Ann	41
6.1	Aaron	126
11.1	Zehava, Barak and Nitzan again	231
11.2	Zehava, Barak and Nitzan (continued)	232
11.3	Zehava, Barak and Nitzan (continued further)	232

Index

ameliorating grief 180–181
atonement rituals and ceremonies
184–185
attachment 16, 54, 63, 69–71
autonomy 69

bibliotherapy 186
biofeedback 173
body image 65
boundaries 10, 54; of body and of self
65–66, 69
bugs in information processing
programs 2, 31–33, 43, 53, 60–61,
67–69, 98–100, 157; fifth wheel 32–34;
flip-flop 32–34; horse blinders 32–34,
164; inability to enlist corrective
feedback 60; see also corrective
feedback; cybernetics; invasion into
programs; non-sense; simplicity
bug-busters 2; debugging 159; of play
therapy 210; sources of in make-believe
play 211; see also make-believe play;
play therapy

case history interview 110–118
Carnap, Rudolph 17, 18
causality: linear and circular 139
changes in sessions and between sessions
227, 233–234
Chomsky, N. 19
cognitive and psychomotor
subsystems 56
comprehensiveness 19, 32, 45; see also
simplicity
consistency 19, 23, 45; see also
simplicity
corrective feedback 1–2, 14, 18, 35,
63–64, 67, 69, 98, 101; inability to

enlist because of bugs 2, 35, 67;
see also bugs in information
processing programs
concretization 186
Context Dependent Componential
Analysis 133–137
creative arts therapies 179, 186, 210
culture 54, 77–93; make-believe play
as a product of 210; see also culture
programs
culture-bound syndromes 80–81; see also
culture
culture change and culture shock; loss
of simplicity in 81–83, 101; see also
simplicity; intra- culture and
inter-culture dysfunction 80–82
culture conceptions, common
errors 78–81
culture programs 77–93
culture programs, classification by roles:
axioms, categories and relations,
explanations, rules 83–84
culture programs, classification by
contents: coping and problem-
solving 89–92; cultural identity
86–87; ecological 85–86; existential
84–86; functional 88–89; structural
87–88; see also culture
cybernetics 1, 14, 18, 20, 34–36, 40, 59,
67, 69, 79, 98, 101, 207–209

daily life interview 118
decision procedure 19; see also
Chomsky, N.; discovery procedure,
evaluation procedure
developmental dimensions 54, 58, 61–62,
64–65, 71–72, 170, 210
developmental lines 54

242 Index

deviation amplification 35, 43, 47, 69, 98, 143
Diamond Model, The x, 1–3, 7, 10, 13–14, 16, 18, 21, 77, 169
directive and non-directive therapy 8
discovery procedure 19; *see also* Chomsky, N., decision procedure, evaluation procedure
dreams, interpretation and manipulation of 196–198
dysfunction 14, 15; in family and group programs 98–100

eclecticism, technical 2, 13, 16, 169
ecosystems 10
(Eye Movement Desensitization and Reprocessing) EMDR 170, 176
emotions 62–64; *see also* emotives
emotion-balancing by means of play 211–214; repetition in a safe environment 211
emotive 62–64; field of associations of 62; core and periphery 63–64
empathy
encouraging internal or external debate and dialogue 189
evaluation procedure 19; *see also* Chomsky, N.; decision procedure; discovery procedure
explanatory 18
explication x, 16–17

fables and allegories 184–188
family and social programs 11, 94–98; bugs in plans 97–100; proximity and control goals and plans 94–97
family interviews 118–120; daily life interview 118; the family puppet show technique 119–120; three requests 118
family puppet show technique, the 119–120
feed-forward 1, 35–98
fifth wheel 33; *see also* bugs in information processing programs
flip-flop 33; *see also* bugs in information processing programs
flooding 185
formalization 1, 17
free associations 58, 189
functioning 2, 35, 88, 153, 207; dysfunctional programs 2, 14, 15, 44, 45, 81, 98; well-functioning programs 2, 14, 44

generative programs 206
Gestalt therapy 186
gradual relaxation 173
guided imagination 178

habituation techniques 185–186; flooding 185; implosive therapy 185; *in vivo* exposure 185; prolong exposure 185
healing ceremonies 177
homeostasis 18
horse blinders 32; *see also* bugs in information processing programs
hypnosis and suggestion 177

idiographic theory 16, 20, 24
induction and modification of dreams 178
information processing: changing patterns of 189–198, 228–229; in family programs 94–97; language of 1, 14–15, 18, 20, 26–31, 39–40, 53, 59, 67, 77
integration x, 13, 18, 20, 169
interpretation and reflection 171, 194
in vivo exposure 185

lacunae 45
language 58–62
learning and development, theories of 55
levels of semiotic analysis 59, 136–140, 206; pragmatic 37–39, 59, 206; raw material 59, 136–137; semantic 59, 206
life events 10–11, 77, 145–149
linguistically uniform 13
locating emotions and cognitions inside the body and changing them 178

magic and sorcery 177
make-believe play 204–211; as a cognitive-affective regulation mechanism 207–208, 211–214; as a cybernetic, social regulation device 208–209; definition of, realification; identication; denying the seriousness 204, 211; development of 210; as a language, a semiotic system 205–206; as a product of culture 209–210; therapeutic powers of massage 174; *see also* culture; emotions; family and social programs
mechanisms of change 159, 164, 166, 169–171; based on influence by

suggestion and magic 170, 176–178; changing body functions 170; concretization 171; enhancing alertness, attention and concentration 170–176; expression and catharsis 170, 178–181; habituation 171; influencing information processing 171; positive reinforcement and support 171; types of 169–171; working through the body 170–172
mentalization 194–195
meta-cognition 194
metaphors, fables and allegories 186
microscopic vs. macroscopic analysis 37–38, 40
mindfulness 174, 186
model vs. idiographic theory 1, 16, 19–21
mourning and bereavement ceremonies 183–184
movement and dance therapies 174–175
multi-systemic 1, 10, 19; diagnosis 107, 137–140
music therapy 179

narrative techniques 193–194
(Neuro-Linguistic Programming) NLP 170, 175–176
non-sense 33; *see also* bugs in information processing programs

object relations 10, 54, 65–66, 121–124
observations 121–133; analyzing and interpreting 125; errors in recording 121–122; recording and transcribing 121–124; videotaping 122
operant conditioning 171
operators in information processing language 28–29; *see also* information processing, language of

paradoxical techniques 166
parsimony 32; *see also* simplicity
part object 66, 69
perception 56–58
personality and social development 11, 65
Peterfreund, E. 18
play bug-busters: arbitrariness of the signifier 216–217; basic duality 216; owning and alienation 214–215; possible worlds 217–218; *see also* make-believe play, play therapy

plausibility 19, 32; *see also* simplicity
play, therapeutic functions: as a debugging instrument 214–218; as an emotion-balancing device; as a means of therapeutic communication 218–224
play therapy: advantages of 204; as a debugging instrument 214–218; family play therapy 222–224, 227–234; functions of 204–205; 222–224, 227–234; group play therapy 224; illusion of alternatives 220
play therapy moves: explicating 219; focusing 219; mimicking 218; obedient actor 220; pacing 219; possible worlds 217–218; providing stimuli 219; the double 219; role of the play therapist 218; willy-nilly 220; *see also* make-believe play; play, therapeutic functions
pragmatics: as level of semiotic analysis 36, 59; *see also* semiotics
presenting problems interview 108–110
presupposition 125
prolonged exposure and repeated exposure 185–186
proximity and control goals and plans 29, 39, 94–96, 101, 125–133
psychodrama and drama therapy 179–180

rational-emotive behavior therapy 192
raw material, as level of semiotic analysis 73, 59, 123–124; *see also* semiotics
reflection and interpretation 194
reframing 192
relations between programs, uni-directional, bi-directional or multi-directional: adverse effects of 142–143, 145–150; as reflected in symptoms 143; distortion 142; dysfunctional defensive response 143; fixation and regression 142; influencing the tempo or nature of change 141, 145–150; insoluble conflict 143; lacunas 141–142; mobilizing defensive responses 141; restriction of choice 140–141; shaping form or content 141; shattering 142; strengthening or weakening 141
reparenting 181
rites of passage 182–183

244   Index

sculpting techniques 187–189
self and body image and concept 10,
    54, 65–66
self-object 66, 69
semantics; as level of semiotic analysis
    36–59; *see also* semiotic analysis of
    recorded observations
semiotics 1, 14, 18, 59, 20, 36–40, 59,
    79, 206
semiotic analysis of recorded
    observations 124–137; formulating
    underlying information processing
    programs 130–133; on the pragmatic
    level 125–130; on the raw material
    level 124; on the semantic level 125,
    133–137
simplicity 2, 15, 18, 20, 31–40, 59, 79,
    100, 206, 214; comprehensiveness 2,
    15, 20, 31–33, 40, 214; consistency 2,
    15, 31–33, 40, 214; defined; loss of 12,
    15, 40–44; parsimony 2, 15, 31–33, 40,
    214; plausibility 2, 15, 20, 31–33, 40,
    214; restoring partially 44–48
strategic and paradoxical techniques
    195–196
strategy 151–156
structures 127–131
subsystems: external 50; internal
    1, 50–54
symbolic objects and acts in rituals and
    ceremonies 187
synchronic vs. diachronic perspectives 2,
    10, 42, 53, 72, 139
systematic desensitization 43, 173

targets of change 159
techniques based on habituation 185;
    see also mechanisms of change
techniques employing positive
    reinforcement and support 181;
    see also mechanisms of change
techniques facilitating transition and
    change 181–184; *see also* mechanisms
    of change
techniques using expression and
    catharsis 178–179; *see also*
    mechanisms of change
techniques using influence, suggestion
    and magic 176–177; *see also*
    mechanism of change
termination: culturally sensitive 157;
    premature 234; signs of 234–235;
    stages of 234–235; techniques of 235;
    therapeutic alliance 156–157
therapeutic contract 156–157; explicit vs.
    tacit 157
therapeutic moves 158–166; auxiliary
    158, 164; main 158, 161, 165;
    preparatory 158, 161, 164–165
therapeutic process 227–234
three requests 118
trance: induction of 176
transition and crisis 2, 14–16, 43–45, 77;
    loss of simplicity in 2, 14, 23–44, 81,
    145–150

visual arts therapy 180

yoga and meditation 174